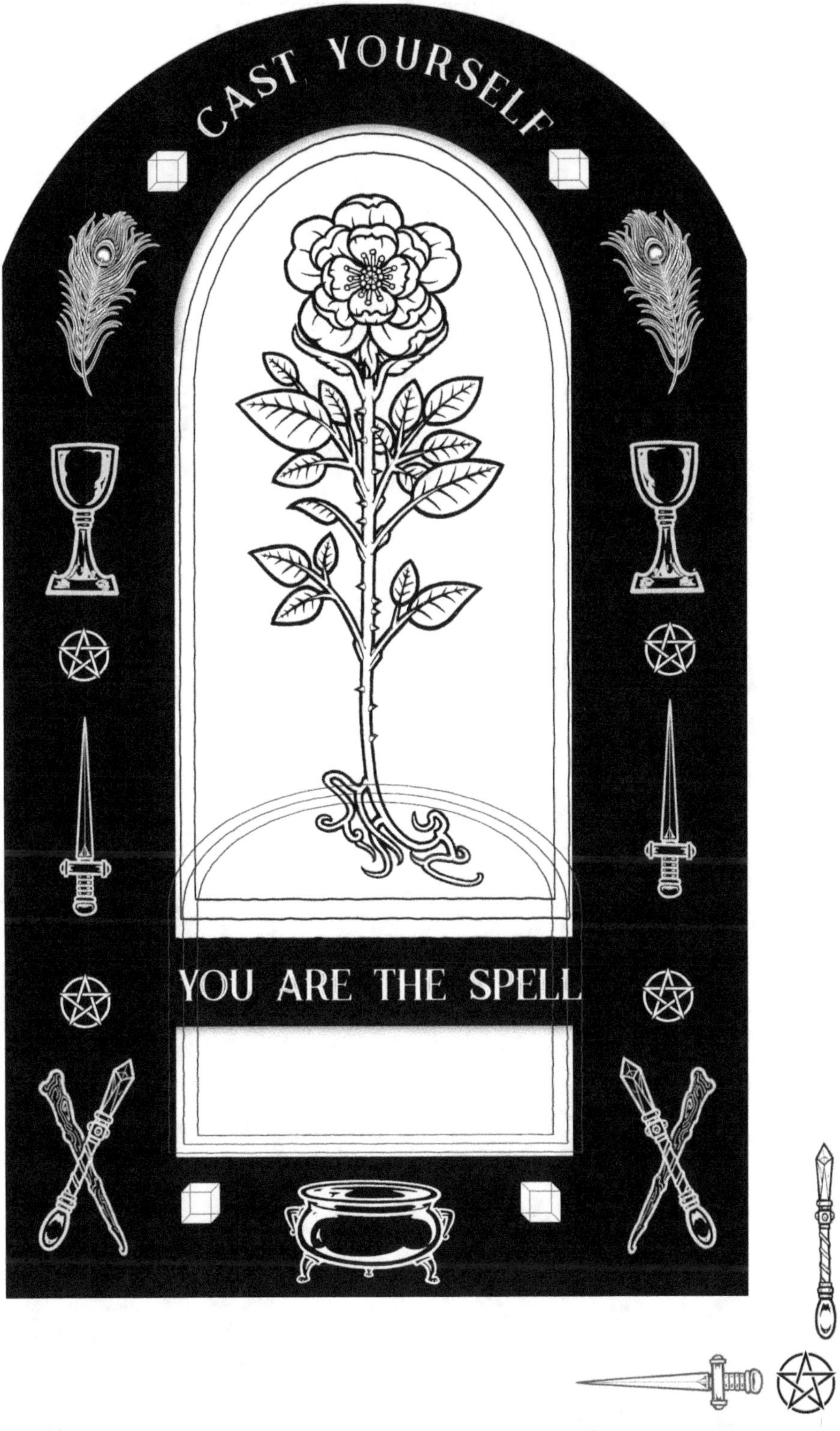
CAST YOURSELF
YOU ARE THE SPELL

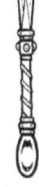

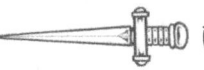

EVOLUTIONARY WITCHCRAFT

THE TWENTIETH ANNIVERSARY REVISED EDITION

T. THORN COYLE

For Victor and Cora Anderson.
And for all my teachers, students, and magical colleagues.

To everyone who reads these words:
Cast yourself. You are the spell.

Copyright © 2025 by T. Thorn Coyle
Cover & Book Design © 2025 by T. Thorn Coyle
Art by Maxine Miller © 2025
Editing: Dayle Dermatis

Paperback Edition ISBN: 978-1-946476-59-3
Hardcover Standard Edition ISBN: 978-1-946476-58-6

This book, or parts thereof, may not be reproduced in any form without permission, other than what constitutes Fair Use excerpts used for reviews or classroom. Nothing here may be used to train Large Language Models, or GenAI. This book is licensed for your personal enjoyment only.
All rights reserved.

Published by PF Publishing,
An imprint of Triple Flame Inc
3439 SE Hawthorne #203
Portland, OR 97214

Printed and bound by IngramSpark.
Australia: Ingram Content Group AU Pty Ltd, Melbourne, Victoria. US: Lightning Source LLC, La Vergne, Tennessee / Allentown, Pennsylvania / Jackson, Tennessee, United States. UK: Lightning Source UK Ltd, Milton Keynes, United Kingdom. Europe: Lightning Source UK Ltd, with facilities in Germany, France, and Spain. The authorized representative in the European Economic Area is Lightning Source France, 1 Av. Johannes Gutenberg, 78310 Maurepas, France.
compliance@lightningsource.fr

CONTENTS

Foreword by Mat Auryn   xv

PART ONE
EVOLUTIONARY WITCHCRAFT

To Reweave the World	3
Evolutionary Witchcraft Twenty Years Later	5
The Roots of Evolutionary Witchcraft	7
What is Evolutionary Witchcraft?	13

PART TWO
CASTING THE SACRED SPHERE

Opening the Teachings	19
Using the Tools	21
Facing the Mirror	23
Loving Your Humanity	25
Self Love Cleansing	27
Preparing to Cast the Sphere	28
Becoming Present and Embodied	30
Creating Keys for Remembrance	33
Stepping Toward the Blue Fire	35
Meditation on the Blue Flame	37
Casting into the Extraordinary	38
Casting from the Inside Out	41
Developing Practice, Committing to Craft	43
Engaging the Sacred Body	46
Learning to Live Tall	48
Following the Energy Flow	50
Opening to Fey Awareness	52
Finding Your Feyness	54
Listening for the Other Realms	56
Unfolding Your Power	58

PART THREE
INVOCATION OF THE DIVINE WITHIN

Deity Magic	65
Encountering Your Soul	68
Sticky One	72
Sticky One Play Date	75
The Wish Bird as Fetch	76
Shining Body	78
Deep, Expansive Attention	80
Creating Aura Colors	83
Sacred Dove	85
Sitting and Listening	87
Collectively Divine	91
Aligning the Triple Soul	94
Prayer for Alignment	95

PART FOUR
EAST: OPENING THE SENSES

The Tools of Air	101
A Magical Worldview	103
Opening to Seeker's Mind	106
The Elemental Powers	108
The Guardian of the East	110
The Wand	112
Wand Listening	114
Charging and Consecrating Your Wand	115
Walking as a Wand	117
Running Wand Energy	118
Asking for What You Want	119
Listening, Visioning, Stepping	121
Global Magic	123
Widening Your Awareness	124
Expanding Your Attentive Capacity	126
Engaging the Breath	128
The Power of Speech	129
The Power to Name	131

Counting Your Breath	133
Expanding the Ordinary World	135
Cleansing the Pentacle of the Senses	137
Feeling the World Inside You	140
Connecting to the Gods	142
Dancing the Sun and the Moon	145
Taking Speech into Action	148

PART FIVE
SOUTH: ENGAGING THE FLAME

The Tools of Fire	151
Touching the Four Fires	153
The Fire of Will	156
Engaging the Core	158
The Guardian of the South	159
The Blade	161
Extending Your Will	163
Holding Choices	164
Walking as a Tool of Fire	166

THE IRON PENTACLE

Discussing Iron	169
Calling Back the Points	172
Sex—Spirit	177
Sacred Pleasure	179
Pride—Fire	182
Automatic Writing	184
Taking Pride Out of the Box	186
Self—Air	188
Questioning Your Sense of Self	190
Cutting to the Core	192
Power—Earth	194
Circles of Power	196
Portraits of Power	199
Passion—Water	201
Saying Yes to Passion	204
Feeding Your Passion	205

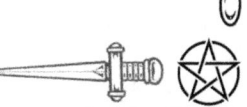

Drinking in Passion — 207
The Fire of Practice — 209

PART SIX
WEST: DIVING INTO COMPASSION

The Tools of Water — 213
The Chalice — 215
Tempering Your Emotions — 218
The Guardian of the West — 221
Consecrating Your Ability to Hold — 223
Engaging the Heart — 224
Heart Breath — 226

THE PEARL PENTACLE

Discussing Pearl — 231
Calling Up the Pearl — 234
Love—Spirit — 238
Opening to Ordinary Love — 240
Polishing the Heart — 242
Law—Fire — 244
Believing and Willing — 246
Knowledge—Air — 247
Clearing the Attic — 248
The Knowledge Game — 250
Liberty—Earth — 252
Freedom from Within — 254
What Keeps Us From Freedom? — 256
Enacting Liberty — 258
Wisdom—Water — 260
Whispering in Wisdom — 262
Drinking Your Wisdom — 263
Spilling Over — 265

PART SEVEN
NORTH: BIRTHING OUR WHOLENESS

The Tools of North	269
The Cube and Pentacle	271
Planes of Stability	273
Being Parent to Changes	275
The Power of Silence	276
Taking a Word Fast	278
Sitting Like a Mountain	280
The Guardian of North	282
The Physical World	284
What Are You Growing?	285
Your Sacred Body	286
Listening to your Body	290
Abundant Earth	292
Opening to Generosity	295
Embracing Death	297
The Tomb of Birth	300
Flowing and Spanning	303
Walking the Pentacles	306
Spell to Become Whole	307
You Are the Body of the Earth	308

PART EIGHT
POWERS ABOVE: RISING AND DREAMING

Calling Above	311
Loving the Face in the Mirror	313
Gazing at the Silver Mirror	315
Resting in the Arms of Love	317
The Guardian of Above	319
Tracking Your Night Dreams	321
Engaging Your Daydreams	322
Rising to Meet Your Desire	324
Seeing Beauty's Black Reflection	328
Balancing Image and Reality	330

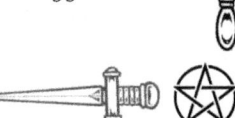

Spirit Journeying	332
Traversing the Blue Sphere	335
Further Astral Travel	337
Looking Up at the Sky	340
Moon Phases	342
Sun Phases	343
Reach	344

PART NINE
POWERS BELOW: LIGHTING THE DARKNESS

Calling Below	347
The Cauldron	350
Cooking Lies Into Gifts	352
Cooking Up Possibility	354
Leaping the Fire	355
The Guardian of Below	356
Engaging Your Fears	358
Naming Your Hidden Emotions	360
The Warrior Ethic	362
Not Coddling Weakness	364
The Stories We Tell	366
Facing the Rust and Gilded Pentacles	368
Reaching Out of Bounds	371
Automatic Writing	373
Rebalancing Passion	375
If Brittle, I Will Break	377
Stepping Forth	379

PART TEN
CENTER: OPENING THE GATES

Calling Spirit	383
Awakening Your Black Heart	385
The Emperor Has No Clothes	388
The Way to Your Black Heart	390
Guardian of the Center	393
Forgiveness as a Path to Power	395
The Rite of Unbinding	397

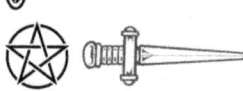

The Violet Pentacle	400
Honesty	402
Using Your Tools to Support Truth	404
Revitalizing Breath	406
Integration and Moving Forward	408
Circles to Love	410

PART ELEVEN
CLOSING THE SPHERE, OPENING THE WORLD

Calling Our Selves	415
Listening for Your Deep Name	418
Engaging Your Whole Self	420
Evolution and Community	421
Rite of Intention and Dedication	423
Remember, You Are Divine	425
Seeking a Third Path	428
Finding Your Work	430
Close the Sphere and Open the World	432
Appendix: Useful Books	437
And More	441
About the Author	443
Also by T. Thorn Coyle	445

FOREWORD BY MAT AURYN

Four billion years ago, a lone cell stirred in Earth's ancient waters, beginning the story of evolution that every living being still carries within. From the silent reach of redwoods toward the sky to the jeweled shimmer of a dragonfly's wings, this lineage has evolved into countless forms, from the smallest bacteria to the vast complexity of the human body. It moves through the unhurried grace of a sea turtle gliding through warm currents and the hidden glow of mycelial networks threading the forest floor, each a testament to life's rich diversity. The living pulse of that Last Universal Common Ancestor still beats in every cell, uniting all life on Earth through an unbroken chain of evolution. This pattern of transformation extends beyond Earth, for everything here and across the cosmos rose from the fires of ancient stars whose deaths scattered the elements of creation through space. The iron in our blood, the calcium in our bones, the oxygen in our breath, each was born in stellar hearts, flung across the void, and gathered by Earth to become the fabric of life.

In witchcraft, particularly the Feri tradition and those whose

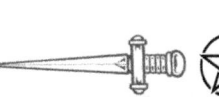

practices have been influenced by it, we speak of our souls arising from the Star Goddess and returning to her, yet our physical bodies also share that same star-born heritage. We are the living continuation of both cosmic and earthly evolution, connected to the stones beneath our feet, the rivers that flow, the forests that breathe, and every creature that moves. To recognize this is to understand that evolution is not only a biological process; it is the ongoing story of the universe becoming aware of itself through us. We are each a burning spark of stellar divinity, cells within the vast constellation of the Star Goddess's living body. Recognizing ourselves as both the children of Earth's long evolutionary story and the star-born kin of the universe invites us to live with intention and agency. It calls us to claim our magick as an expression of that ancient lineage, to shape our lives with the same creative force that shapes worlds.

When *Evolutionary Witchcraft* was released, it wasn't just evolutionary, it was revolutionary. Now counted among the great classic books on witchcraft, at the time of its release it stood apart in a way I had never encountered before. It was the first book I read that placed the empowerment of the self at the very center of the craft and dedicated itself entirely to that work. It wasn't a collection of candle spells or a series of abstract musings on self-development without application. It was filled with somatic practices, meditations, and breath work techniques designed to help you awaken and master your own energy. Every exercise was crafted to awaken the witch's body, mind, and spirit into an alive, charged state where personal power could be felt, cultivated, and directed with intention. It made the work of becoming a witch an embodied, daily practice, showing me that true magick starts in the self and moves outward in every act.

Almost all of my witchcraft teachers and mentors spoke of the

witch's sovereignty as the foundation of true magickal work, and *Evolutionary Witchcraft* embodied that principle completely in a way no other book had before. To the witch, sovereignty is the state of self-governance that unfolds through their inner evolution, built on self-knowledge, self-discipline, and the willingness to take full responsibility for one's choices, growth, and influence in the world. As awareness deepens and the self becomes more fully known, action flows from self-directed intention, and power is wielded with clarity. This kind of authority naturally expands into the wider world, where magick and everyday actions alike become tools for empowerment, confronting injustice, and nurturing collective liberation. In harmony with the Great Work, the lifelong union of personal will and divine will, sovereignty creates a rippling effect, each act of empowerment helping to lift the whole, like a rising tide lifting all boats. In this way, the witch's power serves both personal transformation and the awakening of others, radiating into the seen and unseen with purpose, integrity, and the intention to inspire lasting change.

For the last couple of years, I have had the privilege of getting to know Thorn as a friend. I can say without a shadow of a doubt that Thorn embodies all of these qualities with a level of authenticity, sincerity, and commitment that surpasses most magickal practitioners I have encountered. Beyond that, I have had the pleasure of sharing private ritual space with them, witnessing their psychic ability in action, and experiencing their energy work directly. There is a distinct inner strength, an undeniable inner power, and a deep sense of sovereignty that radiates from them, carrying the presence of someone who lives their magick fully and with purpose. At the same time, Thorn is equally grounded, humble, and most importantly, human. In other words, they carry the rare integration of wisdom, skill, and presence that marks a true adept.

FOREWORD BY MAT AURYN

Evolutionary Witchcraft is the first of several works they have written where Thorn opens the door to becoming that kind of practitioner yourself, not by imitating them, but by uncovering and embodying your own unique power. The teachings within guide you to cultivate the same depth of sovereignty, energetic mastery, and spiritual presence, while always shaping the path to fit your own nature. Thorn offers tools, practices, and frameworks that encourage you to stand in your individuality, awaken your own psychic senses, and channel your magick in a way that feels fully alive and undeniable. It is an invitation to walk with the same strength and integrity, yet to do so in the distinct way that only you can.

Thorn is also an equally committed writer, one of the most dedicated and skilled wordsmiths I have ever read. There is an inner poetry woven into their very soul, and it moves through every sentence they craft. Their words carry rhythm and weight, each one chosen with care to both instruct and inspire, offering clear guidance while also stirring the heart and awakening the spirit beyond purely logical understanding to reach your intuitive self. Whether guiding a reader through a meditation, describing a ritual, or reflecting on the mysteries of magick, Thorn's writing has a living quality that draws you in and holds you there. It is the voice of someone who writes as an act of devotion, shaping language into a vessel for power, beauty, and truth. In this sense, their writing itself often feels like an energetic transmission.

To you, the reader, I offer this foreword as both an introduction and an invitation, especially if this is your first time encountering this remarkable book. Step into these pages with openness, curiosity, and a willingness to be changed. If you commit to showing up for the magickal practices Thorn shares here, magick

will show up for you, meeting your effort with its own living current. The work in these chapters is alive. It is ready to meet you where you are and guide you toward the fullest expression of your magick. Take what speaks to your soul, work with it, and let it shape you into the witch only you can become. This is a journey of empowerment, connection, and transformation, and the current you are about to enter will carry you forward in the great unfolding of your own magickal evolution.

— Mat Auryn, 2025
Author of *Psychic Witch, Mastering Magick,* and *The Psychic Art of Tarot*

Holy Mother, in Whom we live, move, and have our being, from You all things emerge and unto You all things return....

Open our hearts this blessed day. Touch our bodies and our minds. Walk with us through the gates of power, in shadow and starlight, in fire meeting earth, in wind on the ocean and the sweet kiss of life.

Blessed be our journey.

—Victor Anderson and T. Thorn Coyle

PART ONE
EVOLUTIONARY WITCHCRAFT

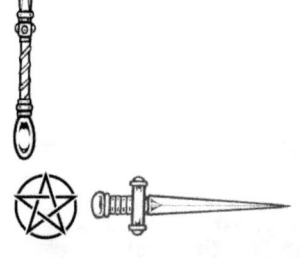

TO REWEAVE THE WORLD

All species can evolve and adapt, humanity included. The trouble is, we've adapted ourselves to far too many things that do not serve us or the planet. We've adapted to greed. We've adapted to harmful growth. We've adapted to technologies that have ended up training our brains and bodies instead of the other way around.

We are living lives out of balance.

Witchcraft, paganism, and animism are pathways that can lead us back toward wholeness, if we let them. Are they the only paths? Of course not. They are simply the paths that I have chosen and that have chosen me.

And before anyone questions whether I am an anti-technologist, I am not. I'm writing this on a computer tablet, typing on a portable keyboard. I'm a user of many technologies, both contemporary and old. What I'm noticing, however, are the ways some of these technologies are altering the human psyche and damaging the planet. I also notice the ways some of these technologies are directly responsible for human oppression.

What I'm questioning are all the ways in which we feel disconnected from each other, from the planet, and the stars.

In my continuous commitment to the ways of magic and the teachings of animism and paganism, I find ways to reconnect. And that is the root etymology of the word religion, isn't it? Religare: to bind or connect.

We are all bound together. We are bound to one another and to every being on this planet. We are bound to things we comprehend and things we cannot comprehend. We are bound to the worlds seen and unseen.

The rugged individualism so prized in the US in particular has led us down a road of disconnection. Witchcraft offers us one way to connect once again.

But what about the evolutionary part? Despite the alarming choices the dominant society has made in the twenty years since this book was first published, I still hold out hope that we can evolve for the better.

By plumbing the mysteries of our own hearts, minds, and souls, we can make better choices. By recognizing our interdependence, we can become better suited to our environment. We can dance with the sacred in the trees, mountains, and deserts, and on the ocean shore. We can remember the sacred in each city, village, and town.

We can call up the sacred together. And together, we can reweave the world.

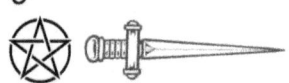

EVOLUTIONARY WITCHCRAFT TWENTY YEARS LATER

The book you hold in your hands today is both different and the same as the one I wrote more than twenty years ago. The world and I have both changed, but the core magic remains the same.

In preparing this revised edition, I went through a printed copy by hand, page by page. In doing so, I realized how much of myself I had written out of the book. So many exercises and thoughts came directly from my own experience, practice, and innovation. And yet, I ascribed them all to my teachers and my root traditions.

This was not wholly false. My root Craft traditions are ecstatic and poetic, changing according to the practitioner. However, with the distance of time and my own deepening magic, I now see the ways in which I could be more honest here, and say, "This came through me."

We all digest the work and bring it forth in varying ways. That is good, it keeps our traditions alive. Traditions can grow stale over time, otherwise. So, in this pass, there are things I have added, and things I have deleted. And there are ways in which I

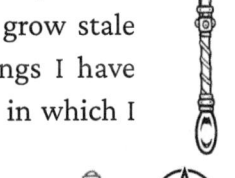

name what came through me, and what came through my teachers or the other traditions I have studied over the years.

My hope is that this makes the book both truer and more accessible.

I honor those who have come before me and also want to honor my own work. I hope that you do that for yourself, too.

May our magic deepen and expand. May we build a finer, more beautiful, more compassionately just world. Together.

THE ROOTS OF EVOLUTIONARY WITCHCRAFT

Since age sixteen, I've been privileged to have had many teachers of the Craft. One teacher, Victor Anderson of the Feri Tradition, once told me that the Craft came out of human suffering. My *own* suffering certainly brought me to Witchcraft, and seeking to find the sources of my strength has kept me here. In Witchcraft, I found my place in Nature, and in Nature, I found my connection to all things. I also found a way into my own soul and divinity, committing to my own unfolding and taking responsibility for my place in the cosmos.

Witchcraft is a significant path during these times when humans need to be responsible, to connect, to find the sacred amongst our lives *right now*, rather than waiting for a day of transcendence and redemption. In a time of global catastrophe, fascism, and environmental devastation, a religion that connects us to the earth is not only understandable, but necessary. As Victor said to me in our last conversation before his death, "It is time for people to wake up. You don't play with the fires of creation and get away with it." Embedded in many Craft traditions are the tools of our awakening.

Modern Witchcraft (known popularly as Wicca) was unearthed, recreated, or founded—depending upon your opinion—in England in the 1940s by Gerald Gardner. Gardner was heir to the Golden Dawn, the Ordo Templi Orientis, British folk societies, naturist groups and, to the best of our knowledge, some actual Witches. Striving to connect the individual to the cycles of nature, Witchcraft as passed on by Gardner and his liturgist, Doreen Valiente, stressed seasonal ritual and a celebration of the Gods of growth and sexuality, rather than the Gods of science and industry, and fostered a kinship with natural forces, rather than attempting to control them.

American spiritual practices weaving folk magic, root doctoring, and Witchcraft were already in existence at the time that Gardner made his work public in the 1950s. And as British historian Ronald Hutton writes, Feri Tradition is "one of the homegrown American strains of pagan witchcraft..."

Founded more than seventy-five years ago by Victor and Cora Anderson, Feri Tradition—though now marked by some influences from British Traditional Wicca—has its roots in the Americas. Victor was a member of the Harpy Coven in Oregon in the 1930s, having first been trained in magic as a child in New Mexico. Cora's training was in Ozark folk and root magic, inherited from her grandfather and strengthened by her own psychic skills, connection to the Faery folk, and her innate house-magic ingenuity.

My Craft is heavily rooted in Feri, though over the years has woven with many other spiritual sources and magical traditions. As I have grown and changed, so has my relationship to the Craft itself.

Like Wicca, the Craft I practice finds connections to the Gods and Nature, but its emphasis is placed firmly on the alignment of the soul of the individual practitioner, and the growth of their power over time, rather than on seasonal celebration.

I honor the sacred elements and recognize the immanent Divine that dwells in the earth, stars, plants, and in our humanity, if only we can learn to recognize it.

My beloved teacher Cora Anderson, when asked, simply said she practiced "the Craft." Someone once asked her what the Craft was. To paraphrase because my memory may not be exact, she replied, "We believe in the earth, the stars, and the grass, and in being sensible."

The Craft is what Victor called a "religion of the human race," and, at its best, echoes the diversity inherent in that statement. Our creativity echoes the creativity of the cosmos itself.

Feri Tradition myth tells us the story of the Star Goddess—whom Victor called God Herself—catching Her reflection in the curved, black mirror of space. Responding to the beauty of this image, She/He/They began to make love to Themself. From God Herself's joy, the Gods were born, and from the joy of the Gods, the worlds were born. The work in this book can help us to catch sight of ourselves, to fall in love and spiral out into our true lives, shimmering with starlight and grounded on the sacred earth. We walk into our souls and are changed.

In the Craft I practice, humans are not subservient to the Gods. Our authority is internal, and gained over time, not bestowed on us from without. No teacher has greater access to magic than any student. What matters is integrity and openness, not title or entitlement.

Unlike some traditions, the Craft I practice also has a queer nature. There is a sense of walking the edges and in-between spaces, of flowing between all genders and holding all possibilities within oneself—one can be human and Fey, male and female or both and neither, fragile soul and divine essence, all at the same time. In looking upon our multiplicity, we find wholeness.

These concepts dovetailed into Reclaiming, an offshoot tradition of Feri. Founded in the late 1970s and early 1980s by a group

of dedicated activists, including Pagan writer Starhawk, it has been a highly public tradition, doing large, open rituals, teaching, and engaging in civil disobedience as a spiritual act. Reclaiming took the joy and beauty of Feri, and the emphasis on internal authority and co-creation, and wed these with anarcho-feminist politics. The tradition still strives to marry social justice, environmental activism, and the shared power of magic, or as its mandate says: "to join spirit and politics."

My work, Evolutionary Witchcraft, springs from both vital traditions, with many other spiritual strands woven into the tapestry of my teaching: Sufism, the Gurdjieff work, Zen Buddhism, and ceremonial magic.

I began to study the Craft at age sixteen, the year I left the Catholic Church. This was the year of my first consciously political act of spray-painting "Reagan Hates Me" on the window of Republican headquarters in my small Southern California town of Whittier during his first term. I also embellished a large portrait of said president with alien antennae. The paint proved so tenacious, the poster was taken down until the glass could be properly cleaned.

What had originated as a peaceful Quaker enclave had become known as the birthplace of Nixon, and I was smack in the middle, between Los Angeles and Orange County, wishing to be free. I moved to San Francisco as soon as I could, and met my first Feri teacher there, at age eighteen, while desperately searching for *something* in a musty old occult shop on Divisadero St. I studied with this student of Victor's for a year, wandered awhile on my own, and then dove into Reclaiming, a natural choice for my magical political soul. The earth was alive, magic flowed through all things, and I had to act from this knowledge. I became activist, priest, and eventually, teacher.

This satisfied me for quite a while. But eventually, revolution put me on a quest toward evolution.

I studied with the Mevlevi Sufis for three years, still doing ritual and teaching, as I whirled, sweated, and prayed in this holy order founded by the mystic poet Jalalludin Rumi. I made peace with my Catholic childhood by observing Lent along the way and living in voluntary poverty with a spiritually eclectic Catholic Worker house that ran a soup kitchen. I studied Christianity, Judaism, and Islam, particularly the mystical branches. My experience of the Gods and my identity as a Witch were present amid all of this as I searched for a firmer foundation to support my soul's work. I was struggling to grow into true responsibility, to be able to *respond* rather than just doing things out of duty.

While whirling with the dervishes and serving up soup with the Catholic Workers, I began to study directly with Victor Anderson, taking notes during hour-long phone conversations or as he worked his hypnotic rocking chair in his small San Leandro living room as Cora fixed me with her penetrating gaze. Later, as Cora was convalescing from a stroke, I visited Victor weekly, to fix him lunch, study, and work magic. My pen and notebook fell away, and the magic washed through me in a rush.

Physically, Victor was mostly blind, but with brilliant insight, and he opened my spirit to the power of the Craft and its tools. He was powerful, funny, and wise, and was also cranky. Still looking, I joined a group that followed the teachings of the mystic philosopher G.I. Gurdjieff, already influenced by "the Work," as his system is called, through years of reading. I learned much of value in my years of immersion there, including learning that once again, I had to leave, though "the Work" continues to influence me.

Amid these searching years, in February of 1996, I received initiation into Feri Tradition itself, passed the power by the Feri initiates in my coven at the time. Feri was tenacious, working in me even as I searched beyond it. Victor and Cora's legacy was holding me.

After my seeking and striving, I had fallen back upon myself, having found "perfection" nowhere. I hadn't yet realized that perfection is wholeness, not the eradication of perceived flaw, but I *did* listen to the line in Doreen Valiente's *Charge of the Goddess* that said: "If that which you seek, you find not within yourself, you will never find it without." I took a big breath and began to deepen into the practices I already had.

What I had gathered from my meandering course was all rooted in the Craft. As a Muslim friend of mine told me, I needed to dig one deep well, not twenty shallow ones. Only then was there a possibility of finding clean water.

I began to study with Victor a second time and later studied with Cora after his death. I took all the techniques of awareness and practice I learned with the Sufi dervishes and from Gurdjieff's teachings, and the compassion from the radical Catholics, and applied them to what I had learned in my years in the Craft.

My work took on a depth and resonance it had never attained before. These changes appeared both in my teaching and practice, both of which I developed over time, always starting with my own soul. I was connecting to spirit, building a foundation, and my teacher was within. My teacher was daily practice and self-examination. My teacher was in my encounters with other humans: on the bus, at work, at home. My teacher rapidly became all my magical tools, applied with diligence. I was taught by other witches. I was taught by music and movement, fire and ocean, and the deep, abiding nature of my breath.

WHAT IS EVOLUTIONARY WITCHCRAFT?

I say that I practice Evolutionary Witchcraft, or Witchcraft as a path toward expanded humanity and divinity. But what does it mean to be a Witch? What does the word mean to people in the beginning of the twenty-first century? Contemporary Witchcraft owes much to ancient polytheism, medieval alchemy, Freemasonry, and an Enlightenment Age skepticism of heavily organized, dogmatic creeds. Yet, unlike many inheritors of the Enlightenment, Witches and other Pagans insist on the sanctity of the earth in the face of mechanization. Witches use magic to pray, to shift consciousness, and to connect with the earth.

What is magic? Magic is the art of evolution. It uses intention, breath, will, and ritual to transform both the individual and her relationship with the world. Magic shifts the balance of power between the worlds seen and unseen, and can affect change individually, socially, and politically.

If I believe in magic, why am I not a Magician? A Witch begins with intuition and the Magician with intellect, so though both practice the art and science of magic, the Witch relies more

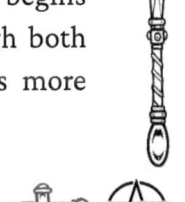

heavily upon the art, and the Magician upon the science. I believe that the Witch could use a little more science and the discipline that goes with it and the Magician a little more art and spontaneity. My practice tries to bring the Witch and the Magician a bit closer together.

Though many Craft traditions are initiatory—including Feri—I have a strong belief that any individual who is willing to do the work of facing themself may make good use of Craft practices and teachings and use them to transform their lives. This is why I asked Cora Anderson for her blessing on this book more than twenty years ago, before publication of the first edition. If one is a serious spiritual seeker, one can apply the practices held in these pages at your office job, in your apartment, in the woods, on the beach, alone, or with others. The work is dangerous, for it transforms.

We can use our work on self as a way to grow more firmly into our own humanity and divinity. If we do this, we will treat each other and the earth better and enter into the right relationship with all beings, seen and unseen. We will evolve. We will become of greater service to each other and this planet, forging stronger, more resilient communities. Together.

The Oracle of Delphi enjoined each seeker to "Know thyself." Some teachers transmit theory or lore, while I transmit practice, because practice changes my molecules and helps my relationships and work.

I am confident that ways will be found to spread evolutionary spirituality and to help us through these times that are desperate for vision, practice, and true change. I hope that those who are deeply interested in this work will seek out further teaching. This book is an entry into your deeper self: may your senses open, your hearts fill, your spines straighten, and your work take on luster and joy.

I offer this book as a tool to those who want more than the basics, to those who are looking for deeper training and those who don't want just another book of spells.

Cast yourself. *You* are the spell.

PART TWO
CASTING THE SACRED SPHERE

OPENING THE TEACHINGS

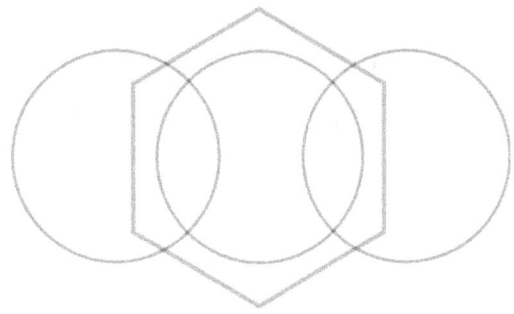

"Do not become that which you resist."
—Victor Anderson
"The master's tools will never dismantle the master's house."
—Audre Lorde

THE AUDRE LORD quote above is graffito in the Kopi Café in Chicago. Her words remind me to ask what I am teaching in this city far from home, and why I am writing this book. I am teaching

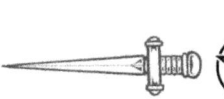

and writing because the tools I've been given continue to change my life. These are not tools of dominance that oppress or enslave, instead, these are tools of liberation. If we all achieve mastery, none will be master over another.

These are tools to slay demons and release your heart. They are tools of revolution and, more importantly to me, tools of evolution. My work is to challenge myself to become more human: to struggle against dehumanizing beliefs and inhumane practices. I want to cease being at war and instead become a peaceful warrior, an activist of heart and body.

The question becomes, how can we not merely survive, but thrive? The tools in this book are part of the answer. These, along with compassion and courage, may just save us. At least, that is my prayer. I also believe these tools can do even more—they can help us to awaken our divine natures. To use these tools well, we need preparation, and that is what we will do in this section—take the steps necessary to prepare for the work of unfolding our souls.

USING THE TOOLS

"*Anything worthwhile is dangerous.*"
—Victor Anderson

THE TOOLS and concepts in this book are our birthrights, yet have often been twisted beyond recognition in our culture. Reclaiming them is both difficult and dangerous because using them goes against cultural precepts and because these tools can change us in significant ways. In turn, this changes all our relationships, how we work, our ethical systems, how we treat ourselves and others, and how we let others treat us.

Changing cultural precepts is a revolutionary undertaking, and the most powerful place to start a revolution is within ourselves. Wiccan author Doreen Valiente said, "Evolution, like charity, begins at home." External activity cannot be divorced from what is happening inside of me and inner work must be balanced by concern for the world outside.

The concepts in this book are potent and can cause earth-

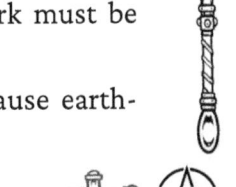

quakes both inside and out. They uncover taboos and buried fears, opening up energies that cannot easily be shoved back into a jar. The tools give us greater access to life force, to pure power.

Power is a good thing, but once this energy is raised, if we ignore the tools that raised it, the energies can twist back upon us, or we can blast others with untrained energy. Fallen into disuse, these techniques can create people who no longer have the disciplined control that is needed to wield their power well. This can cause great difficulties in covens and larger communities, leading to the spread of malicious gossip, high-handedness, or grandiosity. Malice is *not* inevitable if we learn to do our work, fully engaged, and to treat each other with respect. To do this, we must engage in occult activity. Occult study plumbs that which is mysterious and secret. We can apply this definition to the process of looking at our hidden selves.

FACING THE MIRROR

When you begin to engage these tools, please make a concerted effort to be kind to yourself and those around you. When you start running magical energy, it might feel slightly uncomfortable *because* it is so powerful. Magical energy is the energy of pure life force, which can feel overwhelming until we become skilled at handling it. We typically create physical and emotional blockages to keep our life force in check and to keep it from running freely and fully through us. You can listen to your posture and the tensions in your body that twist or strangle the energy and gently begin to loosen that which binds you.

Running life force in a new way may cause you to be irritable with those close to you, or may make you wish to blurt out things that you would otherwise keep silent. Honesty is a good thing but needn't burn everything in its wake. Also, the changes you feel within may make you uncomfortable around those closest to you. You may feel as though you don't want these changes exposed to those who know you best. Be patient with yourself and others. Big changes are coming, but that doesn't always mean the breakup of

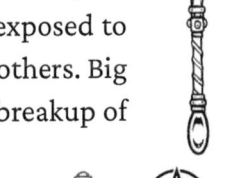

old relationships. In fact, these tools can open us to greater intimacy and trust. The more you learn about yourself and the pathways of these powers, the more likely it is that relationships founded upon falsehood or addiction will begin to fall apart. Conversely, relationships based on respect and trust can strengthen in proportion to your own strengthening.

Below is a helpful exercise that addresses the above concerns:

Every time someone is irritating you, every time you want to say something harsh to someone, whether it is because the energies feel uncomfortable, or you just know you are right, look in the mirror first. Say everything you want to say to the other person into the mirror. You might be surprised at the look on your face, or your posture. What is running through you when you say those words?

Sometimes you need to really say these things to yourself, or sometimes speaking the words is enough to diffuse the energy. If you still feel the need to speak to the other person, this mirror exercise can enable you to speak more clearly and with greater kindness. Before speaking, connect with the earth. Breathe. Practice.

Loving Your Humanity

In contemporary society, we often feel cut off from our humanity. We disconnect from our deeper natures, our animal instincts, and pollute our environment beyond recognition. When we attempt to live only in our heads, our bodies suffer, our emotions become stunted and our other senses retreat from the assault of physical toxins developed by an intellectual ingenuity divorced from that body. We become less and less human, and more and more like machines.

I once asked Victor what the Fey wanted from me, and he replied: "For you to become more yourself. To become more human." These tools help us to engage in the world, to act, and to become more human. In working through this book, we will learn to access and balance greater power, recovering our humanity, making us strong and compassionate. As humans, we can live a political and magical life, no longer divorced from each other, the Divine and the earth. We can cultivate relationships with the realms seen and unseen. Each succeeding section will show us how.

It is my hope that this book will enable you to become familiar

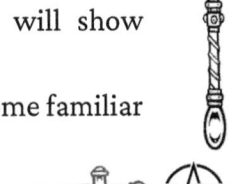

with these concepts, tools, and energies, and begin to work with them in ways that will become sustainable, and that will change your life, your cellular structure, and the way you carry your power. I hope you have a desire to enter your life and emotions fully, and to expand your interaction with the world around you and with the Gods, nature spirits, and the Fey.

SELF LOVE CLEANSING

As you use these tools, old wounds may open up—fear, anger, or shame. You may feel pain in your belly or heart, tightness in your throat. The mirror exercise was to enable you to deal more kindly with others, and this being a lifetime process you may need to look in that mirror many times. As we excavate the layers of our personal archaeology, we need to care for ourselves, too, again and again.

Take a shower, letting all that is bothering you run down the drain. Using your favorite soap, epsom or bath salts, scrub off everything that is bothering you, be it people, events, or feelings. Name them and watch them go down the drain. Then, run your hands over yourself while saying, "Gods and Goddesses, hold witness, I am complete unto myself." Rinse yourself thoroughly, then, turn off the water and stand, breathing, cleansed.

As you begin to breathe more deeply, let your aura begin to pulsate with light, becoming pure, blinding brightness to clean out any last irritants lurking in the crevices. You can then begin to chant your name, over and over, until your aura is full of the sound of your voice, running through your body. Tingle with it. You are full. You are whole.

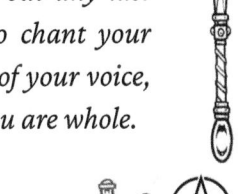

PREPARING TO CAST THE SPHERE

The Self Love cleansing can also be used before for ritual work. Cleansing prepares us for work by releasing thoughts, energies, or emotions that might keep us from being present in this moment, right now. There are many ways to cleanse, through breath work, looking at one's habits, and through the salt-water purification below, which is common to many branches of the Craft.

Fill a bowl with clear water. Say, "Blessed be, creature of water." Breathe across the surface, watching your breath make ripples, connecting you to this element. Pour a small amount of salt into your hand. Breathe across it, saying, "Blessed be, creature of salt." Pour this into the bowl of water, stirring and stirring, counterclockwise, the way of banishing energy, and say, "May I be cleansed." Now breathe out all that keeps you from your work. Or speak it into the bowl, shake it off your body, dance it, cough it out, whatever feels needed.

Once you feel clear enough to do your work, begin to stir the water clockwise, the direction of invocation. "Inner and outer, may all be transformed." Breathe across the water again, and anoint yourself with

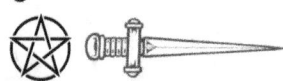

some. Pour the rest out to cleanse the sidewalk in front of your home, or pour it into a sink to clean your drains.

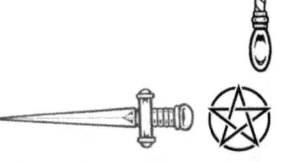

BECOMING PRESENT AND EMBODIED

Once cleansed, there is another important step to becoming more present. This is grounding and centering, a technique to bring us fully into our bodies, calm our minds, and open our hearts to the work at hand. Grounding and centering connect us to the earth beneath our feet and helps us to remember that the center of the earth is always directly below us. This technique also helps us stay embodied, no matter what it is we are doing, and is good preparation for ritual and for life.

I have practiced this technique for so many years that it is now second nature, entering the realm of instinct: my body and energy are trained so well that I no longer have to think about centering. This works to great effect in calming me and making me a more effective and stable person. I use the following when I need to do a nonviolent intervention, really listen to someone, or just walk through a stressful day as well balanced as possible. Over time, this practice has also expanded my ability to be more compassionate toward myself and others.

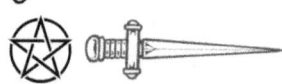

There are many ways to ground and center. One is to imagine a cord of energy moving from the base of your spine and dropping to touch the center of the earth. The following is my own technique, which centers me in my body, and lets my energy expand up and down, connecting me to earth and sky.

Feel your feet beneath you. Take a breath. Feel the soles of your feet open up, stretching to stand more firmly. Feel yourself stable on the earth. Feel your center of gravity resting between your navel and your pelvis. Remember that you are connected to both earth and sky. Take in one full inhalation, feeling first your belly and lower back muscles expand. Then let the breath flow up to expand your ribs. Take another breath, imagining that breath filling you from the soles of your feet to the crown of your head. Breathe in again. As you exhale, breathe simultaneously down and up, "pushing" the breath and energy through your feet and the crown of your head, about one foot above and below your physical body. As you do so, let your spine lengthen and straighten, your chest lift, and your head align with your spine. This can occur in one instance. On your next breath, feel the energy and breath expand out around you, filling your aura, the egg of energy that surrounds you. You are fully in your physical body and your energy body. You are ready to do whatever work is needed.

Students sometimes told me that they had no time for a daily practice, that they had small children who demanded all of their attention and free time, or that they worked full-time and went to school. But when I asked, "Do you take a shower every day?" they most often said, "Yes," so I recommend that they ground in the shower. It doesn't have to take much time, and generally the five or ten minutes you are standing under the water is time when no one will bother you. Once you are used to grounding, you can do it quickly throughout the day.

Busy people who start doing daily practices often find they are able to carve more time out of their day to do spiritual work

because it makes such a big difference in their energy level, their effectiveness, and their presence to self and others throughout their days. It certainly has that effect on me. Even people with small toddlers now tell me how helpful they find daily practice. They have found ways to make practice work, and in turn, it works in their lives.

CREATING KEYS FOR REMEMBRANCE

There are other practices you can do throughout the day to remind yourself to ground, center, and bring yourself fully into the moment at hand. My favorite, inspired by some practices in the Gurdjieff work, is to create "keys" for myself.

These keys are attention tricks that remind me of my spiritual life and my reasons for attempting to work on my self. My most effective key is to pause and really *notice* every time I am about to put my hand on a doorknob. I will take a breath, look at the knob, feel my body, and let a calm space open up inside as I reach for and turn the knob. This can be done in about five seconds. Another key I use is to notice my butt and thighs in the chair as I am sitting at my computer. This reminds me to stay in my body, anchored to my breath, and not let my mind spin off in disconnected fantasies that eat my energy.

You can key your reminders to turning on lights, or opening the refrigerator, or drinking a glass of water. A key should be something simple, yet something you do often enough that it will serve you well as a reminding factor. You are connected. You are not just living in a world created inside your head, but in a breath-

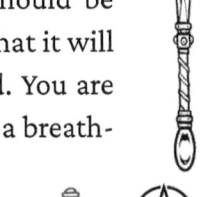

ing, living, functioning multiverse. This exercise is not only a way to remind yourself of your spiritual practice, but a way to notice that you have a place in the larger world. What is your function?

Take one day to try working with the key below. As you do so, you may want to note other keys that might be better attuned to your life. In that case, pick one of those to work with instead.

You are approaching the door to your home. Notice the doorknob. Stand in front of it and take a breath, feeling the air enter your body. Reach out. Touch the knob. Feel it beneath your fingers. Feel your connection. Open the door and walk through.

The above exercise probably took from between one and ten seconds, yet it brought you back to your life. I consider that time well spent.

Students often struggle with this exercise, telling me that they can't do it, that they keep forgetting their key, or that they remember it only long after moment has passed. I tell them that this response is fine and that it provides information about how little we are generally present in our lives. Using keys to remembrance shows us that most of the time we are not conscious at all. We live in a dream state, unconnected to the earth and to life around us, fed only by the fantasies we spin. If you keep working with keys over time, you will better come to understand your states and what drives your thoughts and emotions. It is all information, and information can only help you.

STEPPING TOWARD THE BLUE FIRE

Now that we are fully present, we can enter the next phase of our work, the casting of the sacred sphere. This is a much larger and more holistic activity than simply delimiting a space for ritual. The circle or sphere represents our ability to transform the ordinary into the extraordinary. Casting distills into one moment what we do every time we notice the world—by really paying attention—causing it to become alive and sacred in our eyes.

We will cast the sacred sphere by drawing energy into ourselves and creating a space where the non-ordinary can enter. This creates a virtual temple—joining realms seen with realms unseen—and it prepares us to enter life itself as a sacred process. We integrate magic with life by stepping through the blue flame and into the work of magic.

Magical practices seek the heart, the heat, the core. They raise questions: What is the center of your life? What is the core of your work, your relationships, your spiritual life, and your activism? As our practice raises these questions, the tools can also help us to answer them. At the heart of our magic is the blue fire, which is

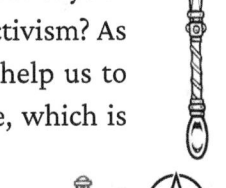

the center of the flame, the base of all the other colors, yellow, orange, and red. It is the space where the fuel meets the fire, creating something in between.

You can gaze at any candle and see the blue fire that kisses the wick. We take this image and use it to shape energy, create portals, and bend time. Magical spaces are liminal, in-between spaces or spaces that skirt the edges. A flip of perspective moves the edge into the center, creating a new sense of the world and opening our awareness to the possibilities that were hidden beyond that edge.

This is the beginning of paradox: the unusual lies in the heart of the ordinary.

You can practice this conciousness by noticing something that hovers on the edge of your vision and turning your head until that thing is in the center. How does this change your view? What would happen if you trained your attention on something you've been keeping at the edges of your life? What might you see then?

The blue flame is the basis for red and yellow. The "cold" blue color dancing in the center is actually the hottest point of the flame, another paradox. The paradox of the blue flame becomes a metaphor for a life of creativity and magical awareness, a fey life. The following exercises will begin to ease you into the magical view of the world.

Meditation on the Blue Flame

This exercise helps to strengthen your attention. This cultivates discipline, commitment and spiritual stamina, which are essential to further work. Spirituality is not just about having a flash of insight or epiphany; it is about building a foundation that will change you inside and out.

Light a candle for your focus, settle yourself comfortably, and begin to notice your breath, rising and falling within you.

Sit in front of a candle and take a deep breath. Focus on the flame, gazing into its colors. Notice that at the heart of the flame—the hottest point, the center, the eye—the flame burns blue. The blue flame is the fire of other worlds, the hottest, most transformational point of fire. It is with this blue flame that we will cast the sphere of working, entering into non-ordinary consciousness, what some Witches call being "between the worlds." Let the flame fill your whole vision. It is all that you see.

When you are done, fill with breath from the soles of your feet to the crown of your head. Thank the blue flame and snuff the candle.

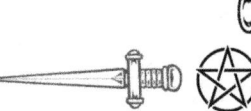

CASTING INTO THE EXTRAORDINARY

Witches often call their castings a creation of sacred space. In a religion where the holy is in everything, what does this mean? To make sacred is to set aside as special. For me, creating sacred space is an attempt to set aside my ordinary, habitual behavior and thought-forms and prepare to enter the extraordinary, more fully myself and more firmly engaged with my own Will.

Casting a sphere is a delimiting of space, another way to help us draw our energy and attention together. By the end of the book, we will open the sphere to include the whole world, but for now, we begin with this exercise by building sacred space one small room at a time. For this you will need a blade, or you can use two fingers of your dominant arm to create a blade-like form. Witches use a knife called an *athame* for this exercise because blades are good at cutting and separating out one thing from another.

You can use the blue fire to cast your sphere for magical workings. The physical flame we gazed at in the previous exercise can now join with a metaphysical flame. This helps us to shift the

actual energy that always runs through our bodies into energy that is charged with the power of the blue Feri fire, the power to shift the edge to center, changing space and time.

Take your time acclimating to this exercise. Sometimes, even students who have trouble "sensing" or "seeing" energy will report that their dominant arm is warm after running the blue flame energy through themselves. I was taught this circle invocation in the Feri and Reclaiming traditions. It was written by Victor Anderson. You may use his words, or come up with your own. I wrote the cantrip at the end.

Take a breath. Draw energy into your body on your breath and up through the soles of your feet. Imagine red, iron earth energy with a flickering of blue at its heart. Imagine that you can breathe into that blue fire, filling it with your own life's force. Let the blue flame run down your dominant arm, into the hand holding the knife you will use to cast our sacred sphere.

Feel the blue fire as it flows easily from your hand into your knife. Face magnetic North, and begin tracing the pentacle of invocation.

Say, "By the earth that is Her fertile body." Move to the East, imagining a trail of blue fire. Drawing an invoking pentacle, say, "By the air that is Her vital breath." Blue fire flowing in a clockwise circle, turn South and draw the pentacle. "By the fire of Her quickening spirit." Moving, feeling the blue fire constantly replenished by your connection to the earth, turn West. "By the living waters of Her teeming womb." And the circle continues, moving back to North, streaming blue fire. The blue fire becomes more and more misty, ethereal. Cast it up above yourself, drawing the pentacle, and saying, "By all the powers above." Cast it across and down, drawing the pentacle, saying, "By all the powers below" Draw the blue flame back up again, sealing the sacred sphere, a glowing, misty bubble of blue fire and light. "And by the Center, which is the circumference of all." The sphere is cast.

You may strengthen the seal by reciting the words below, written by me:

On hallowed earth I walk
With blade of will
In presence of the Gods
Chaos and still.
Blue shining flame of beauty
Marks the sphere.
None cross it but the reverent,
Sacred here.
Into this magic portal
None shall see,
But those who bear the keys
To Mystery.
By breath and blood and bone,
So may it be!

Those of you familiar with magic or Witchcraft may notice that what we have done is cast a sphere, rather than the circle traditional to many branches of the Craft. Rather than just "calling the four quarters," Feri and Reclaiming traditions also call the powers above, below, and center. We will journey to all these places in the course of this book.

We do not live in a flat world. The sacred is not only in front and behind or on either side of me. The sacred exists far above me and below me as well as within. The realms of magic are vast, not limited by the horizon of a circle. Take a risk and extend your perceptions of what can be.

CASTING FROM THE INSIDE OUT

The exercise above was a way to cast the sphere by using energy to create a form outside of ourselves. Here is another way of casting that I developed for myself and my students. It is quick and grows from the inside, from your own physical center. It requires no blade, no words, nor any other accoutrements and, like grounding and centering, can be done anytime, anywhere. You can create your own sphere when you feel afraid or in need of extra protection. I use it when I need a quick sphere and don't have the time or desire to do the more formal casting.

Take a deep breath. Ground and center yourself. Imagine a sphere of blue flame as a tight ball in your belly. As you breathe, feel it expand, growing within you. Keep breathing until it snaps into your aura, a sphere extending out about one foot all around you. There is nothing inside this sphere but you. Breathe again, using your breath to "charge" this sphere with more energy. Feel it thicken and grow in density. You can push this sphere out until it is as large as you need it to be, encompassing a whole room, a city, or the earth.

When you no longer feel a need for this sphere, bring your body and

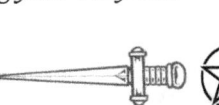

attention to stillness. Stand and breathe within your own sphere of blue fire. Place one hand on your heart and one on your belly. Bless yourself, saying, "I am sacred." Allow the sphere around you to shrink to where it is comfortable for you. You may feel the need to keep it matched with your aura for a while. Then you can let it shrink down to the small ball it began as. See it glow for a moment in your belly and then let it "pop," allowing the energy to dissipate. Take a deep breath. Open your eyes. Say your name three times.

The shift of consciousness you were just asked to make is a doorway to your own expansion. It shows that you have the ability to create and hold energy and to push your edges outward.

Casting the sacred sphere opens us to possibility, to magic, to a world that looks somehow different than we may have expected. By entering the sacred sphere, I am making a commitment to my spiritual path. I am committing to this new world, committing to possibility and to my own freedom and to the freedom of others.

DEVELOPING PRACTICE, COMMITTING TO CRAFT

"*Experience shows us that much is possible, even sometimes the impossible, but the work of craft is too hard for casual interest. Better stay away and have an easier life.*"
—Robert Fripp

WITCHCRAFT IS A CRAFT FOR A REASON. It is not a religion of beliefs, but an art and science. The continued unfolding of the magical world inside and outside of you requires relationship with that world. Anyone who has been in a relationship knows that it requires work, honesty, passion, and patience. As you grow spiritually, your strength, facility, and understanding will grow too, and your relationship with the sacred world will deepen. All of this is based in continual practice.

Making a commitment to practice is making a commitment to my spiritual life, my well-being, and myself. These practices have helped me immeasurably. When I was a teen, I had constant loops of abuse from my childhood running through my head on repeat. Some of the tools in this book were instrumental in freeing me

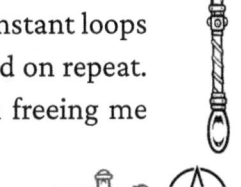

from those loops. The power those old voices had over me was broken as I discovered the power within myself.

A commitment to daily practice gives us the flexibility and strength we need in order to evolve. I'll let you in on an occult secret now: everyone struggles to work. There may always be a fight within you to maintain a regular spiritual practice, especially when it may not feel very good. Work can be hard, and it can also be very fulfilling. Most of us feel a desire to work and a sometimes equal desire to lie back down and ignore what is most helpful to us. The push and pull between these two causes the friction that we need for our growth.

One cannot turn lead into gold without the lead itself, a container for the process, and some heat. You are the lead, inert. Your spiritual practice, your work, is the container.

Gurdjieff talked about working with the Affirming, Denying, and Reconciling forces. These are the places in life where our "yes" bumps into our "no." Sometimes, we must sit with both, until a third, harmonizing or reconciling force arises. And other times? We must choose.

The heat created by the "yes" bumping against the "no" is the source of alchemical change. For example, the "yes" of getting up at 5:30 a.m. to do energy work, prayers, and sitting meditation bumps quickly up against the "no" of wanting to stay in bed and sleep until 8:00. When I get up, something new has the opportunity to awaken.

As you work through this book, I recommend that you choose one exercise to form the basis of your daily practice for one month's time. You can rotate through the exercises, gaining familiarity with each in time. You will eventually find a mixture of practices that work best for you and serve your spiritual life well.

Now, several decades after beginning the deep dive into spiritual practice, I change my daily practice about every six months. This keeps me from getting bored and keeps my practice from

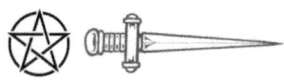

becoming mindless. However, there are two practices that I do without fail, every day, regardless of how my practice changes. These are aligning my soul and sitting in silence. These form a foundation for all of my other work on self.

After studying the Craft for more than forty years I can still observe how these practices change me, and how important it is that I continue to use them. In the first twenty years of practice, when I went through phases where my practice of the tools slackened, I felt less alive and been more susceptible to the influence of advertising, insecurity, and fear. The more I worked these practices, the stronger I become, and the clearer my purpose and intent grows. This in turn makes re-committing easier and easier. These days, the tools are well integrated into my life, but steady practice still increases my equilibrium and keeps me connected to the life that I desire.

Commitment also helps us to grow into responsibility. Accepting responsibility can be hard, because it denies us the option to be small. It is saying: "Yes, I have power," in a world where it might be easier to abdicate power. That "yes" is strong magic. Acceptance says, "There is room in the world for us all. We can shine."

ENGAGING THE SACRED BODY

"*People either feel they can fly or fear they will stumble. Rarely do we sense our ability to walk firm on earth.*"
—Jean Toomer

A COMMITMENT to Craft includes a commitment to embodiment. Witchcraft and Pagan paths do not teach us to transcend the body. Our bodies are sacred, they are our tools, they must be cared for and kept in good working order. In popular culture, the word Pagan is often synonymous with debauchery. Nonsense. While Witches enjoy our bodies and the physical things of life—good food, dancing, consensual sex, beauty—going too far into gluttony or greed does not help us. Rather, physical excess can actually deny the needs of our bodies and senses, leading to a frenzy of emotions or addictions. Try to listen to what really helps your body by way of food and drink, rest, enjoyment, and exercise.

One way to fully enter your body is through your posture. As skeleton and muscles are foundational, I like to begin magical

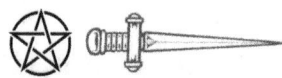

work with an awareness of what they are doing and how I can better work with them.

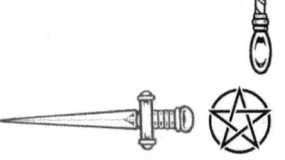

LEARNING TO LIVE TALL

Cultivating an aligned, proper posture helps all of our work. It enables us to begin to breathe naturally and with less tension, and lets our physical and psychic energies run freely, unimpeded by trapped emotions and the actual physical blocks of sternum collapsed on belly or our heads tipping forward and down, crimping the link to our spinal cords.

It takes time to develop good posture. One tendency is to resort to stiff, "military bearing." This is not proper posture either. Good posture means that your shoulders hang comfortably as if on a coat hanger, your knees are loose, and your skull is aligned to rest on top of your spinal column.

Studying dance, martial arts, weightlifting, yoga, or Pilates can help with this practice, and in turn, help all of your inner and magical workings. Fully accessed life force is strong. The more you open up clear channels in your body, the less the energy will become distorted within you. Energy follows breath. If I am able to breathe fully and without impediment, blood flows better, energy flows better, my brain and body function more fully and my emotions become clearer.

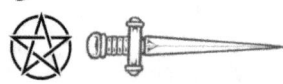

Not all witches practice this. It was my study of dance, weightlifting, and my years studying with the whirling dervishes and the Gurdjieff work that convinced me of this. Posture helps my presence. And my presence helps my practice.

That said, we all have different bodies, with different strengths and abilities. Figure out what posture work means for your life. A person with scoliosis, for example, needs different postural support than someone who doesn't. And a wheelchair user might need different support than someone who uses a cane.

The key is to tune into our bodies, and find the ways that energy flows or feels constricted. Where are your muscles and bones supporting you and being supported?

What physical changes might offer greater alignment to energy, breath, and your life?

FOLLOWING THE ENERGY FLOW

This exercise positions you firmly in your sacred body, and will help you to begin noticing your body, your posture, and your breath, and how energy flow connects to these.

Any of the exercises in this book can be altered to suit your physical needs. Don't injure yourself, but remember that if you have had poor posture for many years, proper posture might hurt a bit at first, until the muscles reacclimate, stretching and strengthening in ways that aid rather than impede breath and energy flow. If you have the means, a body worker might help you work through some tension spots.

For this exercise all you need is a straight chair, or a tall cushion, or simply yourself, standing.

Sit in a chair where you can straighten your spine, or stand with your feet slightly spread. Begin to notice your skeleton. How does your head sit? Does it tilt forward or down or does it rest comfortably, tucked back on top your spine? Next begin to notice your shoulders. Are they slumped forward, forced back, or hanging easily out from you collar bone? Is your chest caved in;

does your sternum collapse on top of your diaphragm? Moving farther down, is your back swayed or does your pelvis tilt slightly forward, straightening your spine? Are your knees locked or comfortable? Begin to make subtle corrections to your posture to try to bring yourself more closely into alignment.

Next, notice your breathing and see where it "catches" in your body. These are generally places where you hold tension. Once you notice this, you can check in periodically throughout the day and send a breath to those tense spots. Eventually they will loosen and grow used to having a proper flow of air moving through. These channels will also open up to the energy of magic and the natural pathways of blood flow, firing synapses, and cell movement. You may find your health improves by doing this practice.

For now, just remember, where breath flows, energy follows. This is the flow of all living things. The more open you are to your breath, the more open you are to life, health, and magic.

Once you have begun to pay attention to your posture, expand the practice to include noticing how you walk, how you sit at your desk, how you kneel to weed your garden, and how you stand when you are engaged in conversation. People who work at computers all day are especially prone to what I call "turtle head," with the neck jutting forward and down, and shoulders slumped or drawn up around the ears. None of this is helpful to getting oxygen to the brain or helping one stay connected to the body. The less connected we are, the less present we are. The less present we are, the less effective we are.

OPENING TO FEY AWARENESS

Once we are fully engaged with our physical bodies, we can open up our senses to other realms and to a broader range of our own magical possibilities. If we do this in reverse order, physical illness or mental instablity can ensue. In other words, it is helpful to set my own house in order before I invite in guests, be they from the fey, sideways realms, the spirit realms, or the realm of the Gods.

Witchcraft works with the in-between—we have already begun to cultivate that sense with our blue fire practice. In the old sense, a fey person was one who was uncanny—psychic, or a magic worker—but more than that, a fey person was one who communed with nature, with Gods, or with spirits and could still live in the world of humans. These people had a foot in "two worlds" so to speak. Are you an artist, a gardener, a poet, dancer, coder, mathematician, or intuitive? You are well on your way to that uncanny sense of being fey and to having the ability to gather information from one realm and offer it to another.

We can communicate with the other realms, should we so desire. We just cannot live there, nor, I feel, should we wish to.

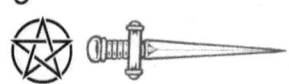

The other realms can be intoxicating to those of us who have trouble living in the here and now. While we can gather information from non-ordinary states and places, we can also get lost there if we wish to use it as an evasion of responsibility. We were born into these bodies, into this world, for a reason, and as we honor nature, we should embrace our lives as humans. It is our work to live where we are, as human beings, doing the very best that we can.

Just as creative humans have different ways in which they are fey, they also have many different experiences with the realms of the Fey, the realms of Faery. The Fey are of help to cooks, poets, artists, dancers, and singers. Gardeners will often work with the smaller Fey, the nature spirits who live amongst the plants. Warrior types, or those involved in the Bardic arts will often encounter the towering Sidhe. If you are interested, you can learn to sense these beings and communicate with them. First though, let us look at our own fey natures.

FINDING YOUR FEYNESS

You too, can be fey. To be fey is to be fully alive in the world you live in right now. Feyness is in the gift of walking down a city street and sensing the trees you pass, and the people, and the sky above. It is to feel connected, rather than lost within your own little world, encased in your thoughts and divorced from your body moving through space and time. To be fey is to be charged with life force, and to see the world with new eyes.

To be fey is to be open. To be open is to celebrate abundance—to see the world as a gift and a blessing. Magic is within us, may we thrive.

I designed this exercise to help us to notice the ways in which we may already have a fey sensibility, a quality of something a little "extra" in our lives, something not quite ordinary.

Divide a piece of paper into three segments and begin to answer the following questions, one for each segment:

What in your life makes you feel "different"? What fears keep you from cultivating the sense of walking "in-between"? What changes

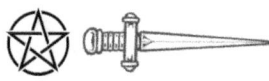

would you make in your life to cultivate the fey point of view—to dance, to dream, to stand tall, to have deep knowing? Make a list of all these things in your three sections. Check back with them in a few months. Are your answers different, or the same?

LISTENING FOR THE OTHER REALMS

The previous exercise showed us our own fey natures and the following will help us to open to the Fey beings who live the unseen realms, often meeting us in wild spaces. Let us listen for those beings who have inspired poets and artists for hundreds of years.

Go to a garden or park, to the forest or a field. Walk slowly, feel yourself open out. Feel your feet beneath you, like you did in the grounding and centering exercise. Begin to notice the small sounds around you. You may begin to notice movement in the corners of your eyes, or to "feel" presences. Slow your breathing. Quiet yourself and be aware. Reach out with your senses. If you notice something tugging at the edge of your vision, turn and make that edge into the center. What do you perceive now? You may ask to be more open to the presence of the spirits of nature, and of the Fey that live in a realm just sideways from our own. This might take time. For now, just appreciate your connection to this living place.

If you wish, you may leave an offering: tie a ribbon to a tree, pour some cream upon the ground, or sing a song. You can leave spit or a strand of your hair. Clean, clear water is also appreciated. Thank the

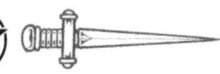

spirits of the place, and any of the Faery beings that may be present. It is good to pick up any garbage you may see. This is a sign of good faith and respect for it shows that you care for all of the realms.

As you cultivate these relationships, you may find yourself wanting to set out offerings in your home or garden. Just make sure any offerings in a natural setting are biodegradable and won't harm animals, insects, or birds. Listen internally for what the beings you are trying to sense may want. Set up a pretty spot and leave your offerings there. You may find that your creative projects flow more smoothly and become more inspired as your relationship with the other realms grow.

Once you have begun this, take care to continue, or you may find that some of the legends about the Fey taking shiny objects or breaking glasses may be true! When such things happen, I pause and ask, "What is trying to get my attention, and why?" Sometimes I have become caught up in my own ideas of how the world *should* work and I need to listen more deeply and take more care with the world that is actually around me.

Through the active practice of presence and attention, I've found that those instances of keys being misplaced or glasses shattering when no one was near them have dwindled to nothing. I am paying attention, and living more connected with the multiverse, so the other realms don't need to grab me by the collar anymore.

This sort of awareness of the other realms also serves to make me more fey myself. I am no longer just locked into an industrialized, computerized world—I have access to nature, to poetry, to wild beauty and a tingling up my spine or a glimmer in the corner of my eye. I am open to the child's imagination and all of the possibilities that holds.

UNFOLDING YOUR POWER

You have cast the sacred sphere and begun to notice your physical body and your own fey nature; now is the time to open the gateways to your power, the power that lies within you and the power you can share with others. This may take many forms and can affect the way you work, or function in your family.

Our power is multihued and multivalent rather than "black" or "white." With multicolored magic, there are no set rules: you must make decisions based upon your inner knowing, self-examination and awareness. In other words, you take responsibility, which is an acknowledgement that you *do* hold power and have accepted accountability for your actions. Multicolored magic also avoids categorizing "white" magic as good and "black" magic as bad, which are concepts that can contribute to racism.

We will begin this process of unfolding power by taking a journey into ourselves. This is a meditation into our own place of power. I recommend that you read this first, then get a friend to lead you through the exercise. You can also record yourself

reading if that feels more comfortable. Take it slowly. You have time.

Set up a space where you can sit or stand or even lie down comfortably. I prefer to do these sorts of meditations—sometimes called trance journeys—standing, so I can engage more of my body by walking or gently rocking, or moving my hands and arms if I need to. I recommend trying this, especially if you have the tendency to fall asleep when you relax. Some people take these journeys without ever really "seeing" anything. This is fine. I myself can take long trance journeys and get a great deal of information while only having flashes of sight. The rest sinks in where it will. Some people "hear," others "taste" or "sense." Still others just "know" somehow. Whatever your experience, don't worry about it. Your way is your own.

The following is a meditation I adapted from the Reclaiming Tradition.

Take a deep breath. Ground and center yourself and then cast the Sacred Sphere. You are safe in the blue bubble of energy. Take another breath, filling yourself with air as you begin to relax. Feel any tensions you carry flow out of your body, imagining them sinking into the earth below the floor you stand upon. Continue to breathe. Continue to relax. Imagine that a path opens up in front of you. Step onto that path. As you travel down it, notice its curves and bends and feel the air around you. What do you see? What do you notice? What do you hear? Take a deep breath. Keep walking until you notice a clearing or opening up ahead of you. Walk toward that opening and step inside. This is your place of power. Feel the air here. Feel the size of the place. Let your feet sink into the ground here. This is your home.

Standing in your place of power, turn toward the East, the place of air, dawn, and intellect. What is there for you? Take some time here. Breathe.

Turn toward the South, the place of fire, will, and desire. What is here? Take your time. Breathe.

When you are ready, turn toward the West, the place of water, emotion, and dreams. What lies in this direction? Take as much time as you need. Breathe.

Turn toward the North, the place of earth, body, and dark stillness. What is here? Take your time. Explore. Breathe.

When you are ready, take another big breath, and turn toward the Center, the place of spirit and connection. What is there, in the middle of the swirl of all of the elements that make up your place of power? Take a deep breath. Close your eyes for a moment. Now is the time when, if an ally or a gift is going to come, it will appear. If you wish for a Faery ally or a gift to help you in your spiritual work, say a prayer for one now. Take another breath. Open your inner eyes. Do you see anything? Or do you feel differently than before? Perhaps your gift lies within you. Or perhaps a Fey ally stands in front of you. Take some time here. Breathe.

Remember that this is your place; you know the way here and can always return. When you are ready to go, thank your ally, or give thanks for your gift. Sometimes it is good to make a promise here by way of thanks. Is there something you can give or offer in return for what you have learned today?

Take a deep breath and thank the Center. Turn North and say thanks. Turning again, thank the West. Turning again, thank the South. One last time, thank the East, and turn toward the entrance to your place of power.

Take a breath and start back on the path. This time the path leads you up, back up into your ordinary self, your waking self. Let each turn take you closer and closer to ordinary consciousness. Walk more quickly. Your sacred body calls your spirit back to the room you started in. Take a deep breath. Feel your body, solid around you. Feel your feet on the floor of your room. Open your eyes. Let breath fill you.

Take a drink of water. Pat the edges of your body. Give thanks for your journey. Thank the Sacred Sphere and release it back, to re-enchant the world.

Standing in the Sacred Sphere, cleansed and open to your power, you are ready for the next step. You are ready to call upon Divinity within you and within the world. Turn the page.

PART THREE
INVOCATION OF THE DIVINE WITHIN

DEITY MAGIC

"**G**od is self and self is God and God is a person like myself."
—Victor Anderson

MANY CRAFT TRADITIONS honor the Star Goddess—the genderqueer God Herself—first, before any of the Elements of Life, Guardians, or other Deities are called into the sacred sphere. She/He/They is acknowledged, not called, for She/He/They is always with us.

Feri Tradition opens all workings with this prayer: *"Holy*

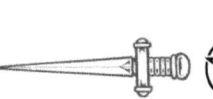

Mother, in Whom we live, move and have our being, from You all things emerge and unto You all things return." This prayer was written by Victor Anderson, though echoes prayers from other religious traditions. I later made my own addition: *"Open our hearts this blessed day. Touch our bodies and our minds. Walk with us through the gates of power, in shadow and starlight, in fire meeting earth, in the wind on the ocean, and the sweet kiss of life. Blessed be our journey."*

Unlike religious traditions that posit a God outside the physical earth, God Herself may transcend the earth, but not our cosmos. With intimate connection, She is woven into the fabric of the natural world, in space, time, stars, and green, growing grass. This is immanence, the Divine in all things. In Her vastness, the Star Goddess may *feel* transcendent, but God-out-there is not separate from the immanent Divine-in-all-things. We see her echoed in Egypt's Nuit, Babylon's Ishtar, Hine Turama of the Maori, and the Welsh Arianrhod, lovers, creators, and Star Goddesses all.

A Craft practitioner's beliefs can range from the pure polytheism of many Gods to an adapted monism, in which God Herself functions as the unifying force of all life. The Gods and Goddesses who embody particular energies that work in the world are said to have spiraled out from Her creative impulse. Victor would say that, "The Supreme Being is God Herself. She needs no-one to help Her. She is male and female. The male is translated out through the female."

As Hers was the first act of creation, God Herself—the Star Goddess—is present in all of creation. Immanent, She fills the interstices of our lives with mystery and beauty: in the pineapple weed pushing through the sidewalk cracks or the flash of lightning shattering the sky. Immanence is the voice of the breeze in the trees and the pounding of the waves on sand. Immanence is a

kiss, a touch, a breath. It is your body sliding across your lover in lust and celebration.

Witches believe that the natural world is sacred, sex is holy, and the human body is beautiful and must be cared for. A witch's sense of self is linked to the earth and this divinity. The Divine in the world is also in us and establishes a relationship with all that surrounds us. The witch, through direct contact with this divinity, becomes an everyday mystic. In Nature, we experience multiplicity: Nature is the face from which our pluralism flows. Things can be one, but they are also many, varied, and beautiful. Thus, there is unity in the connection of immanence *and* the realization that there are many Gods and Goddesses. There are also spirits local to where you live: in the parks, the streams, the fields. The unseen realms are as varied as the seen.

Though there are many realms, our religion does not aspire to some *higher* realm that exists beyond the scope of the material world. The realms are all accessible on earth. For us, the goal is not to leave the human for the Divine, but rather to become more Divine as humans. We are of the earth, and of divinity. Immanence, then, is that within each human that makes us part of the Divine, and ensures the possibility of our becoming *more* Divine. Let us now meet our own sacred souls.

ENCOUNTERING YOUR SOUL

Many Gods have multiple faces or aspects, often three. We, too, have many facets.

From Feri Tradition, I was taught that the human soul is made up of three distinct parts. These can work together in harmony or become disconnected, causing imbalances within. This concept of the tripartite, or multifaceted, soul surfaces in many cultures. The parallels are not exact, changing slightly from culture to culture, yet the similarities are striking.

In some Pagan traditions, the soul has seven or nine parts, in many others, three or four. In his *Republic*, Plato wrote about the tripartite nature of the human being: the appetitive self, the spirited self, and the thinking self. For him, these also correspond to the right structuring of society. The multipart soul is important in the Hawaiian religion of Huna. The Sufis work with seven levels of being, and the ancient Norse, four or more.

The seventh-century Irish document *The Cauldron of Poesy* delineates three centers called "cauldrons." There is also the twentieth-century psychological model of id, ego, and superego, and the ancient Vedic teachings that posit five layers of the human being. Jewish Kabbalistic writings teach of the multifaceted soul, plus the body. From Kabbalah, it filtered into the studies of the Medieval alchemists.

The Golden Dawn—founded in late Victorian Britain by Rosicrucian Masons and home to such luminaries as Maud Gonne, William Butler Yeats, and MacGregor and Moina Mathers—is the progenitor of much contemporary occult practice. This group borrowed Kabbalah from the Christian alchemists, rather than the Jews, and changed the system still further, influencing the course of current magickal groups. Whereas Jewish Kabbalah places five divisions of soul on the Tree of the Sephiroth—with only the first three being accessible and developable during human lifetime—Golden Dawn–influenced magicians placed three souls on the tree.

Anderson Feri Tradition simplifies the soul into three parts. The first division of the soul is often called Sticky One. This is the energy body that most closely follows the physical body. Energy "sticks" to it, drawn in and stored as in a battery. Sticky One carries our animal and child nature, our instinct, and the immediacy of our connections to sex, food, sleep, and exercise.

Then comes Shining Body, which includes the energetic aura, an egg shape around you. This is our human, rational soul. It is the seat of communication and intellect of giving and receiving information intellectually, energetically, and psychically.

Last comes our God Soul, sometimes called the Sacred Dove. Physically, this is a sphere that reaches above your physical head, like a halo, intersecting all the parts of you. This is our own divinity, and connects with all the other realms, including those of the ancestors and Gods.

The Triple Soul is accessed on the human plane and shows us that the physical is woven inextricably with the spiritual. As a witch, I find this most helpful, for I am not so interested in a disembodied spirit or an "after life." I want to live fully and well in

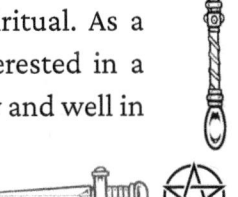

the here and now, on this physical plane, in my sacred body in a sacred world.

All parts of the soul can change, grow, strengthen, and come into alignment. We can begin this work by observing ourselves and noting which parts are most developed. We might be out of balance in one way or another.

For example, while it is unwise to be wholly controlled by our animal nature, it is equally unhealthy to ignore its instinctive wisdom and exist solely on an intellectual plane. The Witch's way is not to leave the body behind and strive for a purely spiritual existence. Our own God Soul is embodied. Our very *spirituality* is embodied. All three souls are one, rooted in our body in this lifetime.

While unaligned—out of touch with the various parts of ourselves—we are more easily prone toward being controlled by random events and emotions or stray thoughts. Disconnection from ourselves, particularly from our God Soul, can lead us into disconnection from our society and the earth and in extreme situations leading to totalitarian governments, serial killers, slavery, billionaires, and human-caused environmental disaster. In less extreme cases, soul disconnection can simply make our lives much more difficult and painful than they need be, keeping us stuck in old patterns and unhealthy work or love situations.

Lack of alignment is a splintering of pieces of ourselves from each other. Culturally, we isolate reason from emotion, and body from intuition, creating duality where none really exists. This causes serious rifts that have long-reaching psychic, psychological, and physical repercussions, causing all sorts of illness and disease, including war. Humans long to be whole.

Soul alignment is a central spiritual practice; it re-knits our spirits and can, in the long term, help us to refashion the ways in which we live with one another. The tools in this book begin this process by mending the unnecessary split between the psychic

and the physical. The following exercises, ending with the most important tool in this book, the Prayer for Alignment, will help you to become whole, balanced, strong, happy, and open to the abundance of the world. For the remainder of this section, we will explore the nature of our Triple Soul, beginning with Sticky One and working our way through all the parts until we are familiar with them. Then we will learn how to balance and align the tripartite soul, making it aligned and true within us.

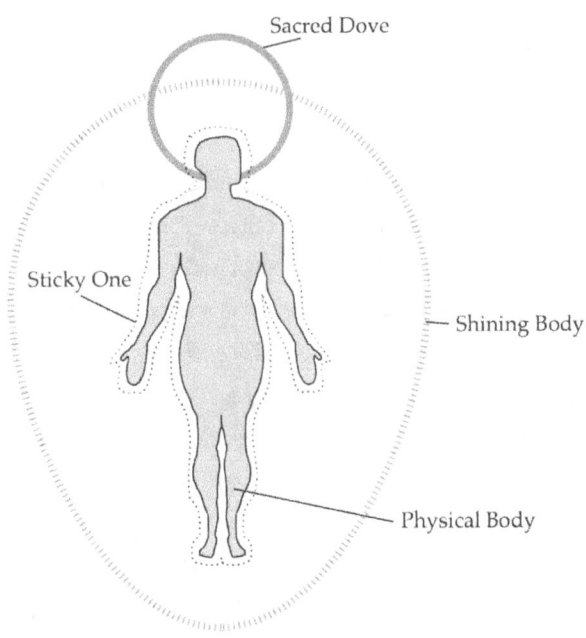

THE TRIPLE SOUL

STICKY ONE

I *want to play. I want to experience the world as it is, unclouded by analyzing, cataloguing terms. I am your innocence and your wisdom. I come to you with wide eyes, and a body supple and free, able to bend over to touch the grass, able to reach the leaves on trees and smell spice and flower. I feel the softness and the rough. I sense the sun on my skin. I know all things, and can show them to you, but I cannot tell you their names. Take me back to when I was happy in a wading pool or playing with finger paints. I do not color inside the lines. I am free. I am new. I am full of life force. Vital. Alive. I am animal, I growl, I run, I glory in my body and the world.*

Think of a child in summer, hands covered in blackberry juice, sticky, sweaty, and full of life. Sticky One, being instinctual and pre-verbal, loves the physicality of symbols, rituals, music, color, dancing, and playing with the lawn hose in the heat. It delights in the silly and in pranks. It likes to play, and enjoys the things of nature best, as opposed to human-made things of formed metals or plastics. It also knows what it needs, whether food, sleep, sex, or quiet. Learn to listen to Sticky One. If you are running out of energy, having slept too little, eaten only junk food, or really need

to be touched, Sticky One will let you know, and grow louder and louder the longer these needs are ignored. If you ignore Sticky One too long, you will likely become ill or accident-prone.

Sticky One can communicate directly to our God Soul. This is why religious ritual is so important and effective. Candle lighting, singing chants, working physical spells, all of these practices engage Sticky One. Sticky One, the deeper consciousness, can then communicate through these symbols to our own divinity.

In developmental terms, however, we can see that children need to grow into their intellect and energetic boundaries. Their animal, instinctive nature is strong, but they need adults to keep them safe. If children don't have this, their development may be skewed and need to be repaired or healed in later years. I have found this in my own life, and know others who have gone through this soul healing as well.

This development is clearly spoken of in the Kabbalistic tradition. The Jewish mystical text, the Zohar, teaches that the *nefesh* comes first, the foundational soul, while *ruach* is built upon it through work, and crowned by *neshamah* only when one has achieved a certain spiritual level. In this system, then, *nefesh* communicates with *ruach,* not with *neshamah*. For those of you interested in further research, look at the writings of Gershom Scholem and Rabbi David Cooper.

Mystic philosopher Gurdjieff—who has had a significant influence on contemporary ceremonial magicians—also taught that a person isn't born with a soul, but must develop one.

Sticky One is the primary entry point to magic and our engagement with the world, with nature, home, and survival. As an energy form, Sticky One is often called the etheric body. Most people experience this energetic body as residing one to two inches from the skin, following the curve of the physical body. Some people call Sticky One the Fetch, a name that harkens to old folk tales where the Witch sent a spirit companion out in the night to do her bidding. These tales may be pointing to a deeper truth: the shaman or Witch had the ability to detach the esthetic body from the physical body to such an extent that a physical part of their spirit roamed the land. This shows up strongly in Norse and Siberian traditions.

Sticky One is a battery, storing life force until the physical, emotional, or psychic bodies or our God Soul need it. Known as *mana* in Hawaiian and *awen* in Welsh, this life force is carried on the breath. It is living essence connected to Divine inspiration. Each breath takes in the life force that exists all around us. As it is connected to all earthly things, Sticky One can also draw this energy up through our feet as they touch the earth. Victor told me that if we die unprepared or with our soul unaligned, Sticky One may stay behind, becoming a "noisy ghost" or "haunting" people. This concept also appears in the Jewish Kabbalistic tradition.

STICKY ONE PLAY DATE

The following gets you in touch with Sticky One and recharges your batteries in a simple, natural, pleasurable way.

Take yourself out for a walk on the beach, in the woods or park, or in a cornfield. Glory in the air, the scents, the way your feet feel on the ground. Or go to an ice cream parlor and order a sundae. Fly a kite. Go to a shop filled with glass beads, fabrics, or bright yarn. Let yourself be fed by sheer sensual beauty. Let yourself play. What in you is fed? What delights in these things? Find what gives that part that is deep within you pleasure.

THE WISH BIRD AS FETCH

This is a practice I learned many decades ago from the late Raven Moonshadow and Akasha Madrone in the Reclaiming Tradition. It strengthens our ability to manifest our will in the world. What do you want or need in your life right now? If your life's force and intent are truly connected with the world around you, as Sticky One is connected, you can bring your will into alignment with the world.

Before you begin, hold a desire or intention clearly in your mind. For this exercise, wish for things close to home. Do not attempt to fetch global justice, for example.

You may want to write your wish down first, to make certain you really know what it is you are asking for. But don't forget to leave room for the multiverse to work its magic. If you want a new job, think of the sort of environment you want to work in, the type of skills you wish to use, friendly people, and anything else you want. Wish clearly but don't pin down the multiverse, as you do not necessarily have all the information at hand. For example, if you ask for a *specific* job in a *specific* company, the supervisor there may actually be a tyrant who forces you to work ninety

hours a week under stressful conditions. Remain open to hidden gifts.

Once you have clarified your wish, ground and center yourself and begin slow, even breathing. Let your breathing come easily. You are breathing life force in and out, calling upon the power of Sticky One to charge this energy. Cup your hands in front of you, leaving space between them, enough for a small animal to rest, the size of a small sparrow or wren. Intention still clear in your mind, begin to breathe gently into the space between your two thumbs. You are breathing your wish, full of your intention and the life force held in your breath. Imagine a bird forming in your hand, made by your breath and intention, growing more solid and strong the longer you blow. Once you feel the bird alive and ready in your hands, throw your hands up and open, and watch it fly away. Notice what direction it goes in, as this might be important information. You may want to light a candle in the color that represents that direction to strengthen the bird's flight.

This technique sends the energy stored by your Sticky One out into the world to do your bidding. In this way, your wish bird is your Fetch, formed by life force coupled with will and intention. It will literally go out and "fetch" what you want. For example, I have used this exercise successfully to find a place to live. I sent the bird off, with a wish for a place big enough and affordable enough for my partner and myself. The next day I saw a sign advertising a house for rent. The bird had flown in that very direction. Despite the fact that four other couples saw the house the same hour we were there, the landlord rented it to us and we lived there happily.

Once you have worked through this whole section, you can begin incorporating the Prayer for Alignment (which comes later, under "Aligning the Triple Soul") at the beginning of the wish bird exercise to bring you into alignment within yourself, with your intention, and with the universe. This will strengthen the ability of your wish to fly true.

SHINING BODY

I am intellect and aura. I reach out and take in information, comparing it to information I have already stored. I am first contact with another. I speak to you. I formulate. I am clever and have knowledge. I am of great use to you in this world you have created. Don't underestimate my ability. When my aura reaches out, I gather and communicate simultaneously, or I hide information. Whatever you need me to do, I am able. Capable. Read me. I will read you. I will speak and connect you to others. I am smart and wish to be respected. I work best when aligned with the other parts of soul.

Now that we are firmly ensconced in Sticky One, and have acclimated ourselves to raising life force, we can use that life force to charge up Shining Body. Shining Body includes our aura, an energy field that creates an egg-like shape around us. This energy field is the first line of communication we have with the world. Shining Body includes my intellectual mode of communication, yet this is not the whole of this part of the soul. My intellectual forebrain is helpful to me, but it is also easily disconnected from my body and emotions. Getting in touch with the rest of the func-

tions of Shining Body gives my intellect a helpful context within which it can function more effectively.

Your first way of gathering and spreading information is psychically, through the use of your aura. I ask urban dwellers who insist they have no psychic facility, "You ride the bus, don't you? Don't you know how to 'read' the other passengers? Don't you know how to take up just the right amount of space and know when you are impinging too much upon someone else, or they on you?" That sense is you, using your Shining Body to communicate with the people around you. Shining Body listens and senses, adjusts itself, communicates out to others, adjusts itself again. The more aware of it you become, the better you can communicate, and the more information you will have to work with.

Over time, the exercises for Shining Body will enable you to be more fully present in all of your communicating centers. The following tools widen attention and help to engage the body and all of the senses. I find that life becomes clearer, fuller and livelier when my Shining Body is engaged. You may find that communication improves because you will be more connected to the world around you, and less locked inside yourself alone.

DEEP, EXPANSIVE ATTENTION

The following is an exercise I adapted from Sensei Wendy Palmer's Aikido work in *The Intuitive Body*. I was introduced to Sensei Palmer's work by Reclaiming witch Cybele.

The exercise below is my variation on the work, honed from years of practice. It enables us to become more aware of the power and skills our Shining Body has. Done over time, it can balance our energy, expand our level of attention and create a still space for us to think and act from.

The first time you try this exercise, it may be easier with your eyes closed. Record yourself reading the meditation, or have a friend lead you through it, slowly. You will eventually be able to do this with no outside verbal aids and with your eyes open, which is a more useful way to go through our everyday lives. This is a potent, ordinary, everyday technique. It should eventually become as easy as breathing, and require little time and effort to achieve the state of dropped and open attention. Once you are familiar with this technique, it can be helpful in many situations, including leading ritual, walking down the street, or engaging in

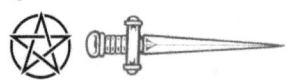

clear communication with someone. This is not a trance technique, but a tool for living.

Sitting or standing in a comfortable position, with your body relaxed, spine erect so the energy can flow, begin to breathe deeply. Imagine a ball of energy in the center of your head, behind the area on your forehead that we call the third eye. This ball of energy is magnetic, and rotates.

Let all of your attention flow toward the ball, sticking to it, gathering from wherever it has wandered. Keep breathing and let the ball do its work. Once your attention is truly fixed on this ball, imagine that it slowly begins a descent through the center of your body, dropping your attention down and down. Let this ball of attention drop through your throat, past your sternum, down into your rib cage until it rests, gently, just between your navel and your sex, in your area of will, your center of gravity. For some of you this may rest a bit lower, for others a little higher. Stay with your attention here for a while, sensing what this state is like.

Begin to let the ball expand in all directions until it reaches the edges of your pelvic cradle. Pause there. If it feels too difficult to hold, let it ease back down to a smaller size.

When you are ready, let the ball of your attention increase out until it is the same size as your auric egg. Feel what it is like to have attention all the way around, three hundred and sixty degrees. You now have eyes in the back of your head. You can now let your aura intersect with that of another, communicating.

Practice expanding this circle even further, letting it shrink back, and then growing until it fills a whole room. Eventually, this should become as easy as breathing. It is your attention and your energy, not something you need to force. It may take practice. Be patient, and keep breathing.

Once you have done enough, let your ball of attention shrink, slowly until once again it fills your pelvic cradle. Let it grow smaller

until it is once again the size at which you started, resting in your belly. Now let your attention move to where it is most comfortable.

At first, you may find that your attention shoots right back up to your head, or even out of your body completely. Do not be discouraged. This is an exercise, a practice, and over time, your attention may more naturally come to rest in your belly and click in with your Shining Body. After years of practice, I am able to gather and drop my attention on one breath cycle, and expand it on another.

CREATING AURA COLORS

This is an exercise I find very useful. After decades of doing aura work, I still return to it when I need to.

You can try it first at home, to familiarize yourself with it. After that, you can do it in a meeting, when you have to speak publicly, or when you need to calm yourself down. I have used it when walking down the street and wanted to change my energy. For example, if I was walking home from the underground station at night and saw people who made me feel unsafe, I could make myself "invisible." Using my aura, I adjusted my energy so those people paid no attention to me.

When practicing, begin this technique by swinging your arms gently outward, twisting your torso so your arms arc in a gentle circle around you. This helps you sense the edges of your energy field. Once you are used to the space you take up, you no longer need that assessment and can dive right into the work.

Still yourself and take a deep breath. Feel your auric egg surrounding you. If you can't feel it, just pretend. Imagine that it is there. On a breath, imagine that egg filling with yellow, for clear communication. Now breathe out pink, for self-love. Next, fill your

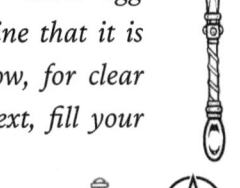

aura with the green of healing energy. Now fill it with grey fog, for invisibility. Let yourself change colors at will. It doesn't take long. Hold each color long enough to really sense yourself surrounded by it. Once you have a feel for this, begin to walk around. As you walk, let your aura change color. Once you are done with this session, fill your aura with whatever color you need right now. Bring yourself to rest, one hand on your heart and one on your belly.

The more you practice this, the easier it will become. Using aura colors can become both quick and practical.. As you grow familiar with this exercise, you can alter it to fit any situation. I have taught it to activists who need these techniques whether in the midst of a big demonstration facing riot police, or at a school board meeting. I used it to good effect in my years at the soup kitchen. It helped me in breaking up a fight or listening to someone in pain. I changed my aura to calm and soothe the situation. I could also make myself larger if necessary, when I am intervening between two angry, six-foot-tall men, or could soften into a more comforting presence.

You can also experiment with this technique in ritual, or during storytelling, enhancing the texture and range of your craft.

SACRED DOVE

I am deep within you, and I float above your crown, like a dove. I am all wisdom, connected to the wisdom of Sticky One. I am in tune with all connections. I am one with everything, ancient. I see with eyes that open on the inner worlds and into the worlds beyond. Trust me. Pray to me. I hear you. I am ancestor. I am inner divinity and deep voice. I am that which draws you and is drawn. I am Goddess, and I am with you. Through me, you connect with other Gods and link with mystery. I am your guide, your inner guide. Feed me. Tell me your troubles. I will hold you and heal you. I am your deepest soul.

We have explored the two parts of the soul that are perhaps most easily explained and experienced. Using these as a basis for understanding, we are ready to link with our own divine nature, sometimes called Sacred Dove, or the God Soul.

The God Soul is traditionally seen resting just above the head and is sometimes pictured as a ball of blue light. When you see a Christian icon, or a painting of the Buddha, you will often see this energy represented as a halo. The orb intersects the auric egg, either physically kissing the top of the head—the energetic opening that communicates to the cosmos and divinity—or

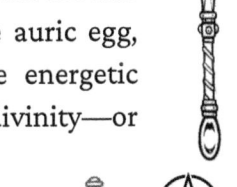

beginning just at the base of the skull (see illustration in Encountering Your Soul). Thus it touches all of your parts: the physical body, the etheric body, or Sticky One, and the aura or Shining Body. Sacred Dove is connected to all, even to things one cannot even know consciously.

Sacred Dove has the ability to distribute the energy stored by Sticky One in the best, most efficacious way and when I need greater understanding, or help with a situation, I breathe the problem up to my God Soul. Whereas Shining Body may talk, Sacred Dove listens, as is implied the embedding of *sh'ma* to "hear" or "listen" in the Hebrew name for this part of the soul, *Neshamah*.

Sacred Dove can also be enlisted to help others. When a person requests healing or help, we can link to our God Soul, asking it to talk to the God Soul of the other person. This way the conscious forebrain, which may have only partial information, isn't trying to make decisions on its own, but is working from a state of connection. This gives new meaning to the Christian saying, "Offer it up to God." That is what we are doing, except in this case, divinity lies very close to us. It is the part of us that is made up of the divine spark, in mystic terms. It also helps when listening or speaking if my Triple Soul is aligned and all parts are in touch with one another, working in concert. Every situation can be improved by this effort.

SITTING AND LISTENING

"*Solitary meditation is when you get in touch with your God Self. You can also meditate in a crowd.*"
—Victor Anderson

"*Do a few minutes meditation every day—find out who you are and where you are going.*"
—Cora Anderson

THE FOLLOWING exercise uses our God Soul's capacity to listen. This has trifold importance. It enables us to become more self-aware, to link up with a larger, deeper part of ourselves whose presence is often buried, and it helps us to slow down. This is a difficult but rewarding exercise, and I recommend that you make a contract with yourself to do this for ten minutes every morning for one month to see how things begin to change within you. You may want to renew the contract several times. This will begin to change your posture, your breathing, and your sense of self. It will help you not become easily distracted and will show you parts of yourself you might not usually see.

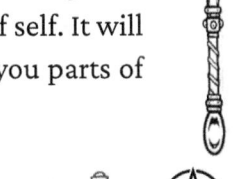

The exercise will bring you into closer contact with your inner divinity as you sit, patiently, while some of your fears, shadows, or demons appear. You may get cranky. Sacred Dove sits in witness. You may grow insecure. Sacred Dove sits in witness. Your back may hurt. Sacred Dove sits in witness. You may want to run out of the room. Sacred Dove sits in witness. Keep breathing. Once you have done this a few times, you can end your session with the Prayer for Alignment (described in the following section).

After doing this exercise for several years, I became more aware of the stories I told myself, the tangents I flew off on, or the emotional states I was prone to spiral down into. God Soul listened to all of these as I sat. Since I sit in the morning, I can then notice the stories as they arise throughout the day and say: "I recognize you." This helps me become less controlled by my impulses and random thoughts or emotions.

Quaker friends tell me that this exercise is similar to Quaker Silence and Listening for the Light. Those with training in zazen, Jewish meditation, or centering prayer may also find this practice to be familiar, though the focus is slightly different. After years of avoidance, I was first introduced to meditation as a simple "sitting practice" through the Gurdjieff Work. Sitting as a form of self-observation quickly became a core tool of my spiritual practice.

I deepened this practice by working for several years with Zen Buddhist Gregory Wood. We often sat together in from of the Federal Building in San Francisco during the second round of the US Gulf Wars. We also sat with a small group in the early morning quiet of his bookshop. I later took this practice to the streets during many actions for racial and social justice. I even sat outside the US Pentagon.

Though our relationship with this practice may evolve over time, let our beginning intention be to simply to sit with ourselves, with God Soul watching and listening, as we breathe.

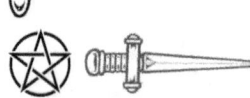

Let yourself settle in. Begin to breathe deeply and slowly. You may want to light a white candle or a stick of incense. If you have bad knees, get a chair you can sit straight up in. Make sure you can comfortably perch near the front edge of it, so your spine is straight rather than resting against anything. If your knees are good, I find it best to pile up a couple of sturdy cushions on the floor. Make sure that your pelvis is higher than your knees and feet, otherwise you can strain your back. You may want to put a towel under your feet to cushion the bones if you are on a wooden floor. Let your breathing slow. It is time to begin.

Imagine your spine floating up from your pelvis and your shoulders hanging gently, as if on a coat hanger. Adjust your head until your skull feels like it is resting directly on top of your spine. You may need to "tuck" your chin back to make sure your head is erect and not jutting forward. Let your hands rest on your knees comfortably, or cup your right hand in your left, letting your thumbs touch softly. Let your breathing fill your abdomen, feeling it expand in front as well as behind as your muscles open to let the breath in. The breath should start low in your belly, rising up and filling your rib cage and finally your chest. Let your inhalation be as slow and steady as you can make it, and let your exhalation match your inhalation. Slow. Steady. Sit. Breathe. Let a still space open up, deep inside you.

There is a still place in your belly. Breathe into that. Feel that stillness open up. Then feel energy rising up your spine—anchored in the still place—flowing up to the back of your skull and opening out to the globe of God Soul. Feel the link between the stillness in your belly and the energy that fans from the back of your skull, embracing the sphere of Sacred Dove like the hood of a cobra. Begin to sense your Sacred Dove: watching, waiting, listening. Every time chatter or worry starts, breathe, and feel your Sacred Dove. It is witness. It is the part of you that can look on all the squirming parts with compassion. Keep breathing. Keep sitting. Be open to all the parts of yourself. Sitting in witness with yourself is one of the hardest things you can do,

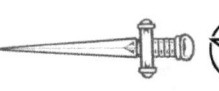

and one of most compassionate. You are sacred. You are loved in all your parts.

Once you have acclimated yourself to the posture of this exercise, you should try sitting for longer periods. Twenty minutes is much easier than ten, believe it or not, because all of the systems that are convinced they will die if they sit still one more moment finally settle down and other, deeper states then have room to arise in the stillness. You may want to work your way up to sitting for forty minutes at a time. This being said, sitting for five minutes is more helpful as a foundation for your day's work than not sitting at all.

COLLECTIVELY DIVINE

"*I am the drop that contains the ocean.*"
—Yunus Emre

I HAVE DEVELOPED the following meditation from my work with the Sufi concept of the "drop that became the sea," meaning the individual soul as joined with the larger divinity. We hold the divine within us and can join with others, creating a sea or tapestry of divinity. Every time you sense the strong connection you have with other people or beings, you are tapping into the ocean of divinity.

This is a wonderful exercise to do as a group, because you all become "drops" that can then interact with each other, melting and melding, pooling and puddling. I have done this in a shallow creek, where we all blessed each other, pouring water from our cupped hands and singing, "I am Goddess, I am flowing water." I have also led this in a meditation hall, where we passed pitchers,

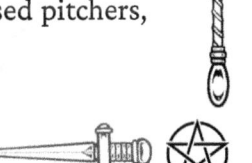

filled each other's goblets, and drank deeply of our divinity, giving and receiving the sacred.

Again, I recommend taping this if doing it on your own, or having one person read it slowly aloud if you are trying this in a group. A light drumbeat can be a helpful aid to taking people more deeply into non-ordinary consciousness. Call upon Sacred Dove, your God Soul, and dive into the ocean of divinity.

Take a deep breath. Drop your attention to your belly and begin to listen, deeply. Listen to your breath, listen to the sounds around you, and listen to your blood flowing within you. Listen to your breathing as it slows, deepening, each breath becoming longer and more full. Feel the edges of your body begin to blur and soften. All the water in your body is softening you, flowing out into your bones, your skin. You are becoming a drop of water. You become softer and softer, your breathing slowing and deepening. The more watery you become, the softer and slower you are. Let the drop that is your being begin to flow out. There are other beings in the world; they too, are flowing. They are water. Your soft edges bump up against theirs. Your edges give way and you merge. Your drop and their drop become one. Out into the world you flow, merging, buoyant and bouncing, soft with the flow of all these bodies, all these beings. Becoming one large pool of water.

On and on you flow, becoming a stream. This stream keeps growing as more and more beings join the flow. It is a stream seeking its source. It is a stream that knows its source like it knows the moment of its birth. It flows with ease. Its course is true. Wandering, bubbling, this stream moves on and on until it hits ocean. Fresh water crashes into salt, in a flurry of ecstatic force, in lust and wild joy. Feel yourself floating in this ocean, this grand sea of salt water, this sea of love. Let yourself be cradled in this water. You are this water. This water is you. Breathe. You will never be alone. You are this sea, the womb of Mother, you are here with all these drops of life, merged with the Divine. Swim in joy. You are buoyant in this sea of love. All fear, shame, anger, and pain are washed away, flowing out of you. They do not matter anymore. Not

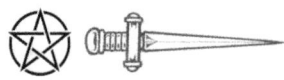

here. Here you are loved. You are one with the sacred. Open your eyes. Look around you. See with the eyes of the sacred. Touch with the hands of the sacred. Dance the dance of sacred love in the world. You are surrounded and you are full of this love. Pass it on. You are part of the cosmos, a drop of divinity. This is the deepest mystery, carried in the water held in every cell of your body. Feel it. See it. Touch it. Dance it. Breathe and flow. Float in the wisdom of your own divine nature.

Once you have swum and danced your fill, get ready to take your leave. Honor those you have merged with. Give your blessings and thanks to the great ocean that birthed us all. You carry the seeds of that birth. Begin to swim back, back to that stream that flowed here. Back to where salt water and fresh meet, crashing together in lust and ecstasy. Begin to flow, easily, back upstream. As you flow, let your edges become more and more distinct, until you can feel yourself once again bumping up against the other drops of water. Flow back and back. Breathe. You are becoming more and more solid. Separate from those other drops. You are your own drop of water. Breathe. You are becoming once again skin. Once again bone. Your body becomes firm around you. Water retreats to cells and blood and spit. You are human. Breathe. Let yourself come fully back into your body. Fully human, fully alive. Pat your legs, arms, belly, head. Take a breath from the soles of your feet to the top of your head. Breathe some of this love and energy up to feed your Sacred Dove. As you do so, feel your spirit flowing fully back down into your physical form. You hold in you the drop of the Divine. Look on the world with new eyes. Blessed be.

ALIGNING THE TRIPLE SOUL

"**W**hen you have all three souls aligned, you can ask anything you want of the Gods and get it. You just have to learn how to ask."
—Cora Anderson

NOW THAT YOU have explored the parts of your triple soul as separate entities, you are ready to work with yourself as a sacred, unified trinity. All three parts can work in concert, creating greater strength and wholeness within you and also opening you up to a state both soft and fierce, ready to act in accordance with each moment. If all of your parts are connected, you are on your way to being more fully connected to the world. This is how we are meant to be, whole and organized by an internal principle. Internal organization bears fruit externally, and thus helps to order the world.

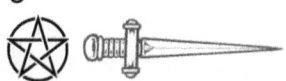

PRAYER FOR ALIGNMENT

Life force, magic, and our relationship to the sacred is available to us every time we draw breath. Life force is the inspirer, part of the Divine breath. The Prayer for Alignment is based on our experience of breath as the great connector and enlivener. This prayer trains your breath, alters your body, and strengthens your spiritual presence. The breathing itself is the prayer, rather than the prayers of words we are more commonly used to. The Prayer for Alignment will help you in all things, especially when coupled with work on posture and your keys to remembrance.

The concept of bringing the parts of our soul into alignment is not unique to Feri Tradition, though Feri is the only Witchcraft tradition that I know of with this focus. Hawaiian Huna teaches this, certain Kabbalistic studies show this, and some branches of ceremonial magic—including Thelema—focus on this, as well, through their work to contact one's "Holy Guardian Angel." The ancient Irish bards could not open to the fires of inspiration if their soul was unaligned.

I spoke about the dangers of remaining unaligned earlier,

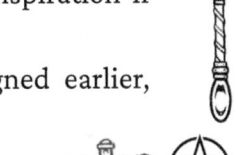

under the heading "Encountering Your Triple Soul." Now, I'd like to talk a bit more about the power that will be made available to you when you begin a daily practice of coming into alignment within yourself.

This prayer is important to all my works of will and intention. When I am using it, I feel better physically and am calmer emotionally, and able to think more clearly. I believe it also makes me more open-hearted and better able to engage in necessary battles—to help others, to help the earth, to stand up for myself. This is why Cora Anderson stated we could ask for anything if we are aligned. Aligned, we are fully present and not acting out of greed, fear, addiction, or any other disconnected state. We are acting from a state of pure generosity, for when we are aligned, we are in tune not only with ourselves but also with the divinity of everything around us. In touch with my God Soul, my personal will can work in harmony with the will of the sacred multiverse. That is the gift of this working. I use the following exercise every day.

The below uses "square breathing" common in the yoga practice of pranayama. I was first taught the prayer for alignment in Feri Tradition in a much simpler form, but find the breath work below to be beneficial.

Quiet yourself inside as much as possible, knowing that more stillness will come as you engage your breath. Align your skeleton into proper posture. Breathe. Let your belly be soft. Breathe fully, letting your back muscles move out with the breath, too. Then feel the lungs expand. Your whole torso expands with air, front, back, and sides. Let your inhalation be full and let your exhalation match that rate. Lightly touch your tongue to the roof of your mouth and try breathing in and out through your nose, deeply in the back of your throat, like yogis are trained to do. It may sound like the breathing of a sleeping person. This breath stores energy very quickly in your body.

Experiment by counting a slow four on the inhalation, pause for

four, exhale for four counts, and then hold for four. This will help expand your lung capacity and raise the energy needed to align. Breathe in, two, three, four. Hold, two, three, four. Exhale, two, three, four. Hold, two, three, four. Take one breath cycle for your physical body. Take one breath cycle for your etheric body, Sticky One. Take one breath for your aura, Shining Body. Take one breath for your God Soul, Sacred Dove. Keep breathing in these sets of four, over and over. If you try this, make sure you are "holding" in a relaxed and open state, rather than tensing your body and closing your throat down. If holding your breath proves too difficult at first, simply breathe in and out as fully and slowly as possible. Imagine that you are filling with life force, which is all around you.

Keep breathing until you begin to physically tingle, until you are so full, you feel you cannot take any more. Then take in just a little more. Once you are tingling and full, on your fourth breath, breathe in, then tilt your head back and exhale up, breathing explosively out through your mouth. Feed the Dove. You may feel the snap of alignment as all three parts of your soul come into their proper relationship with each other, forming a whole. You may feel a rush of energy through your body as your Sacred Dove distributes the energy where it is needed. Feel this energy drop all the way back down to your feet. If you are in need of healing, ask for it now, and God Soul will rain sparks of blue fire around your aura, cleansing you and bringing healing. Your prayer is complete.

The Prayer for Alignment is a powerful tool for health, self-awareness, and integration. I recommend you make it part of your daily practice. As you become more adept at this technique, you can simply breathe up excess energy to align your triple soul and say, "All three souls are one," which is what I do throughout the day, while keeping the formal practice above for my morning work. You can breathe up energy after running or dance class, after orgasm, or at a rock concert, or when you are full of joy. This will help keep you in alignment and keep you from feeling overwhelmed by energy, actually expanding your ability to manage large quantities of life force. It is also helpful to do this during ritual, after singing and dancing for a long time or raising a cone of power for the group's intention. Feed your Sacred Dove and align yourself. Then, if you have energy to spare, you can offer some back to Mother Earth in thanks, or feed some to the Guardians or Deities who have helped your working.

As I stated earlier, you can also breathe up problems, anxiety, pain, or anger to your God Soul, asking, "Can you help me with this?" I find that turning such things over to my inner divinity often gives me insight.

Some people believe that a person must go through convoluted means to ensure that their energy is not depleted by magical or healing work. In actuality, replenishing our energy is as simple as conscious breathing. Just remember, every time we breathe, we are breathing in life force.

Victor taught me a poem that is central to Feri Tradition, and I like to say it when I'm fully aligned: "Who is this flower above me, and what is the work of this God? I would know myself, in all my parts." If a spiritual practice is truly helpful, it always leads to knowing oneself better.

May the light dawning as we turn to the East illuminate us. So may it be.

PART FOUR
EAST: OPENING THE SENSES

THE TOOLS OF AIR

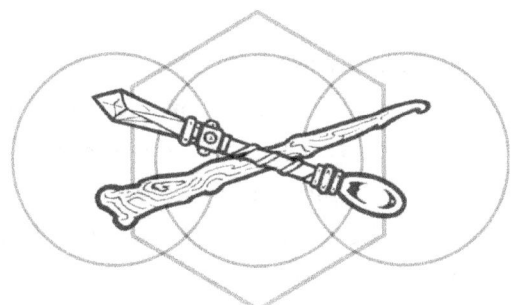

S tep into the East, place of beginnings. Feel the fresh air blowing across your face. This is the place of vision, the morning star. See it glowing in the sky. Turn to greet the dawn. Feel your mind quicken with new thoughts. Feel your breath as it fills your lungs. What is your wish? It can be granted here, in the place of starting over. Our tool here is the Wand, the branch with the ability to bud and sprout new leaves. The branch that dances in the wind. This Wand is tipped with a crystal, shining like the morning star. It holds the power of self and knowledge.

After Deity is acknowledged, the sphere cast, and our own

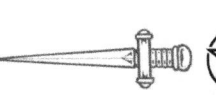

divinity is present within us, we turn toward the directions of the compass. The directions have traditional associations but, depending upon where you live, please alter them to suit your physical reality. I live on the West Coast of the United States, and was taught a tradition based in this landscape: water in the West, dry heat farther South. Luckily, some things remain consistent no matter where you are: the sun rises in the East and sets in the West.

Let us turn toward the East. The tool here is the wand, representing the power of growth, air, speech, and new beginnings. While Tarot and ceremonial magic often place the wand in the south, many traditional Craft paths associate the wand with the east. This makes sense to me. All I must do is think of the wind rustling the branches of a tree to find the resonance of this association.

The wand can be seen as the scepter of knowledge. As the awakening of knowledge is an important place to begin any search, the wand becomes the key for beginning our work in magic. This section will explore many of the powers of air: vision, breath, thought, and the beauty of birdsong at dawn. We will learn about listening and speaking, about the calling in and asking that is prayer, and about studying our thought-forms and perceptions. We will open our awareness and cleanse our senses, opening to the Gods and the world around us in ways that are as fresh as a morning's breeze.

The world expands and contracts, just as our lungs do, inhaling and exhaling. Breath is the source of life. Air is a beginning, rising from the East.

A Magical Worldview

"We don't have to apologize for our reality."
—Victor Anderson

In this section, we will begin to examine the conceptions we hold both about world around us and about ourselves. As I stated earlier, self-exploration is occult activity. By searching out the seldom-plumbed depths of soul and psyche, we shine our consciousness on what has been obscured. We are seeking the hidden: the sources of our strength; our danger; the neuroses that shape us; the power that guides us; our soft and vulnerable spaces. Until we can walk into the deep spaces, we cannot soar into the heights. Balance is the key. Not a static balance, but a shifting balance, with a fulcrum that, through practice, can become both strong and supple. This is part of the dance of our evolution as human beings.

As for our conceptions about the world, for people of the

twenty-first century, religious belief often comes second to skepticism and the religion of science. I tend toward skepticism myself. But as we discovered in our work with the Triple Soul, intellect is not all, and reason is not ruler. We humans are also dancers, poets, singers, lovers, gardeners, and people who feel, psychic people and people in touch with our bodies. Using all of the faculties available to us, we can make space for belief even in the midst of disbelief. The Gods are real forces and the practices in this book do work within us. Do they only work by means that we would term psychological? Perhaps, and I don't discount the strength of mind and emotion, but I also see that there are more subtle processes at work than we may know at first. A serious practitioner can develop emotional connections with her Gods, intellectual rigor and honesty, and physical and psychic discipline, with no one thing cancelling out another.

Witches, spiritual seekers, or priestesses need to be able to hold many realities as possibilities *at the same time*. This is a skill requiring an open mind and heart and the will to think both flexibly and firmly. As a student of religions, I was once sitting in a class where we discussed a theory positing that the Torah was written by many authors, often with conflicting viewpoints, over many years' time. In class, we were reading about the famous Golden Calf story, which, beneath its religious meaning, was also a political piece written by the Southern tribes in Israel against the Northern tribes living in Judah. The more pious Jewish and Christian students were really struggling with this; they had been taught that the Torah was revealed to Moses, not a string of authors with axes to grind.

My professor took a risk that day, and his words have stayed with me. He said, "I usually don't bring my personal life into class, but I feel you ought to know: *I am not an atheist.*" He was trying to explain to us that he held two realities at once. The Hebrew Bible, including the Torah, was an important religious text for him, a practicing Jew, yet he was a twenty-first century academic who had to look at other facts, too. His faith was not canceled out by historical evidence, but was informed by it.

As a Witch, I need to do the same. I may feel awkward describing my experiences of the Gods, feeling that these experiences are irrational, yet that does not mean that they are less real. I have felt the Gods surrounding me, and moving through me, yet I often cannot explain this experience satisfactorily to someone who does not share my language. I can only try to explain that reason is only one way to access information. The Gods can be real to my body or emotions and unreal to my rational intellect. I've learned to live with the paradox and to grow through the pressure of dissonance.

OPENING TO SEEKER'S MIND

We have the ability to function on multiple levels simultaneously. We can call this "spirit mind." For example, if I am leading a trance journey—what some Craft traditions call "path workings"—I need to remain aware of what is happening with the participants, make certain I'm speaking loudly and slowly enough, and keep a loose track of time, all while experiencing the journey myself *and* doing my personal work, albeit on a more shallow level than those being led through the journey. If I am completely out of the path working, I cannot accurately gauge where the journey is going, or what the pacing needs to be. If I am too deeply involved in my personal work, I will get lost and be unable to monitor how people are reacting emotionally, whether they are breathing regularly and are generally all right. Exercising spirit mind uses the same muscles required to hold alternate realities or reconcile intellectual knowing with physical or emotional experiences.

It is healthy to be a believer and a sceptic at the same time. That interplay keeps me questioning and seeking, yet not cynical. It makes it possible for me to begin to think in theological or poly-

theological terms, yet not get stuck in dogmatic belief. I call *this* state "seeker's mind." On a personal level, this helps deepen my religious sense both experientially and intellectually. Seeker's mind also helps me share this deepening sense with my community, so we can explore and deepen as a tradition. Together, we can learn to discuss, argue, and put forth different viewpoints and to take them all into account, building a magical worldview that is holistic rather than fragmentary.

All of that said, you don't have to believe in any *thing* or have faith in any *concept*. Believe enough in yourself to risk opening to a new awareness of the world.

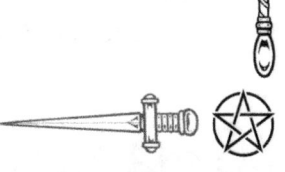

THE ELEMENTAL POWERS

The first edition of this book included work with named Guardians. In expanding the scope of this edition, it felt prudent to allow you—the reader—to form your own relationship to the elemental forces of each direction.

A Magician might call on Archangels in each of the four directions, and a certain Witch might invoke the Guardian of the Watchtowers or the Elemental Monarchs. Others simply invoke the qualities of the element they are calling in.

However you decide to invite the elemental powers into your sacred work, you may find them to be a great help.

There are many ways in which the elemental powers may help our work. For example, I place the Guardians with their directions on the elemental pentacle, by doing this, I can call on the Western Guardian for the energy to help with emotional work, or the Northern Guardian for the energy to help me with issues of power. This is not a matter of the Guardians being personally interested in our love lives, for example; rather, when we are both internally and externally aligned, we can tap into the energies that they hold and use them to great affect.

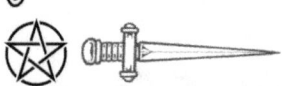

The elemental powers or guardians are beyond gender and name, shifting and changing. They are forces larger than we know; to name them or give them image, form, or gender are ways we can touch and try to comprehend them. I provide some associations that come from my own experiences, but you must develop your own sense of the Guardians, because they may come to you in different forms than they do to me.

You may use the cantrips I wrote to call these entities, or find your own way to honor and call the elemental powers.

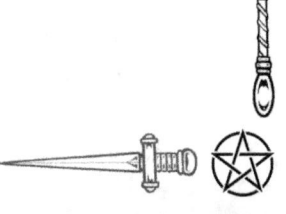

THE GUARDIAN OF THE EAST

Now it is time to meet the Guardian of the East, the bearer of the Wand of Air. This Guardian helps with all the powers of East. It brings the fresh energy of birth into the sacred sphere, and gives new insight and knowledge into your work.

Align your Triple Soul. Center yourself and cast the blue sphere around you. Light a candle on your altar, pale yellow or lavender. Turn toward the East, open yourself to the elemental power there. Feel a breath upon your forehead. Open to the Guardian of the East. Begin to feel the presence coming closer to you. What does this Guardian feel like? Can you get a glimpse? "Guardian of the East, ride the winds and join this rite." Feel the Guardian of Air, the holder of the budding Wand of Knowledge, tipped with a crystal that touches the morning star, the place of new beginnings, self, and focuser of memory and intellect. Feel the presence. Introduce yourself.

Guardian of the East
You who are the first breath that kisses dawn,
Ride the winds and join our rites.
Teach us the powers of Knowledge,

And fill us with the breath of life.
Let us begin, together.
Let us begin.
Touch our eyes, our ears, our lips.
May we speak your name.
May we know the truth.
May we know ourselves.
Welcome.

How does this Guardian manifest to you? Write or draw whatever information you are given.

Take a deep breath. Stay in this presence for a while—feeling, sensing, gazing. You may wish to write what you sense. When you are done for this meeting, say:

Thank you for your presence
Thank you for the gifts of air and knowledge.
May I listen, may I discern, may I grow.
Go if you must, stay if you will.
Hail and farewell.

The invocations are my own. Use them freely, write your own, or simply speak with inspiration in the moment. The last is usually my choice. All poetry is inspired and sacred. Open yourself to sound and word.

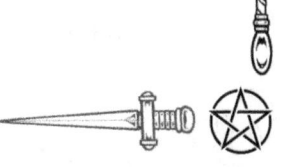

THE WAND

In many Craft traditions, the tool of the East is the Wand. This may confuse people who are familiar with the Tarot, or any other magical system influenced by Ceremonial Magick. If you are accustomed to placing the blade—whether athame or sword—in the East, and the wand in the South, this may feel strange.

You don't need to change your practice if your current associations strongly resonate with you, but I ask that you try to understand this way. The Wand is in the East and associated with air because it is the budding branch of new beginnings. It bends in the breeze and the wind whispers through it; fire would consume it. Even in the depths of winter, the branch holds potential, and the wand is that branch. It is the scepter of knowledge, a tool necessary to begin any study. The East is the place of beginnings. May our knowledge glow like the dawn.

Traditionally, the wand has a crystal tip, like the morning star called by the Guardian of the East. All you really need, however, is a branch. You will find the wand that calls to you. Some people get their wands as gifts, from fallen branches. If you cut any living

plant or tree for your wand, make sure to leave an offering. You may ask a gardener the best time to prune wherever you live.

Those of you who are advanced practitioners may have a wand already. If this is the case, and you have used your wand as a tool of fire, you may want to pick a new wand to represent air.

If you are only familiar with using a blade to draw a boundary, you may be interested to work with the softer boundary of the wand. It is a less brittle demarcation and can be a bit more welcoming. Experiment with this and feel the difference. I especially do this when inviting in the powers of knowledge or creativity, or when I want the circle to be more open, public.

If you are still having trouble imagining a wand as a boundary maker, think of the hedge. Hedges are good boundary makers, broad and lovely, firm enough to keep big things out yet porous enough to allow passage to smaller things. The cattle remain within the fence, yet the birds and foxes come and go.

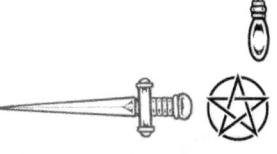

WAND LISTENING

Go into a wooded area or a city park. Feel the trees around you. Imagine you can feel the sap running through them, or lying cold inside, depending on the season. Take a deep breath. Listen to the trees. What do they have to tell you?

Below is an exercise I did with my students for many years. I still introduce myself to new places in this way.

Learn the names of five trees in your neighborhood, your local park, or a nearby wooded area. Bring them some water. If you find a Hawthorne tree, with its strong thorns and bright red berries in Winter, pour a little cream there, or leave nuts out for the animals, for this tree is said to be a gateway into Faery.

After listening to the trees, come to some of your own associations for the wand and the East, the element of air.

Here are some of mine:

Trees reach up into the sky. A hollow wand becomes a flute. Trees give oxygen that helps us to breathe. Trees dance in the wind, rustling and whispering. They are home to the creatures of air.

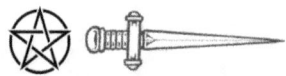

CHARGING AND CONSECRATING YOUR WAND

For this ritual, you will need to gather anything you wish to charge your wand with. You might want to rub oil into it, to keep the wood supple. I do this periodically. Or you may want ribbons to tie on the ends. This may also be the time when, if yours is to be a crystal-tipped wand, you hollow the end, melt the wax, and wind the wire to keep it firmly in place. Take a bath or shower, gather all your tools and get ready to cast your circle. Some people consecrate their tools over time. You can take your wand outside with you to soak up sun and wind before doing the formal consecration within your circle. If you are lucky enough to have a private place outside to do this ritual, all the better!

Ground and center and align your Triple Soul. Cast the sacred sphere and honor the seven directions. Ask for the particular help of the power of elemental East in this working. Light a yellow candle. If there is a type of incense you like, you may burn that, too. Pass your wand over the candle and through the smoke of the incense saying, "I cleanse you with fire and with air, may you be open to receive my intention." Then oil your wand, all the while thinking of the work you want the

wand to help you with—so that it may teach you about air, and discernment and true speaking. Next, raise energy by drumming, singing, or dancing or by breathing in life force as you would for the Prayer for Alignment. Once you feel full of energy, breathe it into the wand, charging it with your breath and intent. "In the presence of the Guardians and elemental powers, may you carry my intention, so that I learn readily, speak truly, and guide well. May my voice be carried in the world and may you represent all things that grow good within me." As you breathe, know that your power is transferred into the wand, consecrating and charging it.

Once you are finished with your consecration, thank the Guardians, extinguish your candle, and send the blue fire back into the earth, opening your sacred sphere. Blessed be.

As we charged our wand with life via our breath, another way to consecrate magical tools is to charge them with the life force in the potent form of orgasm from self sex. You may add that to your consecration if it feels right to you.

Now that your wand is consecrated to magical work, treat it well. Clean and oil it periodically. See how it wants to rest on your altar. I sometimes rest mine on top of my chalice when my communication needs to come more from a heart space. Other times, I will lean it, so it is standing upright, running energy clearly and cleanly, as I want my breath to run through my body. Your tools will speak to you over time, if you make an effort to listen.

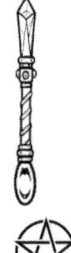

WALKING AS A WAND

When I first started working with these magical tools, I would imagine them in my body, and I would walk around as the wand or the blade. I would feel the energy of the branch, the tree, inside of me, just as we did with the sun and moon. Doing this gives me the "feel" of the tool inside my body and gives me a better feel for the tool when I pick it up and begin to run energy through it. It gives me a clearer sense of the tool and how to use it properly. If you were a wand, what would you do?

Take a breath. Imagine that you are a wand, you are wood or crystal, supple and strong, with a specific purpose. Walk outside, feel the air flowing around you, and notice how you, a wand, respond to the air. Walk, flow, dance in the breeze. How do the trees feel to you? Are you drawn to them? Do they tell you things that they would not tell you in your human form?

Back in your human form, hold your wand in your hand. What does the wand want? Will it tell you its secret name?

RUNNING WAND ENERGY

Now, let us practice running the energy through our wands.

Hold your wand in your dominant hand. Ground and center yourself and draw up some energy through the soles of your feet. Call in a golden-yellow/white energy. Feel that flow into your body. Let it flow through your heart and down into your wand arm. Let it pour through your hand, out your wand, and into the earth. Practice starting and stopping the energy. Key it to your breath at first, and then just imagine the energy flowing on its own, directed by your intention. Once you are through, let most of the energy sink into the earth as an offering and imagine the remainder of the energy pulling itself back to rest inside your wand.

If you feel yourself full of excess energy, you can breathe it up to your Sacred Dove to align yourself. You can also send a breath out to feed the world.

Though this exercise asks you to run golden-white energy through your wand, experiment with this and with the blue fire, sensing which feels best suited to your tool.

ASKING FOR WHAT YOU WANT

We have seen how the East holds the powers of air, the powers of speech. Now that you have a wand, you can use it to ask for what you want. I developed the following exercise to help us with this task.

When you ask yourself what you want, what is the first thought that leaps into your mind? Hold your wand in your hand and draw an invoking pentacle with it, top point to bottom left to upper right, across left, down to bottom right, and back up to the top point. Then draw a clockwise circle around the star. As you draw, say "I invoke _____ into my life. This is my wish, on this my star."

It is very useful to ask yourself what you want from your life, especially your spiritual work. Some people want to evolve, some are committed to self-awareness and discovery, some want community, some want a way to feel more empowered, some want to feel closer to the earth. Clarifying what you want from your spiritual work will help that work immeasurably. Not only is this a good piece of self-knowledge, it reveals your path. You will encounter fewer frustrations and dead ends if you can assess your

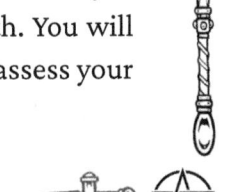

wishes early on. You should re-examine this every few years or so. As you change, your answer to the questions will change as well.

Sit quietly, with your wand resting in the palms of your hands. Let your breath sink to your belly. Relax. Align your Triple Soul, breathing easily and fully. Once you feel centered, raise your wand to an upright position and ask yourself, "What do I want from my spiritual path?" Listen for an answer from your God Soul. You may not get your answer right away. Once it appears, again draw an invoking pentacle, letting your energy flow out through the wand, forming the star clearly in front of you, flaming blue in the æther. Say "I vow to _____" or "I call _____ to me."

LISTENING, VISIONING, STEPPING

Once you have done the preliminary work of asking for what you want, you can do some further work of deep listening for who you wish to be and what life you want to step into. Remember, on the pentacle of the senses, hearing rests in the place of air. We will transform our listening into vision and then step forward into that vision, allowing it to enter our bodies and begin to work its changes there. We won't wait for fate to give us life's allotment; rather, we will listen deeply and step into our own destiny.

I designed this exercise to be done with a witness, as too often what we want for ourselves feels embarrassing to us, as though we don't have a right to our true potential. Even if you do not speak the words aloud (though I recommend doing so), a witness helps to confirm the process and lend support. If you cannot find a human witness, ask the Star Goddess and your own Divine nature to bear witness.

Cleanse yourself by breathing in through your root, the base of your spine, and out through your sex. Then breathe in through your sex and out through your belly, your place of will. Breathe in through your will

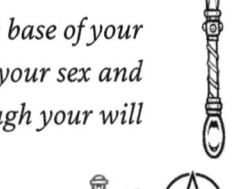

and out through your heart. In through your heart and out through your throat. In through your throat and out through your third eye. Then breathe in through your third eye and out through the crown of your head. Now take a full body breath. Drop into your belly and your heart. Begin to listen to what your soul wants for you. Who do you wish to become? Once an answer begins to rise in you, even if it is only a feeling, let it form into a vision you have for yourself. Again, this might be a sense of self, of posture and moving in the world, or it might be very specific information. Take your wand and this vision and draw a body-sized invoking pentacle in the air in front of you. Say what you are invoking (for example: "Artist, Teacher, and Healer"). Then, step forward into that pentacle, stretching your arms out to meet the points. Feel the energy as you and it interpenetrate. Say, "I accept this into my life. Blessed be."

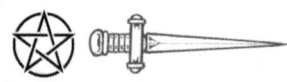

GLOBAL MAGIC

At various times, I have used my wand to send spells off long distances. Most recently, after my class had done the above exercises, we went outside and faced each other, standing in a circle. Drawing energy into our wands, with the intention to cast it out, across the circle, and around the globe, we shouted, "I invoke Compassion and Clear Sight!" Then we sent the energy out, shooting in great arcs to encompass the earth.

I only do this practice with things I am willing to also invoke within myself.

WIDENING YOUR AWARENESS

"*Perceive first, believe later.*"
—Victor Anderson
"*I don't need faith. I have experience.*"
—Joseph Campbell

THE EXERCISES in this section all attempt to expand our awareness and develop seeker's mind. Doing these practices will gives us a greater capacity to hold all things human—intellect, heart, awareness, pain, pleasure, empathy, and satisfaction—and help us to enter non-ordinary, or magical, consciousness.

Magical consciousness is an expansion of our regular senses. It is an entryway into the Sacred, which exists all around us, but can get covered up by our busyness, self-centeredness, depression, self-importance, or simple lack of awareness. Entering the non-ordinary enables us to employ attention, rather than focus.

Focus can be narrow—a tunnel vision that encourages myopia—while attention accesses all 360 degrees. Attention enables you to take in information from the back of your arms,

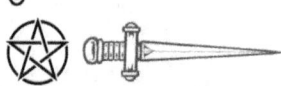

from your neck, your feet, the top of your head, with your peripheral vision and your energy bodies, as well as through your nose, ears, and eyes. Attentive capacity can make you more effective, with a greater ability to process information and communicate beyond the surface levels.

The following exercise is similar to "Deep, Expansive Attention" in section three, but is simpler and quicker. I find it helpful to practice this while walking, or sitting in meetings, as that gets me used to doing this often, wherever I am, which helps me see that I can access these larger senses at any time.

EXPANDING YOUR ATTENTIVE CAPACITY

Though I have written this as a walking exercise, you can alter the following to suit your own physical needs. The important thing is to breathe and open to the world around you. This way, you become more effective in the ordinary world and more powerful in the non-ordinary.

Take a deep breath. Begin walking. Let your eyes soften. Feel your spine straighten and lift as you breathe. Feel your feet pressing down into the ground and, simultaneously, feel lifted from the top of your head. Notice the angle at which you are walking. Notice your center of gravity and try breathing into that spot, feeling the low swing of your hips and your belly riding above them. The more you press down, the taller you stand. Notice your shoulders and the swing of your arms.

Keep breathing, softly and deeply, imagining that your breath fills your whole body. As you breathe, sense the back of your skull. Let your awareness—your vision—expand to include the back of your head. Let it expand to your shoulders in back, and your breastbone in front. Continue to feel your feet, pressing into the ground, and the top of your head, opening to the sky above. Keep breathing, aware of the world you are moving through, sensing it 360 degrees. Let your peripheral vision

widen. Now let texture enter, and scent and sound. Try not to focus too hard on any one thing. Rather, let the information enter your whole awareness. You are moving, aware, expanding your capacity to engage the world.

Once you begin to have a facility for moving into and out of non-ordinary states of consciousness, you will find that even your ordinary state will expand and your horizons will widen. Making love will open out into even more ecstatic sharing and your effectiveness in the workplace will increase, for you will become a better "listener," more able to read what is needed in every situation. You may find yourself taking on the role of mediator because you can sense what is happening, with less emotional static. The longer you engage and breathe with this practice, the less closed in upon yourself you will be become. You will be more open to abundance, more centered and sure, and more aware of the world and its gifts.

ENGAGING THE BREATH

You have probably noticed that all the work we've done so far begins with the breath. In ordinary life, without the help of expanded awareness, sitting, or posture work, breath is often constricted and taken for granted until it is almost gone. I'd like you to begin to cultivate the worldview that all magic begins with the breath. Know that you can change almost any situation, *just by changing your breathing*. That is magic.

We have already begun to experiment with our breath patterns, noticing how breath runs through our bodies and where it is blocked. The following exercises show other ways to become aware of your breath, and to learn to engage it with attention, rather than spending it profligately.

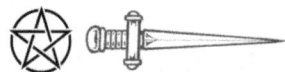

THE POWER OF SPEECH

"*Words are the ambassadors of our intentions.*"
—Susan Harrow

Speech is an important power of air and the East. While the "Expanding Your Attentive Capacity" exercise helped you begin to listen to the world around you, now I'd like you to begin to listen to yourself. What are your patterns of speech, how do they affect your thought patterns and vice versa? What do you think other people hear when they listen to you? What, or whom, is talking underneath the words? Let us find out.

Begin to ask yourself, "*What do I want to grow with my words?*" This question holds the power of the East, the power of the wand. How do you use speech? Do you throw your words away without thinking about them? Do you hoard them, swallowing them even when speaking would be a sharing of your power? Do you tear others down with your words, spending all of your energy being concerned with the actions of *others? Do you not share information when it is needed, or conversely, do you share an overabundance of information, talking more than is necessary?*

Begin to look at your words and your speech habits. Notice your patterns, your tone of voice. Do you speak sarcastically, or always with a questioning tone? How do you speak with intent? Next time, before you speak, practice taking a conscious inhalation, notice your spine, how you are sitting or standing. Feel the words build within you, gathering power. When they feel that they must be spoken, open your mouth.

Listening to myself in this way has helped me to speak more clearly, to engage in malicious gossip less and less, and to speak with more intention and authority. You may notice that when you speak with more intention, your voice becomes slightly deeper than usual and is peppered with less verbal garbage such as "umm" or "you know." People may begin to respond to you in surprising ways. If you begin to listen to yourself, people may actually listen to *you*.

The following is an introduction to the wand work we will be doing later. This exercise is another way to move toward integrity and grace.

Before speaking, take a deep breath and imagine a wand, a branch shining in your hand. Holding this magical tool in your mind's eye will help you to speak as a person of deep breath and sound intention, for it will remind you that your words are magical tools. What words do you want to grow from your wand? Speak those words.

THE POWER TO NAME

"*Three days you may have, to discover my name.*"
—*Rumplestiltskin*, as retold by Tasha Tudor

NAMING IS another power of speech, a power of air. In fairy tales and old myths, we often read that once a sorcerer or magical creature found your true name, it had control over your soul. These stories give us an important clue: that names establish relationship. As children, we learn that to name something is a step toward having greater knowledge of its nature. "Dog" is different from both "grass" and "sky."

Conversely, once a thing is named, its power over *us* ceases to hold sway, as in the tale of Rumplestiltskin, when the revelation of the magic man's name enabled the miller's daughter to keep her child. This power of naming can establish relationships with our "no zones"—that area truckers and lorry drivers cannot see via their mirrors—which are the habits and the emotional screens that keep parts of ourselves hidden. By using our sitting exercises

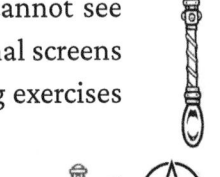

and keys for remembrance, we can catch quick glimpses of our states. By becoming aware of barely conscious activities—like a phrase we repeat to ourselves—we can begin to see into our psyches. Once we begin to get these glimpses, we can begin to track them, layering this impression today with another from last week, until a picture slowly begins to form. Then we can attempt to name our formerly hidden habits or screens.

Once we name our tendencies, they no longer have such control over us, for they are not working solely in the shadows. We gain some measure of control over *them* and can observe them, remark on them, and perhaps not always act according to their wishes. For example, once I realized that I was extremely impatient, and saw even that one part of my brain seemed to be wired in this way, wanting to jump from square one to square four, I could begin to exercise greater and greater amounts of patience in my life. My impatience is still present, but it no longer has such a large amount of control over my behavior. Rumplestiltskin cannot run away with the fruits of my labor.

Use the awareness exercises we've already begun to practice and start to watch for those parts of you that are as of yet un-named. It might help you to begin to keep a journal to chart your internal work. Naming something by writing it down is powerful. It will also help you three months or a year from now, to look back on your work and see how you have progressed and what you may have missed.

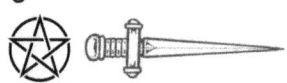

COUNTING YOUR BREATH

This is an aid to your sitting practice that can develop greater opportunity for God Soul Listening. A variation of a practice used in some Buddhist traditions, this exercise will help to quiet your brain and increase your ability to remain present. However, it is important to not get caught up in doing this, thinking "Oh, great! Now I don't just have to sit still, listening to myself."

Therefore, I've designed it to only take you part way through your sitting. Then you let this technique go, and sit, letting Sacred Dove deepen and rise, watching and listening.

Hold the image of the blue flame in your mind's eye. Let it float just in front of you, out from the space of your third eye. Now, begin to notice your breath. Try to make your long inhalation match your exhalation. Begin to count your exhalation. Inhale. Exhale. One. Inhale. Exhale. Two. Attempt to do this up to the count of thirty exhalations, keeping the flame in your mind's eye all the while. Half-thoughts may bubble up, like the need to adjust your posture, for example. If you get stuck on a thought and notice all of a sudden that you are at nine when last remembered counting five, start your count over. Inhale. Exhale.

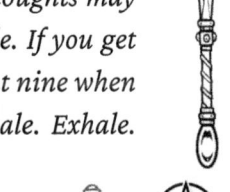

One. Inhale. Exhale. Two. Start this over as many times as is necessary, until you reach the count of thirty. Once you have done so, let the counting and the visual of the blue flame go. Sit in silence with yourself.

I like this practice because it shows just how quickly thoughts can enter, trapping us in a loop. All it takes is the space between one inhalation and exhalation. Thoughts are quick! If they are keyed into emotions, they are much more tenacious, as well. If we sit while in emotional upheaval, our thoughts will catch on these emotions, plunging us into detailed, though phantom, conversations in our minds. Counting can help reorient us, enabling our emotions to slowly quiet themselves. We can sit, breathe, and observe instead of being taken over.

Some people have related that they become frustrated at not being able to get through their count. They continuously have to start over. I pointed out that this is information about themselves that they did not have before! Everything can inform us.

If we can say, "Oh, I get frustrated if I cannot do something perfectly," then we have remembered a piece of ourselves. We can then look at this part more deeply and thoroughly, beginning to map its connections to other parts, forming a more holistic sense of self.

EXPANDING THE ORDINARY WORLD

The pentacle is a tool of the North and earth in most Witchcraft traditions. A tool that has been borrowed from ceremonial magick and alchemy, the pentacle represents the human body, balanced and beautiful. It represents the five senses, the five stages of life and the presence in our bodies of the five sacred elements: Earth, Air, Fire, Water and Spirit or Æther. Da Vinci's "Vitruvian Man" is a good example of a pentacle using the human form as a template of sacred geometry.

As a Witch, I prefer to act, rather than react. The pentacle, with its encapsulation of energy building from point to point, is a good symbol for this move toward action. In Craft Traditions, the upright pentacle sometimes represents Goddess energy, and the downward pointing pentacle, God energy. I like to look at these as descending or rising energies, or expansive and chthonic energies instead. There may be other pairings that make sense to you.

We will visit many pentacles throughout subsequent sections, beginning now with the Pentacle of the Senses, which is rooted in the Elemental Pentacle.

Different Craft traditions place Aristotelean elements in different parts of the pentacle. This particular configuration, however, is a building block to the pentacles to come in this book.

ELEMENTAL PENTACLE

CLEANSING THE PENTACLE OF THE SENSES

"The senses are of the earth, the reason stands apart from them in contemplation."
— Leonardo da Vinci

I PLACE this pentacle in the East because it is a pentacle of beginnings, initiating our relationship with everything outside of ourselves.

I work with the Pentacle of the Senses because the witch is part of the world, and our relationship with the world is grounded in what our senses perceive. Some of us are more attuned to sensory input than others, depending on how our brains are wired. For example, I tend to be very sound sensitive, and also have a keen sense of smell. Some of us have access to all five senses, while others adapt and deepen their relationship to the senses they do have access to.

The Pentacle of the Senses connects us to the rest of the world —seeing, tasting, touching, hearing, smelling—and like all of the pentacles, it is founded upon the Pentacle of the Elements. For

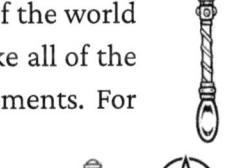

example, spirit connects with sight because we have different layers of sight—both physical and what I call the eyes of the spirit, the psychic or intuitive. Air brings sound waves to our ears and fire carries the smells of fruit ripening in the sun or bread baking in a hot oven. The water in our mouth spreads taste across our tongues, carried on saliva. Our bodies, bone and flesh, solid as earth, are the houses of touch, and our skin is alive just like the bark of a tree. Touch the earth, for of earth we are.

I developed the following exercise to activate our sense, each in turn.

Sight, Smell, Sound, Touch, Taste. Take a deep breath. Feel it fill you. Now imagine that you are breathing through your eyes, clearing your sight. Breathe through them again, asking for new vision, for a new, fey way to see the world. Let your eyes open to the magic in the world, to a secret landscape full of hidden beauty. Send a big, clearing breath through your nose. Now breathe again, asking for a more subtle sense of smell, a way to catch the scents of life and death, of animals and plants, of perfumed breezes. Your ears are also connected to your throat and air passages. Send your breath out through your ears, feeling them open. Ask that your ears be more attuned to sound, to music, sighing wind, rustling branches, truly spoken words. Send your breath out along your skin. Blow into your hands, across your fingertips. Pray for a sensitive touch, for depth of communication through your body. Breathe across your taste buds, feeling your breath float on the top of your tongue, clearing out old tastes and drawing in cleanness. Ask now for an expanded sense of taste, so keen you can almost taste the smells drawn in by your nose. Taste the wonder of the world, open to every bite.

As your facility for full awareness increases, the world itself will open up to you, showing itself to you in all of its sacredness. Some of what you sense with your newly awakened faculties might be discomfiting, startling, or even frightening because you are not used to seeing the world this way. Take a breath, connect

with Sacred Dove, and know that you are powerful and alive. When your senses become more heightened, try to engage them, rather than going back to your ordinary ways.

Cook yourself a meal, or go out to your favorite restaurant or café. Smell the fragrance of things that are fresh, live. Let your eyes really watch every movement you make. Touch the vegetables as you cut them. Listen to the sounds of the steam rattling the pot lid. Don't let the lift of a fork to your mouth become automatic. Feel the heft of it. Feel the temperature change against your lips as the food draws toward your mouth. Then let taste open upon your tongue. If you are eating with others, take them in with your senses, too. Take a breath, engage in conversation, and be aware of the feel of your napkin and the taste of the food on your tongue. Life is good.

FEELING THE WORLD INSIDE YOU

You are connected to the world. The cycles of life move, flow, and continue, daily and monthly, with projects, relationships, and changes throughout your lifetime. In this way, you are like the seasons, like day moving into evening, birds pecking at the jellyfish washed up on shore, and like the ocean itself, tide flowing in and out, filling up and emptying beaches, basins, and pools.

The Craft traditions I trained in are ecstatic, rather than fertility-based, traditions of Witchcraft. This means that we, as humans, have direct connection to the elements of life, to Nature, and to the Gods. We may develop liturgy, and there are beautiful poems, castings, and rituals within my traditions, but the important thing is that, through the use of our tools, we can become more open to a direct connection to life, and can create new rituals, and invoke spontaneously.

Fertility traditions in Witchcraft tend to look for sexual polarity outside of the individual person, developing ways to work with sex and gender by seeing men and women as representatives of specific qualities that are deemed masculine or femi-

nine. In my experience, each person can balance sex and gender qualities within themselves, both energetically and physically. All Gods and humans, whether male, female, or beyond or in between genders, hold the energy of creation, lust, love, and a connection to beginnings. We can celebrate humanity in all its forms.

Some people feel very male, and others very female. Those designations—man or woman, butch or femme, masculine or feminine—are social constructs, and shift from culture to culture. Other humans don't relate to gender at all, and work with blending or heightening polarity in a variety of ways.

I've been genderqueer since childhood. Even during the times I tried to fit in or pass as a woman, I tended to telegraph all the ways I didn't quite fit. I'm grateful that the generations younger than mine settled on non-binary, agender, or genderqueer as descriptors for now, though I am sure future generations will find other ways to express themselves, as well.

Notice how "male" or "female" you feel in any given moment. What qualities make you feel this way? Does this sense change according to different situations in which you find yourself? Or do you always feel very much one way or another? How does this sense of gender energies and qualities within you form your identity?

Notice how often you feel in between, beyond, or simply uninterested in societal constructs of gender. What helps you explore this? When do you feel most comfortable in your skin?

How do you celebrate yourself?

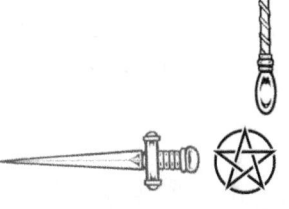

CONNECTING TO THE GODS

In the previous sections, we considered immanence and our own divinity. Within this connection, there exists multiplicity. In the midst of the dance of immanence, specifics stand out, forming around ideas, emotions, natural forces or places, and specific cultures. These are the Gods, and we can experience them in our everyday lives, at any moment. Because of the freshness of attitude required to encounter Deity in this way, I place the following exercises in the East.

Our perception of the Gods begins in the half-light between night and morning, as the Gods live in the place of poetry and shadow, as well as in the glints of sunlight so bright human eyes cannot quite see. They inhabit the areas in between space, time, and consciousness. Our links to the Gods can be tenuous, mostly emotional, sometimes physical—a tingling in the back of the skull, a feeling in one's chest, a finger's touch on the forehead. This is why altered states of consciousness brought on by chanting or casting the sphere are helpful for contacting the Gods. This contact is not part of ordinary consciousness for most of us, but requires training, a getting-used-to.

Talismans help us as focusing tools: Thor's hammer, Mercury's wings, Athena's owl, or Brigid's cross; a budding branch; an antler found on the forest floor; a peacock feather or a statue. These objects can help focus our consciousness by giving us a symbol system as a way to enter into relationship with the Gods.

Open your windows and let some fresh air blow through your rooms, filling your lungs and opening your eyes. Prepare yourself to set aside your preconceptions and, instead, open to experience. Gender is fluid, as changing and varied as the Gods, though I will sometimes use gendered words to describe Deity energies because our culture at large doesn't hold words that encompass the totality of experience of genders, sexualities, and Gods.

Let us try to sense the Divine in nature, in its different guises.

Go to a place in nature where you can see, feel, touch, or taste one or more of the elements. As you move through space, feel the air on your skin: Is it hot, is it cold? Feel the earth beneath you. Begin to breathe deeply, bringing yourself further into a state of non-ordinary consciousness As you breathe, slow your motion down. Your attention should be all around you, 360 degrees. Let yourself sense what is behind you, above and below you. Now allow your attention to fall on something smaller: a flower, a tree, a bird, some water. Breathe. Open to that small something. Ask to be made more aware. Ask for Divinity to come to you. Feel the Divinity that flows through Nature. Try to sense the Spirit of the Place as well as the larger immanent presence. Feel how your own divine nature responds to this.

Next:

Sit at your altar in front of an object that represents a Deity. This object can be human-made or come from Nature. Using the same method you used out of doors, begin to slow your breathing, and move into a non-ordinary state of consciousness. Let the object grow larger. Ask for the presence of the Deity. Let the presence grow around you as you breathe. Let yourself feel. Open to hearing or seeing something non-ordinary.

Spend some time in this Divine presence, then open to the still space that resides in your belly and send a breath there to center you. Thank the Deity and let the energy recede. Bless yourself and your own God Soul.

DANCING THE SUN AND THE MOON

Inspiration is core to magic. Learn to listen with your bones. Learn to speak with your synapses. We will begin this practice by opening to two large forces that affect our lives on earth: the sun and the moon.

Were I with you now, we would drum and dance and I would invite you to the center of the circle to invoke the sun and to dance the sun's energy, to feel its heat on your skin, to work up a sweat and to call it into you until you were running with it, hot, vibrant, vital.

If it is a sunny day, go outside once you are done reading this section if you are able. If it is not sunny out, remember a day when it was, when the sun burned bright above you and warmed your shoulders. Feel it even on a rainy, snowy, or foggy day. It still adds brightness behind the clouds or fog that obscure it. The sun is out there, steadily flaming as we move in an arcing dance around it, drawn by its warmth and the turning pull of gravity.

Take a deep breath. Close your eyes for a moment and feel the sun. Turn yourself so you face it. Begin to breathe. Imagine that you can breathe in the power of the sun, its heat, its power. Take it into your

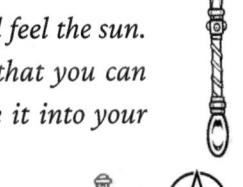

belly. Let yourself begin to move with it. Dance the dance of the sun. If this feels uncomfortable to you, being outside, just take this in, storing it for later, when you can dance the dance of the sun. Call the sun down, call it into your circle. Dance the sun in. Dance it. Sing it. Drum it. What does the sun feel like? Call it in, call it down. You are full of the sun. It is not longer outside of you; you can communicate with it. You can dance with it. You have touched the sun just as the sun touches you. Dance with the sun for a while. You are radiant beauty, powerful, life-giving, and strong.

Take another breath. Begin to slow down. Feel your skin become your own, and feel the sun recede beyond your reach. It still warms and feeds you, but it is far outside of you again. Feel your body, human and alive. Breathe in and out. You are beautiful. Thank the sun. Blow it a kiss. Align your Triple Soul with the energy running through you. Blessed be.

Were I with you now, we would sing and dance and I would invite you to the center of the circle to invoke the moon and to dance the moon's energy, to feel it shining on your face, to feel the night air around you, calling the brightness in the midst of dark into you until you were flowing with it, clear, radiant. and deep.

If it is a night where you can see the moon, go outside or sit near a window where it can shine upon you. If you cannot see the moon, feel its pull on the waters of your body. Know that it is moving in the sky, beyond the earth. Begin to breathe in the radiance of the moon and its silvery white light. Feel it in whatever phase it shines: Is it a promising crescent or is it gibbous, pregnant yet not quite full? Is it on its way to darkness and shadow, or does it shine fully above you, holding all the strength of beauty, distance, and desire?

Take a deep breath. Close your eyes for a moment and feel the moon. Turn yourself so you face it. Begin to breathe. Imagine that you can breathe in the power of the moon—its stillness, its promise. Take it into your belly. Let yourself begin to move with it. Dance the dance of

the moon. If this feels uncomfortable to you, to dance outside the safety of your home, just take this in, storing it for later, when you can dance the dance of the moon with abandon. Call the moon down, call it into your circle. Dance the moon in. Dance it. Sing it. Drum it. What does the moon feel like? Call it in, call it down. You are full of the moon. It is not longer outside of you; you can communicate with it. You can dance with it. It glows inside your belly. You have touched the moon just as the moon touches you. Dance with the moon for a while. You are the subtle beauty, shining, glimmering, and glistening.

Take another breath. Begin to slow down. Feel your skin become your own, and feel the moon recede beyond your reach. It still shines on you and feeds you, but it is far outside of you again. Feel your body, human and alive. Breathe in and out. You are beautiful. Thank the moon. Blow it a kiss. Align your Triple Soul with the energy running through you.

The dance with Sun and Moon is not only a way to work with energies outside of yourself in an inspired and physical way; it is the first step toward the advanced practices of aspecting and possession, in which the Gods can actually speak and move through your body in varying degrees of intensity. This is something done only by trained priests and priestesses. However, anyone is encouraged to open to inspiration.

TAKING SPEECH INTO ACTION

H aving breathed in the powers of air, examining our patterns of speech and invoking our visions, it is time to turn to face the fire. Fire lends the powers of will and action to our words, enabling us to move more fully into the lives we wish to live.

PART FIVE
SOUTH: ENGAGING THE FLAME

THE TOOLS OF FIRE

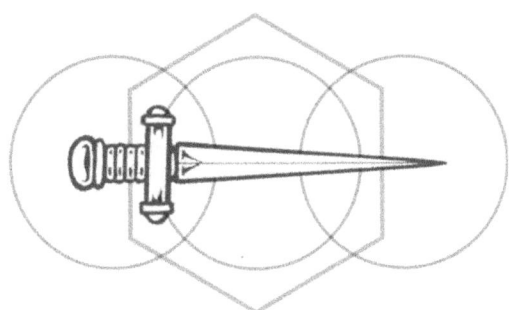

E nter the Southern Quadrant: the place of fire, will, and desire. Our tool here is the blade, the Athame or the Sword. The blade, forged in fire, is tempered by our will and by the world. The more it is tempered by our will, through our connection to Deity, the less it will be forged by the surrounding culture. Make the blade your own; feed it with your fire. Get clear on what you want; hone yourself. This is not a cold, intellectual blade, this is a warm blade, full of sex and desire and the life force that runs through all things. The stronger this blade becomes, full of the confidence of Pride, the more it brings with it the power of Law.

Air feeds fire, and we turn from the East to face the South. Traditionally, this is the place of flame, heat, rising energy, and action. The time is noon, with the midday sun at full power; this stands in opposition to the North, which holds the dark mystery of midnight. The tool here is the blade, forged in fire. The blade—whether the sword or the Witch's athame—represents the strength of will and the power of choice. How will you wield your abilities? What sparks your energy? What feeds your life force? Step toward the fire.

TOUCHING THE FOUR FIRES

Victor Anderson once told me about four kinds of fire energy—coal, flame, arc, and star—and asked me, "Which kind are you using?" Then he sent me on my way to figure it out on my own. That was it. The question was the teaching. The following is my personal exploration of the four fires.

"What kind of fire are you using?" is an important question. *Coal*, or *ember*, is the most sustainable, yet it needs outside fuel to get anything going and even to keep burning itself. Embers will not burn forever if not given more fuel to become flame. This fire is the basic level of health and well-being we were born with. *Flame* is the product of our work, our intention, and of physical food, sex, and exercise, all things fed by a base of steady coal fire. In turn, flame keeps the bed of embers burning strongly and steadily. *Arc* is the power of lightning, the flash of inspiration that is hard to sustain, but that can give us the insights or extra burst of energy to bring back to feed creativity or action. It is also the connecting flame of the welder's torch, and can help to put

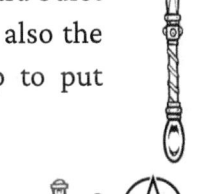

disparate pieces together, but it cannot do the work of forming the pieces themselves. This is the energy we run when newly in love or when working on an exciting new project.

Star fire is the ecstasy of the Gods; it holds those points of communion reached during intensive meditation or prayer, in wild dancing or joyous sex, where I feel so open and so on fire that I am almost consumed. I can gain valuable insights in these spaces, but they are not sustainable. Star fire is not an energy in which to remain. If our work is to become more human, we must bring the ecstasy home, into our daily lives. Though we can touch the realms of the Gods or of Faery, we are not to escape into them. Star fire and arc both can raise the general levels of the more basic fires of coal and flame. They do this by lending vitality and inspiration. And without strong coal and ember, running arc or star fire can quickly burn us out.

Life force fuels more life force. We need to learn what feeds us and how to not fear the fires that will, in the long run, stoke our ability to be healthy, happy, sexy, creative, and productive.

If we are used to living at a low level of energy, well-contained and safe, a rush of new energy can feel overwhelming, causing us to want to stop. Or if we are used to using high energy only in short bursts and burning out, like getting really angry and then feeling exhausted, or going out dancing and being unable to get up the next day, we may distrust this energy and have a hard time finding ways to make our lives and work more sustainable.

Begin to look at where and how you expend your energy. Are you high-energy, frenetic, easily burned out, or low-energy, withdrawn, ill? Do you over-schedule yourself? Do you have trouble getting out of bed? What could help bring you into balance? Ask yourself: How can I best do my work on earth? How can I feed a sustainable fire? What can I feed that will also keep me fed? What is my baseline of energy and how can I raise that level to hold more energy in a healthy manner?

Patterns that I have found helpful to sustain coal and flame as well as creating easier access to arc and star fire are regular physical exercise and daily sitting practice coupled with Triple Soul alignment. Satisfying, healthy food, and satisfying, healthy sex are also effective.

THE FIRE OF WILL

Will is an important facet of our being. Without will, one does not move in the world, but lies around, boneless, as if we have no spine. We need will to make decisions, to be affective outwardly and to make any changes within. Our very commitment to doing spiritual work relies on our will, otherwise we resort only to habitual behavior and spin our wheels aimlessly. To be a Witch, one must engage will. It is the first act of esoteric rather than exoteric religion. If we want to open to our spiritual lives ourselves, we must strive to study the inner—the esoteric—rather than relying on a set structure outside of ourselves to teach us the exoteric, or external qualities.

The Craft demands our full attention to the esoteric because we, as individuals, are going to have to make our own ethical and magical decisions. We can have guides along the way, but no one can give us absolute answers. I appreciate this emphasis on ethical behavior rather than prescribed morality. It puts the responsibility firmly upon my shoulders, requiring me to engage all of my abilities and to cultivate peers in order to check myself and to attempt to discern truth and right action more clearly.

The center of will resides in your belly. It is the center of strength and energy in many traditions. In Hinduism, this is the nabhi chakra. Those of you who study Asian medicine or martial arts will be familiar with chi or qi. There are Celtic traditions of the "fire in the belly" that also correspond. The muscles in the abdomen physically hold our ability to move out and to hold back. As these muscles support a strong back, the seat of will supports our ability to carry responsibility. It is good to get to know this part of ourselves.

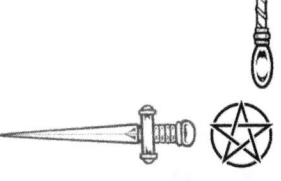

ENGAGING THE CORE

Do you have the will to continue? Is your interest engaged? Are you breathing and present? Let us continue now that we've made that choice. Below is an exercise to help you engage your will by using your abdominal muscles.

As you move through your day, notice your belly. Try to engage its muscles while walking. Tighten and release them while standing in line somewhere. Experiment with both the muscles below your navel and those higher up, near your diaphragm. Take a yoga class, do sit-ups, learn qi gong, or simply try to walk as upright as possible, engaging your stomach muscles as you move. As you strengthen your muscles, let it be your intention that you strengthen your will. As you breathe in, imagine the golden yellow growing clearer and stronger, reflecting the presence of your will and willingness. Let your belly muscles hold you firmly yet gently, just as you hold your will.

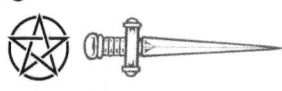

THE GUARDIAN OF THE SOUTH

Now it is time to meet the Guardian of the South, the Guardian of Fire and the Blade. Make whatever preparations you will need to do this work. Align your Triple Soul and cast the sacred sphere. This Guardian can help you with workings needing high energy, or courage, or clarity of will.

Light a candle, red or orange. Turn toward the South. Begin to open to the presence of the Guardian. Breathe deeply. Take a deep breath, connecting to your grounding cord. Cast the blue sphere around you. Light a candle. Face the south. Call to the elemental presence. Feel the warmth in your belly. Open to the Guardian of Fire. The wielder of the Sword of Law, forged in the flame of the will of heat, of noonday sun, the energy of Pride. Feel the presence. Introduce yourself.

Guardian of the South,
You who are the flash of heat in midday's sun,
Light the fires and join our rites.
Teach us the powers of Law,
And fill us with the heat of purpose.
Let us rise, together.
Let us rise.

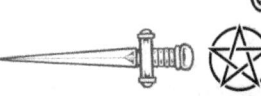

Touch our skin, our sex, our hands.
May we learn our will.
May we know the ways of justice.
May we speak with pride.
Welcome.

How does this Guardian manifest to you? Write or draw the information you receive.

Take a deep breath. Feel the presence guarding the Southern quadrant, huge and beautiful. When you are done for this meeting, say:

Guardian of Fire,
Thank you for your presence
Thank you for the gifts of fire and law.
May I catch the scent, and learn my will.
Go if you must, stay if you will.
Hail and farewell.

THE BLADE

"*Freedom is a two-edged sword of which one edge is liberty and the other, responsibility.*"
—Jack Whiteside Parsons

IN MY PRACTICE—AND in many Craft traditions—the blade is the tool of the South. It is forged in fire, and can conduct heat. It represents the strength of your will, which rests in the fire of your belly. Traditionally it is a black-handled, double-edged blade of steel, although some priests use non-steel blades because of the legends that the Faery folk are allergic to iron. We must remember, however, that *we* are human, and the iron calls to our blood, making it a proper substance for a human tool. It is as humans that we wield this tool, to cut cords and draw boundaries and to come to know the edges that we walk upon.

I have seen blades made of flint, obsidian, copper, silver, or sharp wood. I personally have a steel blade and one made from jet. Steel is a classic for a reason, though. We want our will to be

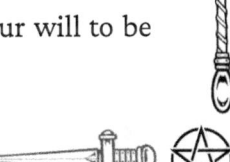

honed, sharp, and able to make clean cuts, and set clear boundaries.

See what feels best to you and think about what qualities in a blade best reflect your will.

EXTENDING YOUR WILL

Hold your blade in your hand. Ground and center. Call the earth's fire into you. Breathe in life force. Fill your belly with life, with fire, with will. Touch your abdomen and feel your will growing beneath your hands. Is your will strong or weak? The fire that flows down your arm and into your blade grows and is refined in your belly. Imagine the blade is an extension of your will. Feel it in your hand. Hold it. Move with it. When you extend your arm with your athame in it, you are extending your will into the world. Each breath can strengthen it.

Set the intention of your will. Begin to move with this will, letting your body shift and turn as your blade cuts the air. If your will is in your blade, what are you putting out into the world? How does this feel? Notice if you move clearly forward, feint sideways, or back up before you move the blade out. All of these movements can teach you something about how you use your will. It can bring passive/aggressive qualities, force, inner strength, anger, fear, or timidity to light.

When you are done, bring yourself to stillness, one hand on your heart, knife flat against your belly. Breathe. Kiss your blade in thanks. Any excess energy can be breathed up to Sacred Dove.

Holding Choices

The power of choice goes hand in hand with the power of will. The basis for all magical acts lies in our power to choose. A key Feri Tradition tenet is "do not submit your life force to anyone or any thing." As long as you are in touch with your life force, you are in touch with your divinity and your connections to the Gods and the world around you. You can call upon the power of your will and your ability to choose. In this way, the Craft has an existentialist bent: even if the choice is to die, you have a choice of how you go about it.

The more you learn to exercise will and choice, the less you can blame others for your situation. When I blame another person or circumstance for my own problems, rather than looking at how I can take responsibility for my part in the situation, I am submitting my life force to another. When I say, "It is her fault," I am giving my life force over to that person. All of a sudden "she" holds the power in my life. Is that what I want for myself? Not at all. I'd rather have choice in the situation. I'd rather say, "I made a mistake here," and keep my life force flowing through my words,

my body, and my actions, strengthening my integrity and my ability to be an ethical person.

I often call upon compassion when doing this work. Strength and compassion need to grow in equal measure for a person to be balanced and whole. That, too, is a choice.

Hold your blade in front of you. Look at its edges and breathe in the idea that the edge of the blade is where your life's choices reside. How closely can you hold all of your choices? Look at them, sense them. Feel them meet at the tip of the blade. When your choices come together, does a third choice appear? Hold the tension of each side, and the meeting place. Engage the muscles of your belly. Take a deep breath. Call upon your will. Now use your blade to choose, letting the non-chosen fall and sink into the earth. Blessed be.

WALKING AS A TOOL OF FIRE

I like to sometimes imagine myself as my blade. I walk down the street as a blade, creature of fire. I notice how that feels in my body, how it feels to be tempered by life, magic, sorrow, and laughter. When a friend felt she was getting metaphysically cut by her own sword, I encouraged her to imagine it inside her, cross guard hanging along her collarbones, sword pointing down. I asked her to begin turning it in a circle, up and down within her. Over time, it ceased to cut her, and she grew more comfortable as bearer of a sword. Get to know your blade, as you get to know your will, both inside and out. Consecrate it, much as you did your wand, with a ritual and sex if that feels correct. Sharpen and hone it, rub it with clove oil. Treat it well. This is another tool that I sometimes rest on my chalice, to temper it with compassion. Use it wisely.

THE IRON PENTACLE

DISCUSSING IRON

Although in Witchcraft, pentacles in general are located in the North, I place the Iron Pentacle in the South, because it uses the fire of red, iron earth energy as a catalyst for transformation and rebalancing. This energy, when run through the points of the pentacle, is basic flame energy, for these are basic human qualities. When the energy within these points is released for use, we can be healthy and living in right relationship. The flames from Iron Pentacle feed the embers of our life's energy. When we call on the Guardians or Gods for help with our work, we are engaging the energies of arc or star fire to help make connections and inspire us. But the energy of Iron always comes back to our humanness, which lives in the realms where coal and flame sustain life and movement.

The Iron Pentacle is a core tool developed and passed down from Victor and Cora Anderson and is foundational for the work of becoming more fully a human being. Found only in the Anderson Feri Tradition and its offshoot, the Reclaiming Tradition, it is both a conceptual and energetic tool, making use of potent words and freeing their energies for our use. They have

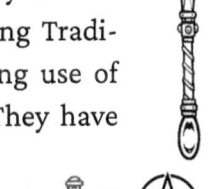

been bound up for far too long. Use this tool and start a revolution within yourself.

If you would like more in-depth work with this pentacle—as well as Pearl and two others—please see my *Stars of Power* book.

IRON PENTACLE

IN RECLAIMING the energies of Sex, Pride, Self, Power, and Passion, we reintegrate that which has been taken from us by the dominant culture or twisted beyond recognition. The energies run through our bodies as though God Herself was drawing an invoking pentacle upon our bodies. If you look at it on the page, imagine lying on your back on top of the pentacle: your right foot will be on Pride, left hand on Self, and so on. The containing circle is drawn around you in the clockwise direction: from Sex to Self to Passion to Pride to Power. This is your personal boundary and you, the individual, are in charge of keeping this boundary. No one can keep it for you—remember, submit your life force to no one and no thing. You contain and run the energy of your life force, and the more you train yourself to do this, the easier and more natural it will become.

Just as learning correct physical posture can feel painful at first, so can running the energy of these points. We must clear out old habits and encrusted thoughts and emotions before the energy can run strong and true, before we can truly feel our Pride or Passion or a strong sense of Self. Our culture has overlaid so many messages upon what are truly our birthrights that they can be difficult to face. What does Sex mean to me? How is Pride different from arrogance? Am I allowed to be my Self, fully, in the world?

All things begin with the life force, Sex. Look at the illustration and notice all the connections that flow from that. There are six triangles of influence, starting with Sex, Pride, and Self. Look at these. What do the relationships mean to you? How does the connection of Self, Power, and Passion play out in your life? How could it help or strengthen you? Notice also the flow on the outside wheel, how Sex feeds Self, which fuels Passion, which supports true Pride and creates our Power, which then flows back into Sex.

The Iron points map onto the Elemental Pentacle. Sex is infused with Spirit as the first impulse of life, Pride is informed by Fire, Self by Air, Power is formed in Earth and Passion in Water.

CALLING BACK THE POINTS

These points, Sex, Pride, Self, Power, and Passion—are all energies that the dominant culture has perverted, twisted, or attempted to wrest from us. It is our job to call them back, to fill ourselves with these energies so we can begin to better work with them. In the sections following this one, we will examine each point to see how they can work in our lives. First, though, it is important to have the energies within us and in front of us, so we can viscerally *feel* what they hold. This feeling can then inform and guide our thoughts, and give us the energy to draw on as we do our work.

So let us begin the process of calling back. Remember, if you cannot *believe* or *feel* any of this, you can imagine the work. Whatever you can imagine, you can begin to manifest, opening to changes energetically, physically, spiritually, or psychologically. That is powerful work.

I will lead you into a meditation, which you can have a partner read to you, or which you can record and play back as a guide. You can do this meditation lying on the ground in a star position, or

standing. I have written it for a standing meditation, because that is my personal preference. Both forms are effective.

Drop down into yourself. Breathe deeply, as fully as you can, bending your knees slightly and straightening your spine. Let yourself rock a bit, feeling your feet firmly beneath you. Now imagine that you have a glowing cord emerging from the base of your spine. This cord is always connected to the core of the earth, molten and hot, shifting and moving beneath you. On your next breath, release any fears you may have about this work or any tensions in your body, and let the earth take this and transform it into energy you can use.

On your next breath, begin to draw up the red, iron energy from the center of the earth. Breathe it up, imagine it rising swiftly up your cord, entering at the base of your spine, filling you with energy. Feel this energy throughout your body, beginning to warm and tingle. Let yourself stand in the Star position, legs apart, arms outstretched (knowing that if your arms get tired, you can bring them down and put them up again as needed). Let yourself feel what it is like to be a pentacle of light and energy.

The energy of iron begins to focus itself into a point, a ball, in the center of your head, behind your forehead or third eye. Feel this point, and name it Sex. Begin to call its energy back. Call Sex back from all the places you may have left it.

Call Sex back from anyone who tells you what your relationship to sex, life force, and creativity should look or feel like. Call it back from your lovers, your partner, call it back from people you wish were your lovers, call it back from disappointment in not having the sex life you wish. Call Sex back from former lovers, from people who make you feel not sexy or from those who make you feel full of sexual energy. Call Sex back. This is your energy. This is the life force that runs through all things, making the world vibrant and alive. Begin to feel this energy running up and down, through you. When sexual energy is yours, and yours alone, it runs up and down, connecting you to earth and sky, filling you with life force. Let yourself be full of the energy of Sex. Blessed be Sex.

The red iron energy flows through your body, running down in a glowing line until it reaches your right foot, pooling into a ball there. Name that point Pride. Feel the connection between Sex and Pride. Does this line run clear and strong? Is it muddy or sluggish? Return to Pride. Let the energy of Pride begin to fill your body as you call Pride back to yourself.

Call Pride back from all the times you told yourself you couldn't do something. Call it back from all of the accomplishments you feel good about. Call Pride back from all the times you were arrogant. Call Pride back from all the times you felt shameful or not worthy. Call it back. Call Pride back from the people who told you pride was wrong. Call Pride back from anyone who tried to belittle your sense of worth. This is your energy. Let the energy of Pride run through you. Blessed be Pride.

The red iron energy flows up through your body, into your left hand, glowing, pooling into the point of Self. Name it. Self. Feel the line connecting Pride with Self. Does this line feel like it runs quick or clear? Is it bright or dim? Now cast your attention back, and see or feel the tripod of energy as Sex feeds Pride and Pride feeds Self. Sense this triad of connection.

Begin to call back the energy of Self. Call yourself back from all the things you ever wanted to be. Call Self back from any expectations other people have of you. Call your Self back. This is your energy. Call Self back from feeling that you cannot be yourself, that you must play some role in life. Call Self back from any person or institution who told you that you don't belong. Call it back. What do you feel like, when your own energy fills you, fully and completely? Feel that. Full. Complete. Feel the energy of Self. Take your place in the world. Blessed be Self.

Let the red, glowing Iron energy move through you, across your heart, connecting Self to Power. Feel that line within you. Is it hot or cold, quick or slow? Does the connection between Self and Power feel strong or barely present? Feel too, the tripod between Pride, Self, and

EVOLUTIONARY WITCHCRAFT

Power. How do they support and balance each other? Pride feeds Self, which feeds Power. As the energy of Iron pools in your right hand, name that point Power.

Begin to call Power back to yourself. Call Power back from all the times it has been used against you. Call Power back from all the times you have used Power over another. Begin to fill with Power. Call it back from all the times you felt powerless. Call it back from brutality. Begin to fill with the power of life, of the earth. Feel the shifting balance of Power grow and move within you. Feel the strength in thigh and shoulder, feel your spine, supple and strong. Breathe in Power. Be full of strength and beauty. Blessed be Power.

The red energy passes through your body again, moving down to your left foot. This is the line joining Power to Passion. Sense this line. Is it running clear, sluggish, quick, or muddy? How does Power feed your Passion? Sense the triad of Self, Power, and Passion. Feel Passion as a ball of red light in your left foot. Name it. Passion.

Begin to call Passion back from all of your dreams. Call Passion back from that book manuscript languishing in your desk drawer, from the paintings you haven't completed, from the garden going to seed. Call it back from every cause you are working for. Begin to fill with the energy of Passion. Feel it rising up from below and spilling out into the universe, a gift. And feel the universe answer back, energy flowing back into you, reciprocal. Feel yourself full of glowing Passion. Breathe that in. Blessed be Passion.

The iron energy flows back up to Sex, to that point in your head. Feel the connection between Passion and Sex. What does that look like, or feel like? Sense the tripod between Power, Passion, and Sex, as one feeds into the other. Stay with that for a moment. Now feel the tripod between Passion, Sex, and Pride. All the points feed one into another, running in the cycles of life force, health, and abundance of energy and creativity.

And now, God Herself draws the circle around you. Draw that circle with Her, creating your own boundary, moving from Sex to Self to

Passion to Pride to Power to Sex, the way the sun moves across the earth, revitalizing, invigorating. Breathe. You are the Iron Pentacle. You glow. Breathe any excess energy up, aligning your Triple Soul.

We run red, iron earth energy through ourselves to connect the Iron Pentacle points together. Now will look at each individual point via the element that corresponds to it. Let us enter the fiery Iron Pentacle more fully, beginning, as all things do, with the power of Sex, based in the potency of Spirit.

SEX—SPIRIT

Sex is the rush of sap into the tree. It is the caress of bee leg on rose petal, the rooting of the mole into the earth. It is the line of my flesh etched into space by my breath. It is the line of our flesh etched by another's hand. It is the heartbeat of the earth and the sun raising sweat beads on our skin. It is the shock of ocean water and a tingling deep down, from genitals to grasping toes. Sex is connection to all of life, built on the Elemental Pentacle; it reaches the Spirit held in all.

In our culture, sex is tricky. It is glorified in strange and twisted ways yet simultaneously swept under the rug. To reclaim Sex, we must reclaim the power of the life force, which is in all creative acts. We must enter into the realm of worms aerating the soil so the roots can better grow. Of the roots thrusting into that earth, caressing it in the darkness. Imagine, birds in flight, coupling, plummeting toward earth in a dizzying spiral. Feel that power. Imagine lightning arcing down and earth rising to kiss it. This is a power connected to all things, not divorced from the flow, not ruining our surroundings by being all too much inside our heads, prone to building more and more boxes to protect

ourselves from the elements and from each other, slowly destroying the earth.

In ordinary life, we either suppress sex energy so deeply we can barely feel it, or we run it in such a way that it spills out of us and onto other people. We can learn to run this energy up and down instead of out. By running it up and down, we become full of vital life force and can use this energy to fuel all of our endeavors, be it studying, working, gardening, dancing, painting, blockading while protesting injustice, or even, surprise, surprise, having sex. When I am full of the life force and know that my sex energy is *my* sex energy, I can use it in the whole of my life.

Calling Sex back is also an acknowledgement that I cannot place responsibility for my sexual self upon any other being. It is up to me to be connected to all growing things. To all of life. It being *my* energy, I need not fear it anymore. It is energy I can draw on. I can feel sexy for myself and enjoy my own pleasure in sexuality. Letting life force run freely is not common for those of us who live cut off from what we call the natural world, where the life force is unimpeded by concrete and electrical interference.

It doesn't matter if a person is asexual, pansexual, or anywhere else on the spectrum of sexuality. We can all find ways to connect with life's burgeoning energy and the energy of sex.

SACRED PLEASURE

As I have said before, to Witches, sex is holy. You can use your sexual energy for many things: charging tools and spells, aligning your soul, opening up to abundance, feeding Deity. Here we will explore the mystery of sacred pleasure. This exercise begins to repair some of the damage many of us have sustained by cultural concepts of physical beauty and by sexual abuses or sorrows.

Sacred pleasure is a reentry into Sex, for and of yourself, as a pure celebration of life, where we use sex energy to bless ourselves, our bodies, and our spirits. This means *all* of ourselves, those parts that try to run from either sex or from confronting the self at its most naked. Many of us have ingrained patterns around sexuality or giving and receiving pleasure. What can these patterns teach us? Just as our sitting exercise can show us the patterns of our thoughts and emotions, we can look at what this exercise brings up for us around sex.

If you are a person who does not feel sexual desire, please adapt any of the below to facilitate your connection to life and pleasure. What might help you do this? Eating a favorite piece of

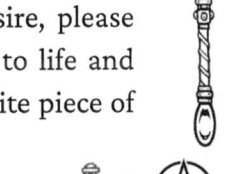

ripe fruit? Dancing? Swimming in clear water, feeling it caress your skin? How can you connect with life force and pleasure, right now?

I invite those who do experience sexual desire to look at any of your sexual habits—fantasy, avoidance, things you always do, things you never do—and see how they disconnect you *from* or connect you *to* sex energy. Try an experiment: notice the usual patterns of your mind or body as they arise during sex and, as in the sitting exercise, try not to latch onto them. View them as information and return to your breathing, trying to really just *be with yourself* in this moment. Be with yourself, just for the length of this exercise. If you find this difficult, or it brings up emotions of anger, frustration, fear, or sorrow, know that you can do the "self-love cleansing" exercise. Surround yourself with love and know that you can try again another time.

Light some candles, or lie in a scented bathtub. Begin to breathe in the life force, as though you were beginning the Prayer for Alignment. Begin to feel the sacred sphere growing around you. Breathe into it. Relax into the energies. Let yourself open to them, floating on them. Kiss your hands and touch your eyes, ears, nose, mouth, breasts, genitals, and legs and feet. Say, "Blessed are you who see, hear, smell, taste, and speak the Sacred. Blessed are you, formed in beauty and strength. May you walk the path, guided by the Gods." Run your hands over your beautiful skin, your sacred body. Say, "I am beloved and beautiful. I am sex and sacredness." Bring yourself to orgasm—or allow yourself to feel pleasure—in this sacred sphere. As you reach your peak, breathe the energy up to feed your God Soul and align yourself. Bask in the sense of wholeness this gives you. If emotions come up, feel those too. If any energy is still left, breathe that to any Guardians or Deities you may have called upon, or release it into the sphere. As the sphere dissipates, say, "May life be blessed."

If you had trouble with this exercise, I recommend aligning your Triple Soul as shown in section three, and running the Iron

Pentacle through your body. Both of those will help to bring you into right relationship with your sex energy, and with all the energies of the human being. Then, by all means, return to what you like about sex, to what suits you. I recommend periodically checking in, returning to look at your sexual patterns and noticing the effect they have on you, and how they may change over time.

Sex is holy, you are sacred, and the life force is always available to you.

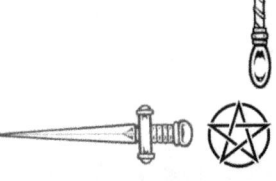

PRIDE—FIRE

The fiery energy of the Iron Pentacle runs from Sex down into Pride. Pride enters when my spine aligns and I stand tall, when I speak my piece and my chest opens to the resonance of my voice. Pride enters when I am fully immersed in the dance of life: proud to be human, proud to be alive, proud to be about my work, proud to know you, and proud to begin to know myself. Built upon the fire from the Elemental Pentacle, Pride emerges when our will is engaged and we stand upright in our truth.

We are often misinformed about what pride is. What is called "pride" in our culture is often merely arrogance, or what I call "false pride." Arrogance has its flip side in self-deprecation, which is just another face of the arrogant posture. Whenever we do not measure our own worth truly, our Pride point is out of balance. We will explore this further when we look at the Rust and Gilded Pentacles.

Do you carry yourself with pride, or do you hunch forward, hiding yourself, head pitched down, arms tucked, trying to take up as little space as possible? Taking up space is a good thing. This

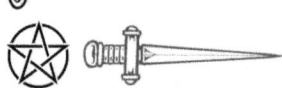

is not arrogant insecurity, where we enter a room, demanding attention from all the inhabitants. Instead, this is a feeling of rightness, a sense of belonging to yourself and being proud of who you are.

The world needs for good human beings to stop skulking around and to take their places, do their work, and do it well. How do you serve the world in this way? What are you proud of?

What are you really good at? Step into the circle and tell us. Are you a kind-hearted listener? Are you patient with children? Do you leap into the fray to battle injustice even though you might be afraid? Are you a fine dancer or a sensitive musician or a dedicated gardener? Do you know the best way to scrub a hundred pounds of potatoes for soup at the local shelter? What makes you a human being?

AUTOMATIC WRITING

This tool may be familiar to those of you who work with writing coaches. Victorian occultists used to use a similar method to contact disembodied spirits. I use it to commune with the Gods, my guides, and with my own intuition. We will use automatic writing to contact our own spirit, which lives, sometimes buried, within us.

For this exercise you will need unlined paper, a fast-writing pen, and a timer. You will write in two segments, one up until the clock rings and then for another few minutes following that. I suggest unlined paper because your handwriting can get big and loose once you have warmed up and things start flowing.

Light a candle and take a breath to call to your soul. Set the timer for six minutes. Begin to write, starting with the words "What is Pride? Pride is..." Don't worry if you can't think of anything to write. This exercise isn't about thinking, it is about uncovering the images, words, and feelings we have been taught about Pride. Depending on where you are in your life and your level of confidence, anything may come up, from "Pride goes before a fall" to "Pride is dandelions standing yellow in the

summer." Don't delete words or try to make sense. Just write. If you get stuck, just go back to writing "What is Pride? Pride is..."

The clock is set. Take a deep breath. Let the pen begin to move across the page. Don't stop. Keep breathing. Pride is. "What is Pride?" Pride is. Let the words flow from your pen faster and faster. Don't think. Let your body relax and your writing grow larger and less contained. Pride. Words of pride are flowing from your pen. Everything you have been taught, all you have learned about Pride. What is it? Keep writing. Keep breathing. Let it flow from you, like flame etching words in the paper. Potent. Black as smoke. Blue as the heart of the flame.

Once the clock rings, don't stop. Start writing the words: "I am proud of..." Take a deep breath. "I am proud that..." Keep writing. "I am proud that..." "Pride is..." "I am..." Flame, words, paper, pen. Take a deep breath. You are writing from a place of Pride. You are writing from deep in your belly. Keep going until you cannot go anymore. Write. Write. Write. Soon you may find phrases repeating. One phrase. Two phrases. Maybe three. "I am proud that..." Keep writing. The phrases will tell you what you need to know. They will tell you when it is time to stop. Don't give up. Push through. Keep going. You are racing. You are writing. You have crossed the finish line. You are human. You are proud.

Stop. Put down your pen. Take a deep breath. What have you learned about the Pride point? Read the first section. What rings true and what sounds a false note? Moving onto the second section, what came forward to tell you what you are truly proud of? Did things repeat? Did a theme emerge? Pick the strongest phrase that you wrote. Read it. Now say it aloud. Say it to your mirror, looking unflinchingly into your eyes.

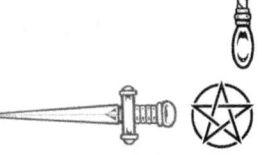

TAKING PRIDE OUT OF THE BOX

I designed this exercise as an exploration of internal risk. It requires us to speak to others about pride. Part of what keeps energy tied up is not talking, of keeping things hidden out of shame, fear of ridicule, or fear of being seen. In consequence, we don't always speak honestly to ourselves or to other people. The next exercise can help us to admit to our curiosity and to speak without fear. Ask yourself whether you have boxed your pride in to keep it small or hidden from the public. Sometimes we have boxed pride in so well, it is hidden from ourselves. Let it loose and see what happens.

Ask your friends, coworkers, family, and circle mates. Ask the grocer on the corner, the postal worker or your librarian. "What are you proud of?" Don't ask them, "What do you think of pride?" Ask, "What are you proud of?" The question might catch them off guard and both of you will be surprised at the answer that pops out! Or you may find that they have thought about it for a while and have a reasoned answer. Start a casual discussion in your neighborhood. Get folks thinking. This spreads pride around. Just the fact that you are willing to ask the question will plant the seed that pride is a natural thing.

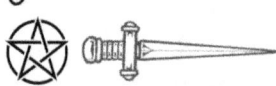

As you take pride out of its box, it will begin to grow around you. You will be working magic in the world and doing us all a great favor. The more people realize what they have to be proud of, the more that people will begin walking tall, the more we will do our work gladly, fully, and with a feeling of generosity for the world. Abundance grows along with pride. Love does, too.

SELF—AIR

Deep in the Iron Pentacle, the red-hot iron energy flows upward, connecting Pride to Self, to that essence, small or large, which cannot be taken from us without a fight. Somewhere in all of us is a surety about who we are and what is important to us. We may bury this, or try to give it away, but with some uncovering or *re*covering, we will find it within us, singing its song. Self is built upon the element of air. Let the wind blow away all that does not belong to you. What remains?

Our sense of self is formed by many circumstances. Much as we would like to choose who we are, this is not always possible. We are molded by our childhood experiences, economic circumstances, or by other people's expectations and desires for us. These desires can include the need to have us remain as small as possible, to not be as smart, talented, or big as we could be. Or they could be the opposite, wanting us to shine in ways we are not drawn to. Either set of expectations could leave us feeling not good enough, for it is seldom that a person can live up to another's expectations, particularly during childhood when we didn't know ourselves well enough to choose whether the expectations

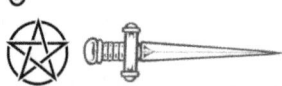

fit. This can play itself out in our adulthood, tripping us up and causing dissonance when our wants outstrip our abilities or when we lack the confidence to forge ahead, knowing that forging ahead means risking the unknown.

At this point in your life, while walking the ways of magic and spirit, it is good to begin to use your tools of air, of thought and discernment, and apply them to the subject of Self. You can begin to look at how your sense of self has been formed and notice whether or not that sense suits the deeper purpose of your actual self, your core essence, or what some traditions call the "I am." Begin to breathe into that "I am" whether you can fully sense it at this point or not. This will strengthen your sense of your true self.

QUESTIONING YOUR SENSE OF SELF

The questioning attitude is a good one to bring to magic, because as long as we can ask questions, the unexpected has room to appear.

What is your sense of self? When you think of who you are, what do you think of? What is truly your essential self and what has been heaped upon you by years of expectations or lack of encouragement? What stories do you tell yourself about who you are? Drop into one of these stories...how true does it feel to you?

Ask yourself who you could be if you allowed it. What would you be doing in your life if you weren't riddled with fear or misplaced ambition, anger or complacency? And who are you now, beneath your job, your family, your schooling? Are your dreams for yourself so outlandish they can never happen, thereby keeping you in your place? Or do you expend all your energy dreaming them so you never have the power to be? Conversely, do you tell yourself your dreams are unrealistic when perhaps there is some truth in them? If you were to write a mythic tale about yourself, with you as the hero, what would that tale be? What exploits have you engaged in? What is the story of your birth and grow-

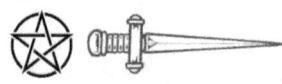

ing? What monsters have you battled, living to tell the tale? Do you face demons at work every day? Who wins?

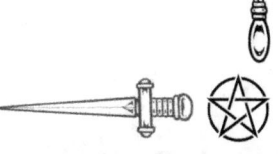

CUTTING TO THE CORE

For this exercise you will need three candles and your *athame*, your knife consecrated to magical, spiritual work. This tool represents the fire and strength of your will. If you don't have such a tool, use your favorite kitchen knife, or for gardeners, pruning sheers. You can also use your hand, fingers held out like a blade. Just know that for now, the tool represents both your will and your ability to cut a boundary around what is yours and what is not yours.

Take a deep breath. Light the candles to lend strength to your work. Use what you have, but I recommend warm colors: red for your connection to home and the earth's power, orange for your connection to the life force, and yellow to represent your will and lend you confidence. There are three of them to remind you that there is not one source of help and strength, but many. If the work grows difficult, you can gaze on one of the candles, breathe in, and then continue into the next phase.

Take a deep breath. Breathe up some of the blue fire energy to charge your blade for this working. Breathe across your blade, and down the tip. Center yourself. You will use your athame to demark the

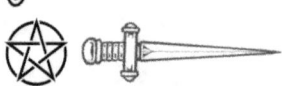

boundary between where "you" begins to intersect with that which is "not you." The "not you" can take the form of roles or identities that have been put upon you, or the ways in which you have mutated yourself in order to fit in. All of these suck away your sense of self.

Begin to peel down to your essence, your core. Let all the selves, the masks that have been put upon you or that you put upon yourself, drop onto a pile by your side. Keep looking, feeling, cutting away. "Is this me?" "Is this not me?" Parent, lover, child, teacher, failure, success, worker, dancer, priestess, mathematician, programmer, gardener, builder, the graceful one, the clumsy one: let all those names and identities fall away, dropping to the floor around you. When you think you are done, try to go down one more layer, paying attention to your face, your heart, your back, the soles of your feet. Sometimes there are masks on my face that are hard to see because I've held them so close. Is there any place you've forgotten that may hold another name, face, posture, or belief about yourself? Cut it away.

Feel what it is like to be down to the core of you. What is there? Are you a color, a scent, a band of light, a pure tone? Glory in this sense of yourself. Breathe it in. Bow to it in honor. Stand within it. What is a posture you can take that will remind you of this state? Anchor this feeling to that posture, knowing that even if you forget who you are, it is there in your body. Every time you stand this way, you will be brought back to your true nature.

Now, turn to your pile of masks and stray energy. If there are any identities that you choose to keep, take them from the pile and put them back on, like clothing. How does that feel? Feel the core of yourself beneath them. Know that this is work that you can do again. Right now, imagine the remaining masks turning to neutral energy and sinking into the earth, becoming compost to feed new growth.

The more years you practice this, the less disparity there will be between your masks and essence. You will become truer and truer to who you are.

POWER—EARTH

Feel the fiery iron energy flowing through the pentacle, connecting Self with Power. What is Power? I feel it when we sing together, or when I sit still and feel strong in my stillness. Power is the ability to keep silent, gathering energy. Power is the ability to speak, to shout, to scatter. It is mutable, not static—power must change in order to remain powerful, otherwise it becomes brittle. Power is in our muscles and bones, built upon the strength of the element Earth. Power is the sun, giving life to plants and people, and power is the dark potential of the buried seed.

I used to fear my power, for I didn't understand what power could be. During my childhood, "power" was illustrated by an out-of-control temper and a slide into irrationality, violence, and betrayal. I have grown to see that power does not have to work this way. I now have ample evidence that when I work with others who feel powerful, our work connects and takes on life in interesting ways. Power shared is power magnified. When I am full of my power, I am more secure. The more secure I am, the more generous I am able to be.

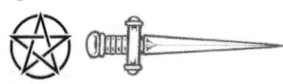

Insecurity breeds a mentality of scarcity. It becomes easy to feel there is not enough love, food, money, attention, or work to go around. Therefore, we can feel we must scramble for it, using power over others to get what we want. Conversely, we might fear that we'll get used and abused because we don't step forward enough in the competition for power. These are lies perpetuated by systems of dominance. Unfortunately, they work on us in insidious ways. We can feel squashed in such a system or feel like we must claw our way to the top.

There is no top, for there is no ladder. We strive instead to stand in circular forms, passing our power hand to hand. We are not the same, for I have skills you don't have, and you have ones I don't, but we can work together and learn. We can strive to bring each other into shared power, not by assuming instant equality of skill, but by passing on what we know to one another. By bringing each other into the circle of shared life, our power grows. We can listen to those who have walked the spiral paths ahead of us, and we can practice, becoming strong.

CIRCLES OF POWER

Some of us may have a lot of power in the world and others of us may have too little. Look at that now: What is your definition of power and how do you use it? I firmly believe that the greater our capacity to hold power is, the greater our capacity is to use it wisely, compassionately, and in a balanced fashion. I designed the following exercise to help us expand our capacity for power, life force, and energy in general.

For this exercise, remember how the fiery energy from the molten outer core of earth flowed from Sex into Pride and Self and now into Power. Though you are now in an Iron Pentacle point associated with earth, the impetus for movement nonetheless comes from fire. We will move backward and forward in circles of increasing and decreasing degrees of power.

EVOLUTIONARY WITCHCRAFT

-1   1   2   3   4

Take a deep breath. Connect with your grounding cord. Imagine that you are standing in a circle that fits your body comfortably (Circle 1). Let the circumference surround you approximately three inches wider than shoulder width. Close your eyes for a moment and sense yourself: your feet, your skin, your breathing, your heartbeat. Take another breath and feel power flowing around you, in the circle where you are standing. This is the amount of power you live in, walk in, work in. This is the circle you are most comfortable standing in. Stay here for a little while, taking this in. When you are ready, take a step backward (-1). You are stepping into a circle of diminished power and diminished capacity. What does this circle feel like to you? What happens to your posture here? Breathe.

Now take two big steps forward, moving through the circle you started in and landing in the one in front of that (Circle 2) a circle of greater power. Feel power tingling around you. What does your body feel like here? How is your posture? Breathe this in. Feel it. When you are ready, take a step back into the circle you started in (Circle 1). Stay there until you are ready to move again.

Now take two steps forward, moving through the circle you in front of you and into Circle 3. This circle holds still more energy and power. How does this feel to you? Is it better or worse? Does your posture change? Breathe this in. Stay in this circle for a moment, really feeling the energy swirling around and through your body. Take another breath, and step forward once again. Ahhh. Circle 4. Feel it surround

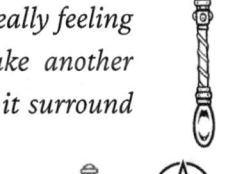

you. Feel your body. What happens to it? Breathe. Let yourself stand here for as long as you can.

Work your way back to your first, beginning, circle. Rest there for a moment. Now step into whatever circle you choose to work with. Step into a circle of power. It may be one step ahead, or three. Or you may decide to remain where you are for right now. Breathe in that circle of power. Claim it for yourself. It is now your territory. Expand in health, balance, and wisdom. Enjoy. Blessed be.

The circles may feel incredibly intense, or the intensity may just drop away. The last time I did this exercise, I discovered a trick I was playing on myself. I had the capacity for a far greater amount of power than I was letting on! When I stepped one step behind me, I caved in. When I stepped into circle number two, I felt good, but had to really concentrate to take the power in. It altered my body a lot. When I moved into circles three and four, however, the intensity dropped away and I felt simply great! I ended up claiming the fourth circle of power, even though when I began, I thought I would only be able to claim circle number two. Play around. See what happens. Perhaps you will surprise yourself.

When I lead this exercise in groups, I have found that when we all stepped into circle number four, we were standing side by side in a large circle of shared power. That is the magic of working together: when I step into my own power, I make room for others to share power alongside me.

PORTRAITS OF POWER

The next exercise takes us to look at "portraits of power" in galleries, museums, cafés, or city walls. I love looking at art in this way: Caillbot's *The Floor Scraper*s shows people working together, sharing the power of sheer muscle and common work. Georgia O'Keefe's shells and flowers show the power of color, form, nature, and sex. Mary Cassatt shows the power of mothers and children. Emory Davis celebrated the power of people in community.

The most potent portraits of power I have ever seen were by Wolfgang Leib. I was confronted by a thrumming, throbbing, pulsing, glowing, powerful piece of art. It was a square of about five feet, flat on the ground, bursting yellow, goldenrod. There was movement flowing across square, yet it was absolutely still. It was pure life force: the power of sex and of all living things, captured in this white room. What was it? A square of pollen, held to the floor only by the heat from the lamps above. It was wildness held captive and potency held waiting.

I once saw a piece by Glenn Ligon that was simultaneously an expression of power and a critique of systems of power-over. The

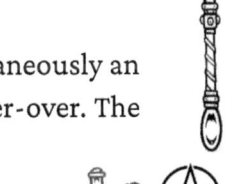

artist used coal dust to map out a page of James Baldwin's writing in relief on a canvas. The blackness, the artist's intention, the intensity of the coal and Baldwin's words all had their own power. Many of the words had been obscured, blurred by the coal, by the very blackness that gave them substance. This was the critique of the power-over of racism and a culture that sees blackness as a cause and source of erasure and subordination. Yet through all of that, the sheer power and beauty of the blackness itself shone on that canvas.

Take a trip to an art gallery, café, or museum. Or search for art on city streets or on the Internet. Look for images that you associate with power. Look first for what you think the dominant culture associates with power: military pictures, statues of generals or statesmen, photographs of ships, the rich and famous. Look around. What do you see? How do these images make you feel? Is there variety in the portrayals of power? Breathe this in.

Next, begin to focus on other forms of power. Are there photos or paintings of the ocean? Of old trees? Strong animals? Dancers? Are there portraits of people working together? Are there portraits of peace activists? Artists? Are there any images, even abstract ones, that just speak power to you? Breathe that in.

What is the power of a Japanese brushstroke? What power is held in a piece of wood, smoothed and polished to reflective brilliance?

What do these visions of power say to you? What do you want to cultivate, to draw out of yourself and others?

PASSION—WATER

The molten, red iron energy traces its way through you, mapping a line from Power to Passion, the last point on the Iron Pentacle before the energy completes the circuit with Sex. What is the source of your passion? What drives you? What do you desire more than anything? Speak it, feel it, sense it. Do you fear it? Passion flows from water, on the Elemental Pentacle. Do you fear being drowned by it?

What would you risk for your passion? I sometimes need to risk fear and comfort. For example, with my writing, I might come up with a million emotional blocks to doing it that are so subtle and strong, I don't even notice them. I am all of a sudden too busy to write or am going to take a short break and end up taking a two-hour nap or I just decide, in the middle of the first page, that it isn't going to be very good anyway. So, I stop. I thwart my passion. This again ties back to the Pride point, to feeling powerless and to losing sense of self. It also links directly to Sex, to whether or not I am full of life force and whether or not I am willing to channel even *more* life force without shutting down.

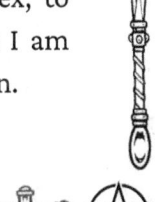

Passion flows from emotions, and emotions can also block our passion. When I'm stuck, it is helpful for me to remember that passion can work with *com*passion. If I have compassion for my needs and desires and my blocks and failings, it creates a sense of ease in my life. With ease, energy can flow. If I can unclench fear or judgment, my passion can grow something strong and lovely.

It is also helpful to notice when I *do* avoid what I am passionate about. Once I've acknowledged this, it becomes easier to notice those times when it is happening. At first, this may come an hour or even a few days later, when I realize, "Oh, I started that project…what happened?" Over time, I get better at noticing the urge to quit or delay while it is happening. Then I can notice, "Hmm, there seems to be some fear here, and some sadness around that…"

This practice lets those non-rational, and often emotional, parts of myself know they are being seen and gives them less ability to control the situation. I can have my fears and still do my work. It makes it much more likely that, rather than walking away from my passion, I might go make a cup of tea, or take a brief walk, or even just draw a deep breath. Then I can go right back to writing, sending out applications for a new job, going to that planning meeting, tending the garden, or arranging that date. I can take a breath, allowing ease to enter and passion to flow once again.

Of course, the converse of this situation can also be true. You may be the sort of person—as I sometimes am—who dives headlong into a cause, project, or relationship. You may then surface a few days, weeks, or months later and think, "What did I ever see in that?" This may leave you and others feeling bewildered and hurt.

Over time, I have learned to devote more time to my long-term, abiding passions, even when they are feeling a little tepid. These passions sustain me. The sudden passions might excite me

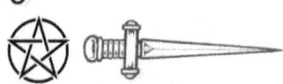

in the moment, and can feed some good creativity, but I don't want to devote all my energy to them any longer. If I do, they end up drowning my other voices, leaving nothing for my sustained work, the work that waters my garden for the long haul. Sustained work leads to true mastery.

SAYING YES TO PASSION

I have developed two exercises for cultivating balanced passion. Both have to do with ingesting something. I need to literally take my passions in so that they can work within me, before I offer the fruits of my passion to the world. This is also a way of making the source of my passions more tangible and of the physical rather than strictly metaphoric realms.

FEEDING YOUR PASSION

Take some time to look at how you stop yourself from fully feeling your passion. Make a list of different ways in which you feel thwarted in your attempts to have the sort of life, work, and love that you desire. Now make a commitment to feed your passion.

Take a deep breath. Every day for a full turn of the moon, you will commit to feeding your passion. Gather twenty-eight seeds, nuts, raisins, or whatever it is that you can eat over the course of twenty-eight days. It should be something significant to you but not require an elaborate effort. You want to reinforce for yourself that feeding your passions can be simple and easy. Perhaps each week you will want to gather the most luscious fruit you can find and eat a piece every day. What do you desire? What will feed you in taste, color, and nutrition? The crunch and slight resistance of the protein-rich almond? The luster and sweetness of a peach? Listen to your desire for passion and follow its lead. This is a way in which Sticky One can help you. The child self knows what they desire!

Hold the food you have chosen—your sacred sacrifice to passion—in your hand. Feel the life force in it, gathered from sun, water, earth,

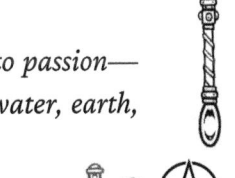

and air. Ground and center yourself. Say, "I commit to feeding my passion. I am open to the energy of passion in my body, my soul, and my life." Breathe into your food, filling it with your intention. Take another breath. Now eat, feeling the power of all the elements gathered in that food as it enters you. Let yourself begin to fill with passion. Give thanks. Blessed be.

Each week, as you have done this exercise of eating, begin to meditate on what positive actions you can take to cultivate your passion: start a journal, take a dance class, fight for justice, make art, initiate sex, do one thing you've always wanted to do.

DRINKING IN PASSION

This exercise acknowledges your power to free your passion and to make your desires manifest in the world. It uses the life force held in your breath, the spiritual power that grows inside your being the more work you do on yourself. For this exercise, all you need is imagination, breath, and your chalice or an ordinary cup.

Fill your chalice with clear water. Take a deep breath. Begin breathing in life force. On each breath, drop more deeply into your center. Dive into your belly like you would dive into the ocean or a still pond. Dive further. Reach for your passion. Feel your passion bubbling up from within you. What is it? Name it. See it; smell it; taste it. Does it move across your skin or burn in your toes? What do you desire? What have you so longed for yet been frightened to name? Do not be ashamed. No one is here to judge you. This is between you and the Gods. What is your passion? Allow it to form within you, growing in substance and strength. Breathe. Dive deep. You are swimming in your passion. It caresses and feeds you. It is your heart's desire. It is what you truly want, have always wanted.

Let yourself fill with your passion. Let your heart's desire take you

over, just for this moment. Fill with it. Passion. Now, charged by your passion, by the invitation of God Herself, witnessed by the Gods, open your eyes. Hold your cup in your beautiful hands. Gaze into your cup. See the surface of the water as it moves. This is a reflection of the ocean, of the deep pool within you. Take a deep breath. Feel the life force fill you. Feel your passion rising within you. Exhale into the chalice, charging the water with your life force, with your passion. Gaze upon the water. You have the power to manifest your dreams and desires in the world. Open yourself to passion. Drink it down. Drain that cup. Be full. Know that you can embrace your desire. Drink in your wisdom. Blessed be.

THE FIRE OF PRACTICE

Continue to revisit the points of the Iron Pentacle and notice how they play out in your life. Running the Iron Pentacle through your body on a regular basis is a quick way to see which points feel strong, weak, or overbalanced. Let the molten energy that flows around the earth's core fill you, revitalizing your will to practice. With feet planted on the ground and arms outstretched to hold the world, breathe the fire and ignite your life. Sex, Pride, Self, Power, Passion.

You are now ready to face the quenching pool and slake the thirst brought on by your inner work.

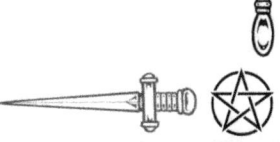

PART SIX
WEST: DIVING INTO COMPASSION

THE TOOLS OF WATER

C up your hands. Fill them with clear, cool water. Let it trickle over your skin, running down your arms. Raise your hands to your face, feel the water cascade across your cheekbones, bathing your eyes, your nose, your mouth. Breathe deeply. Feel water filling you. Flowing. You are clear, cool water. You are clean. Our tool here is the Chalice. You are the cup, the vessel of wisdom and bringer of compassion. Drink.

. . .

THE BUILDING of the sacred sphere continues as we turn our attention toward the West. In many Craft traditions, the West is traditionally seen as the place of water, the repository of dreams and deeper visions, of the flow of emotions and the pull of the moon on our own physical tides. Here, the time of day is twilight, the gloaming, in between day and night, opposite of East, where the in-between time is dawn. The tool of water is the chalice. Water spills, pours, and flows, and in watching and experiencing water, we can notice these same patterns in ourselves.

In this section, we will explore the tools of water, both physical and metaphysical. We will hold the cup of compassion and drink. We will breathe into our hearts and live. We will become the oyster, seeing the pearl wrought from our own pain

THE CHALICE

The chalice represents the sacred wells that were gateways to other realms—to dreams and the Underworld—the wells where the salmon of wisdom swims, the wells over which grew the sacred trees from which people hung wish cloths and prayers. The cup is also the ocean, life-giving and life-taking.

There are many cups in the world: big drinking bowls made of white porcelain to hold *café au lait*; delicate crystal goblets for champagne; sturdy water glasses, tinged with green. What sort of cup are you? How do you see yourself? What do you hold for the world? Another question is, what sort of cup attracts you most?

I have a beautiful chalice of mosaic glass made by an old friend. I fill a cobalt-blue goblet with water for my ancestor altar, and a sturdy green ceramic bowl I use for cleansing. All of these serve me in different ways. I also have an Irish teacup that I fill with offerings of tea for our household spirit every day.

Cups represent my ability to hold things. I like to be able to hold many different things, many emotions, situations, and types

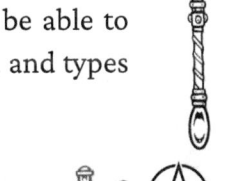

of energy. By using my cups, I expand my capacity to drink in healing, love, calm, peace, courage, life force, and compassion. What do you want to hold in your cup? What do you need to drink into your life?

If I could drink the world, I would drink sunlight and roses and all the varied hues of faces that I pass in the street. I would drink the moon, and love, smoky whisky and sweet cider, black tea with honey, and the clearest water I could find. I would drink in the ability to continue, to greet each day with a breath, to speak, to love, to dance, to work. I would also drink in the ability to pour. To pour out compassion and wisdom and a soothing balm upon an aching body. I would pour my heart, for my heart would be full from all this drinking, with plenty to share. I would pour out abundance.

You can read the following through once and then imagine yourself as a chalice being filled. If you like, you may record it and play the meditation back for yourself.

Take a deep breath. Imagine yourself as a cup, a vessel. What is your shape and color? Are you sturdy or delicate, bright, dark, or clear? Send a breath through your heart, opening yourself to receive. Imagine the Star Goddess above you, full of infinite love. In Her hands She holds a pitcher, pouring liquid stars, pouring love and compassion. See the pitcher tilt and feel the liquid cascading down. Let this water of life and love fill you. Take another breath, and as you exhale, imagine that you push the boundaries of your cup still wider. And still the Star Goddess pours, and you are filled once again, deeper and wider. You have a great capacity to hold love, life, and compassion.

And still She pours. Let yourself fill to the top, liquid spilling out from the top of your cup. Imagine that you stand on top of the globe of earth. Let love, life, and compassion spill from you, cascading over the earth, bathing all it touches.

Open your eyes. Try to hold the sense of yourself as a cup, filling up

and sharing your gifts with the world. Send a breath through the soles of your feet and the crown of your head. As you are blessed, so do you bless the world.

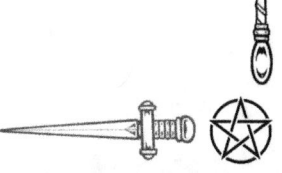

TEMPERING YOUR EMOTIONS

Emotions are the metaphysical base of water, just as will was for fire, or intellect for air. Tempering our emotions is an interior process akin to physical forging. Tempering brings opposites together to make something true. In forging metal, fire and water come together, along with the air of the bellows and the earth of the anvil. The following exercise helps us to blend seeming opposites, represented by two cups of water. I encourage you to bring this concept to your sitting practice. Sitting with conflicting ideas, emotions, or desires increases our strength and openness.

The following exercise is one I adapted from an earlier version taught by Reclaiming Tradition witch Hilary Valentine.

My version highlights how things can move out of balance internally. We can use these insights to bring externals in balance, too, slowly working our way out: we first look at ourselves, then at our internal responses to the external world, then at the external world itself.

This exercise requires two cups filled to the top with water. I recommend doing this exercise outside, or in a shower or other

place where you don't mind spilling. We must release some things to make space for greater balance. We cannot expect to hold on to everything; we cannot expect to blend opposites and not spill any water.

Read the exercise and then pick up your cups and begin.

Fill your two cups until the water almost reaches the rims. Take a deep breath. Think about what you most hate about yourself. Let that be the water in one cup. Think about what you most love in yourself. Let that be in the other cup. This is meant to stretch you. We sometimes censor words like "love" and "hate," but pushing below the surface can bring up our deeper, more primal emotions. Really let yourself feel what you love and what you hate in those two cups. Feel the weight of them in your hands. Feel what it is to hold them, with your heart as the balance point in the middle.

Begin to pour what you love and what you hate back and forth. Feel that dance as you rock, back and forth, back and forth. Listen to the sound of the water pouring. What does this do to your heart? When the water spills, know that you are making space for a new possibility. Keep pouring until you feel you have a mixture of love and hate, until they have become one substance. When you really feel this, take a big breath and come to stillness, letting all of the water settle in one of the cups. Look at that water. Hold it in front of your heart. What had to drop away to create this new mixture? Inhale, filling yourself with life force, ready to receive this magic substance.

You can also do this exercise with your feelings about world situations: hope and despair, anger and effectiveness. You can place feelings about your friends or heroes in the cups, putting them in opposition with people you may vilify, especially politicians. What would happen if I put someone I admire—like Dorothy Day or James Baldwin—in one cup and someone I loathe —insert a certain politician or billionaire—in another? Could I allow that mixture to come to a place of balance and a transformation closer to the truth? Could I bring temperance to bear against my prejudices? Could I do this as a magical act to affect change in the world?

This process is more satisfying to me than the simple raising up and tearing down we so often engage in. When I do this exercise in regard to people or situations outside of myself, I drink half of the mixture, to internalize the change, and then pour the other half out upon the ground as an offering to aid and bless the situation.

THE GUARDIAN OF THE WEST

The Guardian of the West, or water, can help us with all the work of the heart, lending us depth and compassion. They can appear to you in any form or gender. Let us go on a journey to meet this Guardian, the bearer of the cup and the powers of water.

Take a deep breath and center yourself. Cast the blue sphere around you. Light a candle on your altar, pale blue or sea-green. Turn toward the west; open yourself to the power of the Guardian there, as you breathe deeply within yourself. Feel a touch upon your heart. Open to the Guardian of the West.

Begin to feel the presence coming closer to you. What does this Guardian feel like? "Guardian of the West, rise from the depths and join this rite." Can you catch a glimpse? Call upon the Guardian and invoke the depths of your heart and intuition. Here flows wisdom, the secrets of gloaming and in-between spaces, opener, reflector of dreams. Here breathes the mist of twilight. Feel the presence. Introduce yourself.

Guardian,
You who swim in twilight spaces,
Rise from the depths and join our rites.

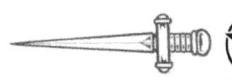

Teach us the powers of Passion
And show us the depths of Wisdom.
Let us flow, together.
Let us flow.
Touch our hearts, our spit, our blood.
May we speak your name.
May we speak our hearts.
May we walk in compassion.
Welcome.

Take a deep breath. Feel the presence guarding the western quadrant, huge and beautiful. How does this Guardian manifest to you? Draw or write whatever information you receive.

When you are done for this meeting, say:
Thank you for your presence.
Thank you for the gifts of water and passion.
May I taste life and plumb my heart.
Go if you must, stay if you will.
Hail and farewell.

CONSECRATING YOUR ABILITY TO HOLD

Your cup represents your ability to hold emotions, to love yourself and to drink in what you need. Consecrate it much as you have your wand or athame. It is a sacred tool of the heart.

Set up the sacred sphere and call upon your allies to bless your cup. You may wish to dedicate it to your ability to hold greater quantities with fluid grace, or you may wish to consecrate it to compassion, or the ability to drink life deeply. Send your cup a kiss of life's love and your passion.

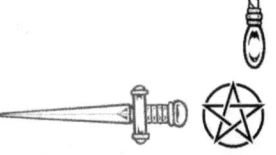

ENGAGING THE HEART

Call upon the cup of depth and compassion. Things can get murky in those depths, yet by bringing compassion into situations with strong and hidden currents, we can plumb what is truly there, rather than cover it up with more rubble or allow it to sweep us out to sea. Compassion offers the ability to listen below the surface. This deep listening allows for right action that varies according to the situation. It does not always mean acting in a way that feels good to all, but it is acting in the way that is most helpful.

I first began to encounter this concept in a deep way while working full time at the soup kitchen. Sometimes people needed a listening ear and other times people needed to have their actions questioned. Sometimes I had to break up fights and escort people out the door. Was this lack of compassion? No, it was a sign of respect. If I respect another being, I treat them as though they have the ability to care for themselves and their world in some capacity. Now, I have to gauge this capacity, for it is not the same for us all. I *do* expect more from those who are able to give it, but to expect nothing from others is a sign that I don't feel the other

person is capable of anything at all. That is not compassion; that is pity that can devalue their life.

Compassion leads to clear Passion and Wisdom, the water points on the Iron and Pearl Pentacles. Here is an exercise to engage, cleanse, and strengthen our hearts.

HEART BREATH

This exercise is not intended to keep us from being angry or sad, but rather to keep us from lashing out in hurtful and unproductive ways. Breathing through the heart comes from a variety of spiritual paths, mostly some branches of Buddhism and various Hindu traditions.

WHEN YOU ARE FEELING ANXIOUS, *overwhelmed, or angry, center yourself with the grounding exercise in section one. Feel your feet beneath you. You are present in your body, not spinning out in your head or pulled under by your emotions. Your body serves as a balance for both. As you breathe, imagine your exhalation moving through your heart. Feel a slight tingling along your breastbone as the breath moves through. Let your heart soften and open, just a little. Let yourself relax as breath washes through you, filling your body on the inhalation and exiting through your heart. If you wish, now, you may ask for forgiveness, patience, and compassion. Feel those enter on each breath, a gift. Feel your heart grow luminous, radiant. Bring the breath all the way*

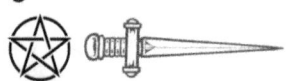

up from your feet and out through your heart. You are calm, grounded, and present. You are ready to face whatever challenges you need to, with an open heart.

THE PEARL PENTACLE

DISCUSSING PEARL

"*There it lay, the great pearl, perfect as the moon. It captured the light and refined it and gave it back in silver incandescence.*" —John Steinbeck

I PLACE THIS PENTACLE HERE, in the realm of water, because it carries the image of the oyster, deep within the sea, coating a grain of sand until a pearl rests, glowing, within the hard shell. This pearl also reflects the moon, which pulls the oceanic tides and tugs on the waters of our bodies. This pentacle shows the fruits of our labors with the Iron Pentacle. Irritation and pain have altered, becoming strengthened and beautiful.

Working with the energies of Love, Law, Knowledge, Liberty, and Wisdom, the Pentacle of Pearl holds the vision of a new society. It is a tool of hope, providing a way to shift the balance of power into a more liberating, joyous, sane, communitarian one. The Pearl pentacle appears when Iron is fully present. If Sex energy is not running clearly within me, I do not have full access to Love. Without balanced Power, there can be no Liberty.

The energies of Pearl vibrate up one octave from Iron; they sing together, the same notes on a different pitch. When I am attuned to them, I vibrate as well, out into all the worlds. One of my early teachers, Pandora, said that Iron Pentacle is the work of a lifetime, and the Pearl the work of many lifetimes. Over time I have come to understand this statement to mean that while Iron is my personal work, Pearl is work I can only do in connection with others. In this case, "many lifetimes" means the lifetimes of many people, all doing their personal work and working with one another.

The Elemental Pentacle is the most basic ground of all, in our blood and breath, building us and creating the world. The Iron Pentacle is about building our psyches, our emotional makeup, and how we face the world on a personal level. Drawing on these two pentacles, the Pearl Pentacle is how we interact, how we exist in relationships and in the larger systems of community, governments, or enclaves.

These Pentacles are not separate; they are inextricably linked and strongly affect all the worlds. I have run the Pearl pentacle through my own body and energy field and I have drawn this pentacle around the Pentagon in Washington DC, which is the heart of a pentacle. I have chanted these points in groups and alone.

PEARL PENTACLE

WE BEGIN this balancing task by shifting the Pearl energies within ourselves, first working up from Iron. For example, if we are confident enough to cease buying into systems of domination and control, we become better able to support and create more sustainable and compassionate systems.

We create the culture that is formed by and, in turn, forms Love, Law, Knowledge, Liberty, and Wisdom. If I understand Law inside myself, I can better aid the creation of just Law in the world. If I have Liberty within me, I can work for Liberty for all. As within, so without.

CALLING UP THE PEARL

The energies of these points cannot be twisted as easily as those of Iron can, but our mental or emotional conceptions of them might need restructuring. They may need restructuring in our society, as well. If you'd like to explore this, my *Stars of Power* book goes into that more in depth.

But for now, we'll keep this introduction simple.

If I am having trouble with Wisdom in my life, I work on it by going back to Passion and seeing what is out of balance or absent there. If Love is a problem, we can revisit sex and our relationship to life force, which can affect all our survival issues: home, work, and money. This holds true for all the points on the Pearl Pentacle.

In the following exercise, we call up and reclaim Love, Law, Knowledge, Liberty, and Wisdom. These points shine out from the Iron Pentacle and live within us, helping us to create societies anew. All the work we do to reclaim the points of the Iron Pentacle bring the points of the Pearl Pentacle forth. Like the oyster coating its irritation, it is only in acknowledging our pain and taking steps to transform it that we can come to the beauty of Pearl. Again, you

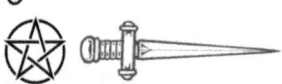

can have a friend lead you through this meditation, or record it and play it back for yourself.

Breathe in. Feel your feet on the ground. Breathe down, then up again. Begin to run the Iron Pentacle through your body, feeling it etched within your form. Let the red, Iron energy lighten and lift, shifting into Pearl, luminescent and glowing. Breathe into that opalescence. Let it form into a point in your head and feel the life force of Sex moving into Love. Call Love back to you. Love. Call it back from every love song you've ever heard. From every time it was whispered to you. Call it back from every time you've felt unloved or unloving. Feel yourself filling with Love. Feel the Gods surrounding you; feel their Love. Feel your God Soul, so in love with you. What does it feel like to be full of Love?

Let the Pearl energy run through your body, connecting to your right foot. Law. Feel that point. Feel the connection between Law and Love. Is it quick or slow moving? Just notice. Begin to call Law back to yourself. Call it back from governing institutions. Call it back from every meeting you've sat through. Call the energy back. Call Law back from the police, the courts. Call it into yourself. Letting yourself be full of Law. Call up the natural balance of things. This is the power of the sword, scything through illusion like the fire scythes through the forest, enabling new growth to happen. Natural Law. This is Law built upon Pride, not arrogance. This is Law connected to Love and Sex, to life force. Fill with it.

Let the pearlescent energy run up through your body, connecting your right foot with your left hand, connecting Law with Knowledge. Feel it shining in your hand. Sense the connection between Law and Knowledge. How does that feel? Does it shine, or is it barely moving? Feel too, the tripod supporting you, the triplet of Love, feeding Law, feeding Knowledge. Breathe in. Feel the glow of Knowledge. Begin to call Knowledge back to you. Call it back from every teacher, every book. Call it back from all the times you've felt disconnected from your knowledge. Call it back. Touch the knowledge of your Self linked to the universe, to the Gods. Call it in. This is your Self, reaching for the morning star. Let yourself fill with Knowledge. Breathe. How does Knowledge shape you?

Let that energy begin to flow across your heart, into your right hand. Flowing from Knowledge to Liberty. Feel the line shimmering between them. As Law feeds Knowledge, so does Knowledge feed Liberty; the three support each other. Feel it. Breathe. Call Liberty to you. Call Liberty up from the exhilarating rush of life's joy. Call Liberty back from all the times you have not felt free. Call it back from fear or envy. Call up freedom. Feel it coursing through your body, your soul. Liberating your being. Liberating the world. Thou art Goddess. Breathe. Feel the forces of Power that enable your liberation. Call it to you, feel it feeding you. What is the taste of Liberty? How does it feel? Is your spirit expanding?

Feel the quicksilver of Liberty running down through your body and into your left foot. This is the point of Wisdom. From Liberty, everything has changed, everything you knew, all your formulations are re-formed, clearer. Feel the line between Liberty and Wisdom. How does it run? Feel the triplet of Knowledge, Liberty, and Wisdom, balancing and feeding one another. Feel yourself becoming Pearl. Call Wisdom to you. Call it back from spiritual teachers and holy books. Call up the flow of compassionate generosity. Call Wisdom back from the mistrust of your passions. Call up your own deep knowing. Let this Wisdom vibrate from your Passion. Drink deeply of the Passion that forms your Wisdom. Let that which excites you make you wise. This is the Wisdom that will reconstruct the world into a new way of being. Breathe in Wisdom. Feel that triangle—Knowledge, flowing through Liberty and forming Wisdom. Let yourself drink in surety. What does Wisdom feel like? If you let it change you, the worlds will change.

The energy of shining Pearl runs back up through your body to your head, connecting Wisdom back to Love. Love spills out, feeding earth below and sky above. Feel that line and sense the connection. What does it look like, feel like, taste like? Feel it in your body. Vibrating. Now

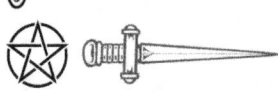

feel the triangle connecting Liberty to Wisdom to Love. See how they feed into one another, are dependent on one another. Breathe. Now turn your mind's eye to the tripod of Wisdom, Love and Law. Love is the Law, fed by Wisdom. Breathe. Feel the whole Pentacle of Pearl running through your body. Say the points as the energy runs. Love. Law. Knowledge. Liberty. Wisdom. Love. Run this energy until you shine, a star in the heavens. God Herself invokes you. And now, let the circle be drawn around you, containing and setting the energies, turning the wheel sunwise, the way of energies growing and gathering. Love, Knowledge, Wisdom, Law, Liberty, and Love. Breathe.

Feel the energy of Iron supporting Pearl. The Earth's mantle is made of star stuff, a nebular cloud called home by gravity's pull. Let your heart be the pull that draws your life into fullness. If there is any excess energy, breathe it up to feed your God Soul.

Though the points of Pearl need Iron to be fully realized, we can get a taste of them even if our Iron points are imbalanced. The following exercises give us a glimpse of what life could be if Iron and Pearl were manifested fully within us. They help us to split the oyster's shell and see the beauty held within. Each Pearl point is connected back to the Elemental point from which both Iron and Pearl grow. So, though we run the watery, pearly light through ourselves to balance all the points, we will also be referring back to spirit and fire, air, earth, and water in the following exercises.

LOVE—SPIRIT

"*Love doesn't just sit there, like a stone, it has to be made, like bread; remade all the time, made new.*"
—Ursula K. Le Guin

WHAT IS love in the context of the Pearl Pentacle? It is not romantic love or the subsuming of one's spirit and life force to another. No. This is the deep love linked to the first act of sex and creation, the act that called on Spirit to infuse all things. This is the respectful caring that underlies all. It is in the breeze on each tree leaf. It is so well connected to the Sex of the Iron Pentacle that it can be hard to differentiate. In fact, they exist in harmony with one another.

Love is that which uses the life force well, and for the good of all. It is not about selfishness or ownership. It is a sharing, the underpinning of life that infuses everything. Love is vast, encompassing cultures, animals, plants, suns, and stars. Without respect, there is no love. Without life force—sexual energy—there is no love. The Star Goddess loved herself/himself/themself and

from that, worlds were born. Love yourself that way, and who knows what will be born? Love yourself that way, and society gains a different foundational force. *That* is magic.

OPENING TO ORDINARY LOVE

I am filled with love for ordinary things, for young people on the bus, faces pensive or flush with longing. I love the moon rising over the city. A raindrop on a leaf. The sudden flight of crows. I am full of gratitude for the world, and for our ordinary lives. We can open to love that is more inclusive than we sometimes believe possible. We can learn to love the wonder of the world as it is: gritty, sweaty, beautiful, and human.

In this exercise, I ask you to make a list of things that fill you with a sense of love and gratitude. Whenever I feel love, it is paired with gratitude, for I am thankful at the world that opens in front of me. What seemed closed just a moment ago unfolds in front of me like a flower. Petal by petal it reveals itself and my heart is revealed to love. I breathe that in.

Make a list of thirty things that you love: thirty things, concepts, people, or qualities. Breathe as you do this. Breathe in love. Breathe love onto that page. Breathe it into the pen as you write. Fill with love. Now read this list. Pick one that stands out, shining like a jewel on the page. "The sun slanting across the floor." Or "Daisies in a mason jar on the kitchen sill." Or "The feeling in my body after a run." Or "The face of

the woman who asks for money on the corner near work." Write that one thing on a small piece of paper. Set it on your altar. Meditate upon this love for one week. Burn a candle in front of it. Let yourself drop into this thing that fills you with love. Love for the universe. Love for life. Let this be your meditation.

The more we meditate on things that fill us with love, the more open to Love we will become. The world will become a thing to love. In the midst of bad news and violence, the world can still rise up and make us gasp in wonder.

POLISHING THE HEART

Polishing the Heart is a simple physical meditation Postneshin Jelaleddin Loras taught during my time with the Mevlevi whirling dervishes. I've adapted it over the years, incorporating it into my practice when friends, students, or clients feel in need for some specific heart clearing.

I find this practice of gently running fingers over breastbone to be soothing and helpful when my heart feels wounded, bruised, defended, or caked over with muck. It is simple and effective, and you can do it wherever you are, rain or shine. The first time you try it, you may want to dim the lights, light some candles, and settle into a private space. But you can do it any time you feel the need: anytime you feel heart sore, angry, sad, or disconnected.

The physical practice comes from the dervishes; the rest is my own.

Feel your feet on the ground and feel your breath moving through your sacred body. Let your shoulders relax, and your center of gravity drop, perhaps bending your knees slightly on an exhalation. Begin to notice how your breath moves through your body, allowing yourself to

grow more and more relaxed as you breathe, opening your heart a little, as during the heart breath. Now gently begin to move your hands over your heart, gently down, cycling past one another. You can use your fingertips for a light touch or the palms of your hands for a firmer, yet still gentle, brushing motion. Imagine that your hands are washing over your heart. They might be water, smoothing rock, sending clarity in where confusion reigns. They might be a polishing cloth, gently rubbing away dirt and debris.

Let your hands continue to flow gently over your breastbone as you breathe. Continue to relax. You may wish to rock gently, back and forth, like a child being cradled. You are loved. You are forgiven if you need forgiveness. Breathe. Love. Breathe. Love. You are slowly made whole again, comforted and held. Bring yourself to stillness, one hand covering the other, resting on your heart. Feel your heart begin to expand. Breathe into it.

Say, "I am increasing my capacity to love. I am open to love. My heart is big. I have love within my heart." Take a big heart breath and say, "I am beloved." Now, cup your hands and imagine them filled with love, like they would fill with water from a clear stream. Tip your hands out, spilling the love onto the ground in front of you and say: "May love be poured upon the earth. Blessed be."

LAW—FIRE

"*The scientist's religious feeling takes the form of rapturous amazement at the harmony of natural law.*"
—Albert Einstein

THE LUMINOUS ENERGY of the Pearl Pentacle runs like water, down from Love, connecting it with Law. Law is a distorted concept in our culture. The Law of Pearl, based on true pride, is natural law. When pride is present, there is a sense of worthiness and belonging to community and the natural flow. When laws are made in response to unworthiness, they can cause isolation, suspicion, and a divorce from nature.

This doesn't mean that natural law always seems nice. Law is built upon the element of fire: a forest fire does not seem nice, but is sometimes necessary. Law is about balance and connection. It is about gravity and the way the stars move. Law is also about my will and my use of it. Am I in alignment with the natural world as much as possible for a person in the twenty-first century? Have I done my daily practice, sat in prayer or meditation, run energy, or

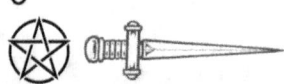

engaged in a physical practice? Have I sought forgiveness for omissions or things committed when I was not in alignment? I cannot live according to natural law if I have caused an imbalance and not sought to rectify it. Right living engages Law: discipline, pride, joy, and revelry.

Thinking of Law in this personal way gives us an idea of how Law works on a larger scale, ordering all of nature through the gentle turning of seasons or through the devastating power of a flash flood. On a human scale, law requires the engagement of individuals attempting to bring their own lives into alignment with each other and with natural law. The power of law, a structure of magnificent scale, is built upon each individual component. It is like one of Buckminster Fuller's triangles, supporting a whole dome. Law is both the triangle and the dome.

Ask yourself: What are the laws that I choose to live by? Which laws have been put upon me? Which of these have I internalized? How do they work in me and through me? Do these laws control me or strengthen me? Do I use these laws to control or strengthen others? What oaths do I willingly take? How is my will acting in concert with the world around me?

BELIEVING AND WILLING

Law requires movement. True law must balance belief and action. Our ideas must be galvanized by our will and our willingness. What do you believe, and what are you willing to do to give life and energy to your beliefs? If we want change, we must be willing to act. That is the power of the law point.

I designed the following exercise to help us live with greater congruity over time. It has certainly helped me.

Fold a piece of paper in half lengthwise. On one side of the paper, write, "I believe," and on the other, "I will." As quickly as you can, write down six things in the "I believe" column. Now go back and look at each one. As quickly as you can, write down what you will do to help bring about each belief. Some of these actions may take pondering, but if you have a first impulse, even if it seems silly or irrational, write it down. You can always edit it out later, but getting the impulse out is good. There is energy there. It is quick like fire.

Here is one example: "I believe nature is sacred." "I will clean up the beach in my town." That is Law in action. May our laws always reflect our beliefs, and if not, may we work to change those laws.

KNOWLEDGE—AIR

Like the reflection of moon upon water, the shimmering Pearl wave flows upward from Law and into Knowledge. Knowledge is often confused with purely intellectual intelligence. It is not simply this, though intellect is included. Knowledge is held in our bones, in our blood cells, in muscle tissue, in emotional memories, as well as in parts of our brain. Information alone does not constitute knowledge. One must digest information, incorporate it, practice it, and make associations within oneself.

Living in a constant wash of information and input can make it difficult for us to sink deeply into any area long enough to grow knowledgeable. It is part of the work of the Pearl Pentacle to bring back an ability to have knowledge: to know myself, first of all, and then to connect to other sources of knowledge, becoming student and, in time, becoming teacher. In this way, we can educate each other, and help with evolution instead of aiding the spiral into less-than-human. Knowledge is founded on Self that is built upon Air. Know yourself, in all your parts.

CLEARING THE ATTIC

Decades ago, I would magically comb my hair because I could literally feel the energy trapped there. I joked with my friends that I had old cars and bedsprings stuck in my crown, the energy got so snarled up in my thick, curly hair. This exercise is an adaptation of that work I used to do. It uses a comb or brush—or our fingers—as a wand to clear the way for clearer or deeper knowledge. Many thoughts, facts, and opinions can clutter up our brains, making it hard to access our knowledge. This exercise is a way to begin clearing out the attic of our brains, creating spaciousness and order and letting the air flow through.

Prepare a bowl of salt water. Set it in front of you. Begin to comb or brush your hair out. Imagine that all the old belief systems that don't serve you are coming out of your mind on the teeth of the comb. Shake the comb—or brush, or your fingers—out over the water, letting the salt water absorb these thoughts. Comb out any thoughts that don't serve your work. Comb out information that doesn't feel helpful or germane to your life right now. Breathe deeply. Keep combing. It doesn't matter if you can name these thoughts or not. Just imagine that

they are floating out of your brain, onto your hair follicles and onto the comb. Shake them into the salt water. Let them dissolve and nullify. They are no longer necessary; they no longer have power over you; they no longer clutter up your brain. As you comb and shake, feel vitality entering the attic of your brain on each breath. Feel the wind begin to blow, clearing out dust from crannies and behind old cases and boxes. When you feel you have done enough for the moment, send one last big breath through your brain. Open a window. Pour the salt water down the drain.

THE KNOWLEDGE GAME

Before entering this game, you may want to do some automatic writing around knowledge. Write for five minutes on "I know" as a warmup. The following is a group exercise I developed decades ago with Reclaiming and Feri priest/esses Gwydion and Patti.

You will need a kick ball or a beanbag—something you can safely throw and catch fairly easily. A small beanbag is easy to make: take a cloth sack and fill it with beans, sewing the edge or tying it tightly with ribbon or string.

Stand in a circle. The person with the ball states something they knows about themselves and throws the ball to someone else in the circle. That person has to immediately say what he knows and toss the ball to someone else. The ball will popcorn around in this way, with the catcher having to speak quickly, from the belly, rather than pausing to think. The game can change after a while into what folks know how to do, or facts about the world. It should begin, however, with self-knowledge.

This game is very revealing. The first time I did it, I was surprised at what I knew! There were things deep inside that I

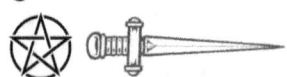

would not allow myself to be certain of if I stopped to think about them. In speaking quickly, I bypassed my usual censor and blurted out the most amazing truths about myself, things close to my core, rather than the usual superficial facts that I presented to the world.

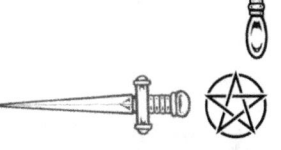

LIBERTY—EARTH

Water flows over the Pearl, carrying a shimmer across your heart on the stream of energy flowing from Knowledge into Liberty. Liberty means freedom on the grandest scale. Liberty comes from having the power to be able to do what we want and to discern whether our wants serve us. For many of us, our wants feed addiction or self-destruction. In these cases, we have no way to differentiate between what helps us to grow in a healthy way and what impedes our growth. When we are stuck, dreaming of a freedom that will never come, we don't have the power to access what we really need. We don't have the power to liberate ourselves.

So again, this point of Pearl is founded on mastery of Iron—Liberty based on Power, which is built on the stable element of Earth. Our personal ability to use the energies of Iron and Pearl will in help others in turn. We can share our liberation, and the tools that brought us there. We can also more readily see the tools of oppression—systemic or otherwise—and help others to see them too. We hold each other; we help each other. In sharing

power, our walk toward liberty comes all the sooner, and with greater surety. In our power, we are less prone to manipulation. Free from manipulation, we can work to improve the lot of all people.

FREEDOM FROM WITHIN

This exercise uses the body, symbol of earth, as a format through which to recognize our blocked power and all the ways in which we are not free, though we may long to be.

Find the places in your body that are tense with fear, indecision, sickness, or greed. These are all places where your power is blocked and, therefore, where Liberty has not been claimed.

Gently stretch every day, noticing where excess tension resides. Breathe into those places. If you can afford to, go to a body worker and really notice all those places as you are being worked on. Send deep breaths through them, helping to begin to ease the blocks and open pathways to liberation within yourself. It is true that the more relaxed you are in your own power, the freer you are. The freer you are, the more generous you can be in working toward the liberation of all beings. Return to your posture work with this in mind. Notice where you have ease and where you carry excess tension. Send breaths through these spaces as you move.

What would it be like to feel your own liberation? How would you carry that? What would it feel like in your body? Relax into that possi-

bility; the possibility of your own liberation. If you were truly free, how would you move through the world? Begin to practice. With practice, the reality will come. Imagine it and it will become a reality over time.

For me, when my Power is present and activates the Liberty point, I find myself to open to being soft and stable, open-hearted and strong in my will

WHAT KEEPS US FROM FREEDOM?

The more we engage with this practice in body and spirit, the better our ability to look at what is constricted in our personal lives.

Make a list of all that keeps you from true freedom in your life. Begin to notice the ways in which you support this sense of feeling dominated, helpless, or trapped. Are you trapped in your job? Do you feel burdened with too many responsibilities that don't really interest you? Do you feel ground down by money issues? Are you addicted to drugs, adrenalin, shame, or television? What do you need to shift toward greater freedom in your life? Recognizing these things is a step into power and toward liberation.

Ask yourself: What three things in me need liberation? What is bound up and locked away or buried beneath oppression? What would liberation feel like, taste like, sound like, look like? Take the sense of liberty inside yourself. Now, how would that look, taste, or sound in the culture you are part of? What is your dream of liberty?

Write down one thing you will do to bring about your own liberation.

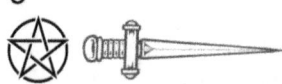

Now that we are looking at issues of power and liberty in our own lives, we can turn our gaze to our communities.

Where do things feel stagnant or trapped in your family, spiritual group, or local government? Being actively engaged in these larger, community relationships can help move energy. Sometimes the acts can be simple: facilitating a meeting, naming subterranean processes, organizing for worker's rights, cleaning up a local river.

How do you incorporate your daily practices into actions that help others as well as yourself?

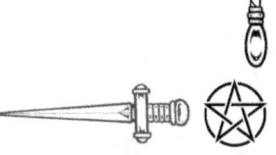

ENACTING LIBERTY

The single most helpful Liberty exercise I found was using my sitting practice as the foundation for daily self-observation. The more scrupulous I became in this practice, the more quickly I could admit to mistakes or see problems, clearing and freeing up energy that would otherwise be spent uselessly in self-justification or worries that undermine my own power.

I also turned this personal practice outward. For several months, my friends and I sat in silent meditation outside our local federal building during the morning rush during a brutal, ongoing war. Our signs read, "May we learn to be peaceful" or "Love, Not Fear," and we just sat, eyes closed, breathing, spines erect, anchoring down one corner of the edifice. We were attempting to be peaceful ourselves.

I've also sat with others during protests, demonstrations, blockades, and encampments to help balance the energy of people engaged in civil disobedience. In this way, we provided a still space for activists and the sometimes more combative energies.

We were often thanked, sometimes shouted at, but mostly, we

just sat. Why was this a liberating act? It is an act that slowly worked toward our personal liberation, and I cannot but help feel that over time, it may have helped spark the liberation of another. It is not enough, of course, but it plays one small part in the whole.

We are rooted in the earth together, using the powers of earth: stillness and silence as we hold the protestors, the struggling families, the Federal Building, City Hall, or the Pentagon within our hearts. In doing that, I felt free.

WISDOM—WATER

"*Compassion is our only hope, wisdom our weapon.*"
—Noah Levine

WATER CONTINUES TO FLOW, and the energy of the Pearl Pentacle sketches a luminous line from Liberty to Wisdom. Wisdom is intuition and integrated knowledge. We are all able to be wise; it is not the purview of teachers, spiritual or otherwise. Wisdom springs from our deepest passions. When we have passionate energy for something, some form of creation, or are seeking justice or some act of love, then we are responding to this deep knowing, this wisdom. When we respond to something like the water responds to the pulling of the moon, we are in touch with Wisdom. We can learn to trust this, in every part of heart, body, mind, and soul.

Wisdom is deeply rational, stemming from passion, emotion, instinct, and digested knowledge. Wisdom gets expressed through painting, music, dance, or any form of communication that draws on more than just our verbal skills. Though Wisdom may often bubble beneath our words, with training we can gain the verbal facility to express it. Wisdom expressed requires a combination of skills. It is activated when Sticky One begins to talk to Sacred Dove.

Flowing from Passion, the heart opens, offering true insight into another's soul. *That* is Wisdom. It runs through the body like water and can be held by our skin or poured out through eyes, hands, or mouth. Wisdom can always be shared.

WHISPERING IN WISDOM

Begin to listen to your deeper self, noticing what flows from your passion.

Take a risk with your passions. If you can cease to fear them, you are well on your way to becoming wise. Wisdom connects to Liberty. Find the place in your body where wisdom is, the place that whispers to you and guides you. Now ask yourself: How am I wise and not wise? How do I act wisely or not wisely? When am I disconnected from my passions and floundering? When do I know so deeply, I can pass it on through my skin, my breath, my words or touch? Wisdom walks, dances, and flows.

DRINKING YOUR WISDOM

Here is an exercise first given to me by Victor Anderson, as a way to drink the life force that connects all things in divinity. I have adapted the exercise for this. As we drank in our passion, so we can drink and bless our wisdom.

Take your favorite cup, or chalice if you have one. Fill it with clean water, filtered or from a well. Pour a small libation, an offering onto earth or into a potted plant. Center yourself; breathe in life force until you are full of it, tingling. As you breathe, gently move your attention to those deep places in you, those pools, those springs of passion. Ask to be shown your Wisdom. Once you have made this prayer, breathe some of your life force into the chalice, with the clear intention that this life force, channeled through your passion, will feed your Wisdom. See the chalice glowing in your mind's eye, luminous with life energy and with the full potential of your wisdom. Dip a finger into your cup, and anoint your crown, forehead, heart, belly, and sex with the water of your Wisdom. Take another deep breath. Drink your wisdom in. Drink it in until the cup is dry and you are full. The luminous energy that was outside of you now dwells within; feel it shining like the moon. Give thanks.

We have now completed the cycle of Pearl. Draw the shining line of energy back up into love, connecting the circuit. Let the energy flow through you once more, from the point of Love to Law to Knowledge to Liberty to Wisdom to Love. Then feel the shimmering circle drawn around you, sealing the energies into your body. Blessed be.

SPILLING OVER

Cleansed, refreshed, and shining with the beauty of the full moon, let the water flow out from your heart—buoyed by all the liquid held in your body—to water the earth. May your love, your hope, and your wish all pour abundantly. Soaking in the lessons of water, let us now turn to face the North.

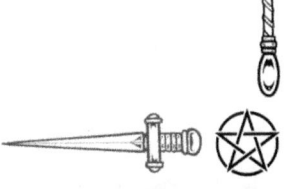

PART SEVEN
NORTH: BIRTHING OUR WHOLENESS

THE TOOLS OF NORTH

N orth. Still darkness and the strength of black midnight. The burrowing badger and the sleeping bear. Tall mountain and deep cave. The tool here is the Cube and Pentacle. Feel the hidden wisdom in the depths of your soul and the beauty of your body, dancing. Claim the power to keep silent. Be still within. Dive into your power; feel it rippling across your muscles and settling into your bones. Be green and full of life. Be quiet and listen, move slowly and with great purpose.

The powers of North are held in Earth, and traditionally found in the physical world and our relationship to it. This relationship

includes the awareness of our own bodies, money, structure, life and death, and our ancestors. The time of day is midnight, opposite of the high noon of South. Earth holds stillness, potency, silence, and mystery.

In this section we will revisit the sacred landscape we live within. We will further examine our relationship to the landscape of our bodies. We will stand upon the Cube of stability and find the flow in the pentacles that shift chaos and reform our lives. We will listen in silence and walk into darkness. Our feet will find their way.

THE CUBE AND PENTACLE

Most Craft traditions consider the pentacle the tool of earth and North. In some branches of the Feri Tradition, the tool of North and earth is a Green Cube with the symbol of the Pentacle carved on its side. I embraced this tool because it made sense to me. I have a green cube on my altar as a reminder of my magical foundations.

The cube represents stability, earth, and the mystery that can be locked away, and the color green denotes a connection to the growing world. The cube holds the power of four in each of its squares and six in the number of its sides. These signify stable balance and the restoration of harmony and are numbers to build from. The pentacle is dynamic change, the five of the human body and our senses. We are not static, but moving. The cube can become stuck in its own square. The power of five held by the pentacle creates new things out of a chaos that may seem to be at war with itself, but holds that shining instance of collaboration when it all comes together, the points of the star touch, and the form is made clear. Order and chaos dance hip to hip.

The cube and pentacle working together hold the paradox of

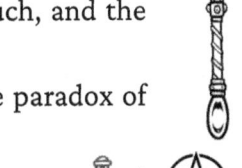

earth for me. My body sometimes longs for secure stillness, but it cannot stay there for long, as movement is necessary for my health, and the body engages its head and four limbs again and dances out to do work in the world. Yet without stable ground to grow from, the human becomes unstable, out of balance, or even sick. Cube and pentacle in concert hold the interplay of hibernation and running in the fields, of sleeping well and working to satisfaction. Solidity must be balanced by dynamism for us to be fully human, fully ourselves. Careful attention to both those needs leads to increased health and soundness. Yes, this can be true for those of us with chronic physical or mental illness or other disabilities. We can all find our way toward stability and dynamic action.

The cube is also an altar. When we examine the altar of our lives, how stable do we feel? And how often are we drawing the sacred toward us?

PLANES OF STABILITY

The Green Cube is formed from the square—the base for so many structures. Within us, the square is reflected in the four-chambered heart that pumps life through the structure that is the body. In the cube, four becomes six, structure and form.

I developed this exercise to help us answer some questions and draw a clearer picture of our lives. It also involves a card reading I designed, so prepare to pull some Tarot or oracle cards—or runes or ogham if you prefer those systems of divination—for further information about how to best allow the flow of life force back into the structure that supports you.

The image is an opened-out cube. Some magical and alchemical traditions work with the image of the Rose Cross. The rose is the pentacle resting in the heart of the opened-out altar of the cube.

The Planes of Stability Reading encompasses six categories that are basic to human life: 1) spiritual practice, 2) home/relationships, 3) body/physical health, 4) emotions/mental health, 5) money/work, 6) nature/earth. What do you build your life upon? What are the founda-

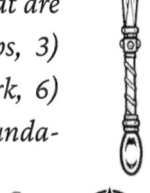

tions of your practice, your relationships, your home and work? Draw a picture of a cube and label it. What kind of support do you still need in your life? Do you need more honest friendships? A more satisfying job? Better health?

Do you not have enough stability in your life, or do things feel so stable that you are growing stagnant? In the second case, you may need to turn the cube over and look at things in a different way. You may need to shake things up a bit, and allow the cube to reform itself in a way that better serves you. Running the energy of the Iron and Pearl pentacles through your body can help you with this work.

Pull one card for each plane of the cube, laying them out in the pattern of an opened-out cube. If the meaning of a card seems opaque, you can pull two clarifying cards to answer the following questions: What can help me with this? What hinders me?

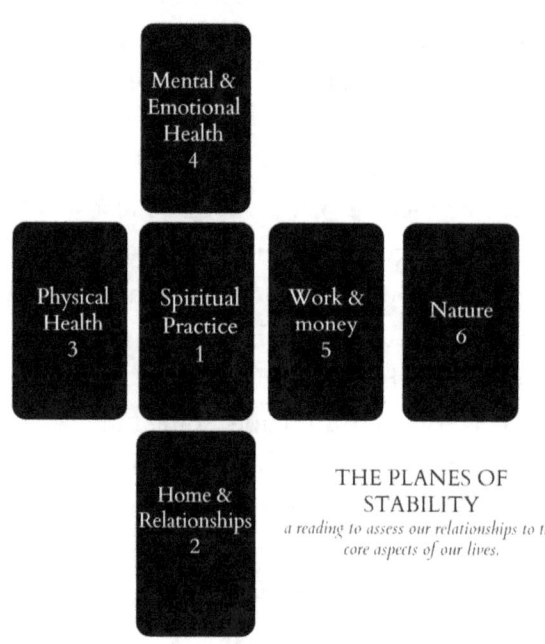

THE PLANES OF STABILITY
a reading to assess our relationships to the core aspects of our lives.

BEING PARENT TO CHANGES

Creativity gives birth from the cave of hibernation, and thus do stillness and darkness bring forth change. The Craft practitioner combines the powers of the Elements with the Iron and Pearl pentacles. What do you combine in your life—the practical and physical, the emotional and psychic, or the creative and spiritual? Bringing something to birth requires grounding and risk, patience and effort. If some of your work is stalled out, perhaps you are missing one of the following components.

Using the categories from your cube reading, make a list of the ways you manifest your work life, your food habits, your emotional awareness, and all the other things that are subheads of the larger categories of the cube. Look at this list. Are all of the things listed satisfying to you? Do they seem healthy and in balance to you? Are some lists much longer than others?

Sit with this information for one month's time. Then ask, "What do I want to do with this information? Do changes need to be made?"

THE POWER OF SILENCE

One of the powers of the North is the power to be silent, the power of stillness, the resonance of no-words. This is the power of midnight, of secrets, and a time for work when others are sleeping. There is potency in midnight, because it is the depth of the fertile dark, when the owl hunts and the moon shines high. In urban neighborhoods, it can hearken the beginning of the hours of business for activities that need to be done under cover, in hidden places. Humans, raccoons, opossums, and foxes roam, seeking out food, revelry, or business. In more rural areas, owls hunt and other creatures burrow.

We can use these times to be still, to drop like a stone in a dark pool, to crawl into a cave of our being and scry into our souls.

I have talked already about the powers of speech as powers of air—this is its obverse. As Witches, it is good to learn when not to speak, when to hold the mystery. The power of silence, used properly, will lend resonance to our powers of speech. One must know the spaces between the notes to value the music itself.

Another power of silence is that of digestion. Let your experiences and thoughts digest in the dark cave of your belly before

you attempt to bring them out into the world as lights for teaching. Undigested words are simply the work of a parrot, not a priest. We need to learn the lessons of slow-moving time and integration instead of the quick spouting of ideas. Digestion is holding true power, with integrity, leading yourself and others, through example, into liberty. Our culture often teaches us the opposite: time moves quickly for us; things turn around at breakneck speed.

This power of slowness and stillness is something that can be hard for some of us to cultivate, but we can continue to try. Continued practice certainly made it possible for me. Stillness is now a powerful ally.

TAKING A WORD FAST

Before one of my initiations, I was asked to keep twenty-four hours of silence. As a highly verbal person, this was a powerful lesson for me, the beginning of deepening, and an integration of my then thirteen years of work and study in the Craft. As I grew in my studies and practices, the power of silence increased within me, lending strength to my magic. I still talk a lot, but I leave a lot more space, too. Things grow in these spaces.

Set aside a twenty-four-hour period where you will not speak. You may wish to go off on retreat to accomplish this, but it is not necessary. You can stay at home. Just warn your family or friends that you will not be speaking, texting, or otherwise interacting. If possible, try to spend at least part of this time in seclusion. This is a good time to take a sacred bath, do some mirror gazing or journaling, or expand your time for sitting meditation, which will help to stretch and deepen your silence. Don't read the news, scroll the Internet, or answer emails. Take this time to be with yourself and the world that exists right physically around you.

When it is time to break your word fast, think of what the first words you want to say will be. Break your silence with magical intent. May your silence be blessed.

SITTING LIKE A MOUNTAIN

The powers of earth include stillness. It is time to look again at your sitting practice. Our God Soul cannot only listen to our stories, it can also open us up to a deeper, more connected stillness. If you have not begun a sitting practice, I recommend that you to try now. My students report that sitting adds stability and integration to their spiritual practice. The following meditation can help bring a sense of stillness and presence that can influence the rest of your day.

Sit with an erect, relaxed posture. Send your attention throughout your body, feeling the bones inside you and the muscles that support them. Feel the skin that encases them, and the breath that moves throughout. As you sit, notice the shape you make, from the spread of your knees to the apex of your head resting on your spine. You are a mountain. Feel yourself, old, solid and still. Feel your energy spread out behind you, forming an anchor for your body, echoing the shape of your thighs and knees in front. You are a cone of earth with a solid base, rising up to meet the sky. You are a mountain.

As you breathe within your mountain shape, imagine a cave of stillness opening up deep inside of you. Within your mountain, there is

the cave of your belly. Feel the stillness open up and deepen into a dark cavern. There is a pool in that cavern that spreads out. A pool of even deeper stillness. You are centered around that pool; you anchor it and you rise from it. You are mountain and deep cave, you are the pool of stillness. You are contained, yet fully part of the ecosystem. The mountain is supported by earth, sky, and wind, and in turn the mountain supports plants, animals, and fungi. You are alone and still. You breathe with the earth, expanding and contracting

As you close your meditation, try to rise from your seat with an awareness of your bones and muscles, with an awareness of the deep cave and still pool.

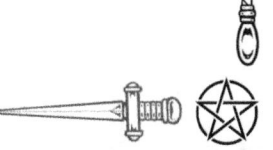

THE GUARDIAN OF NORTH

The Guardian of the North helps us with all of our work of earth. This Guardian lends us stability, fecund darkness, and the ability to sense on a deep level.

Take a deep breath, connecting to your grounding cord. Cast the blue sphere around you. Light a candle on your altar, dark green or black. Turn toward the North, and open yourself to the power of the Guardian there as you breathe deeply within yourself.

Feel a breath upon your forehead. Open up to the Guardian of the North. Begin to feel the presence coming closer to you. What does this Guardian feel like? Guardian of the North, walk the earth and join this rite." Imagine the Cube of Power, carved with the five-pointed star, stability and change joined together, the paradox of human strength and beauty and the road to liberation. Feel the silence of midnight blackness. Introduce yourself.

Guardian of the North,
Dancer at dark midnight's cusp,
Walk the earth and join our rites.
Teach us the ways of Power
And show us the strength in silent darkness.

Let us deepen, together.
Let us deepen.
Touch our bones, our muscles, our skin.
May we move in balance.
May we stand tall within the world.
May we walk towards liberty.
Welcome.

Take a deep breath. Feel the presence guarding the Northern quadrant, huge and beautiful. Stay in this presence for a while—feeling, sensing, gazing. Write or draw what you sense. When you are done for this meeting, you may say:

Guardian,
Thank you for your presence.
Thank you for the gifts of earth and liberty.
May I touch the mystery, and learn silence.
Go if you must, stay if you will.
Hail and farewell.

THE PHYSICAL WORLD

North represents the physical world—the human body, the animal realms, the trees and plants, food, and cycles of growth and rest. What is your neighborhood, town, or land like physically? Do you live amongst mountains or plains? Are you bounded by water or high desert? Are buildings made of wood, brick, or steel? How do your surroundings affect you emotionally or psychically? Do some wandering in your vicinity and try to sense this. Look at the bushes or trees and listen for the animals, insects, or birds. Send a breath out to cleanse your senses once again: breathing through your eyes, ears, and nose, across your tongue and your fingertips. Feel yourself alive, walking, standing, looking, and listening. You are part of this land, this town, and this neighborhood. You are part of the earth.

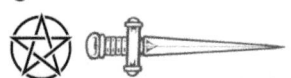

WHAT ARE YOU GROWING?

What do you wish to nurture in your life? Let us revisit the exercise we did around matching will and belief under the Law point of the Iron Pentacle. Do your actions reflect what your heart finds important? Do you live in ways that are sustainable or are you consuming too many of your personal resources, or the resources of your community or the earth? Are you cultivating love and right livelihood? Try to sense what you can be doing to nurture your own growth and to nurture the earth you live on, and the communities you live within.

Ideas: Volunteer at a soup kitchen, hospice, animal shelter, or community garden. Organize a trash pickup at your local beach or park. Teach a child to ride a bicycle. Plant some trees. Ride the bus or a bicycle. Learn how to compost organic material. Give back to the earth that sustains you.

YOUR SACRED BODY

Your body is part of the sacred earth.

Before we begin this section, please remember that what I write below are only suggestions to help us pay better attention to our physical needs. You know your body better than anyone else. Be honest with yourself and make your choices accordingly.

Revisit the work you began when you started to notice your posture, but this time check in with your whole body. How does your body feel and how do you feel about it? What *is* your posture like these days? Are you aware of it at all? How are you eating—are you getting enough of the good things that feed you well; are you taking time to cook? Are you eating on the run, or eating too many things that do not give you what your body needs? Are you not eating enough? Do you deny your body good food? Food is mass and energy, and mass and energy are life. If you haven't already, take a look at your eating habits and notice whether or not they serve your work.

Our dominant culture can skew our relationship to our bodies. We are often told that we are either couch potatoes or

exercise addicts, skinny or fat, weak or strong. In reality, we come in all shapes and sizes that can be healthy and beautiful. Some of us are thin and some are large. What matters to me is this: How healthy do I feel? How much walking, dancing, or other movement am I doing? Am I getting enough protein, vegetables, and water? Am I able to enjoy my body, food, and physical movement?

Examining our relationship to our bodies may seem obvious to some and painful to others. Regardless of our feelings about it, this practice is helpful to us as both humans and magical practitioners. We need to be as healthy as possible to do our work. We are embodied for a reason and must not seek to deny the body. What we sometimes forget, however, is that denial can come in many forms. Denial is not just the starvation of asceticism; denial can also be eating donuts and chips all day or longing to run off into more "spiritual" realms instead of living in the here and now.

As with changing our posture habits, those of us who have had years of eating that does not nourish us, or exercise habits that punish rather than support us, may need to reset our habits for a while before we can clearly hear what it is our bodies need. I had to do this when my autoimmune disorder was finally diagnosed. Medication only did so much to stabilize my symptoms. For the rest? I had to figure out what foods supported my health and which actively made it worse. Sometimes we need outside help with changing these patterns, and family, friends, or support groups can aid us in this work.

Clearing out the less nourishing foods can also help us get rid of some of the cravings that keep us from listening to what our bodies *really* need. For example, I sometimes crave tortilla chips—and they are frankly delicious!—which can cause inflammation in my body and leave me exhausted and brain-fogged. What I most likely need is some salt or electrolytes, instead.

One common craving is for sugar and fat, which can mask a need for protein. This is especially important to remember if you are doing a lot of magic and running energy fully. You may need to eat a little more than usual to recharge, but make certain you are really giving your body fuel, not foods that will further deplete it. Dessert is good, but not at the expense of vegetables and protein. If sugar or fat are the first things you reach for after expending energy, try to listen a little more deeply. Listen to what foods sustain and grow energy.

Similarly, if all you want to do is lie around and read all day, you might go for a short walk and see how that feels. I find that a walk often recharges my batteries and gives me the energy I thought I lacked when I was lying about. I am more productive, healthier, and mentally and emotionally happier if I get a decent amount of exercise. But I still need to listen to my body's cues, because sometimes what I truly need is deep rest.

On the flip side, some people become addicted to exercise or to severely controlled eating. These tendencies can also be signs of imbalance. No one but a professional athlete or dancer needs three hours of intensive exercise every day and a body starved means a brain starved and emotions that may crumple in a ball within you.

Again, there are no absolutes here. No "one, true way" that suits every body or environment. As a person who lives with an autoimmune disorder and the aftermath of a brain injury, my physical and energetic needs are different than they were in my early twenties. This makes it even more vital that I support my body in its needs.

Look at your patterns, just as you might gaze upon the patterns leaves make at your feet, or waves upon sand. Learn to read your physical body as you read the stars in the sky. You are part of the natural world, not separate from it.

Live in your body. Live in your world. Grow and thrive. Know yourself in all your parts. This is your charge.

Unless it is triggering, for one month, look at your eating habits.

Are you eating things that nourish your body or only things that feed some of the emotions that you may be coddling to your detriment? Notice how you carry your body and notice whether you can choose to walk short distances or always use the bus or a car. Notice how helpful using a mobility aid is and how embracing that might help your life.

If you are afraid of movement, put some music on when you are alone and move or stretch a little bit, letting yourself warm into your body. Revisit the Sacred Pleasure exercise. If you ache, trade a massage with a friend or seek out a body worker. Take a luxurious bath. Cook yourself a beautiful dinner.

LISTENING TO YOUR BODY

We can make commitments to the sacred earth, to our communities, to our practice, to work, our Gods, and to service. Our first commitment is to ourselves. None of the things on the list above will be truly served unless we take care of ourselves, as well. This is something that I grappled with, and something you may have heard a million times. If you are like me, it is something you may not quite believe.

One morning years ago, I was lying in bed, not feeling well, thinking of all the things I had to do before my shift at the soup kitchen began. For the previous week, I had a feeling in my brain and belly that I was doing too much and perhaps needed to take a break from a few things. Well, here I was, having not made any moves toward giving myself a break. I finally had to say, "Thorn, you feel sick! You are a Witch! Listen to your body!"

Years before, my autoimmune disorder was undiagnosed, and I was chronically ill and fatigued. I made the changes necessary to support my health through use of herbs, exercise, meditation, and acupuncture. However, this did not mean I could sustain juggling too many things that fractured my energy and attention. My body told me that quite clearly. It still does. That one morning, I needed a break. I had begun getting sick a bit more often; nothing dramatic, but enough to let me know that it was time for a winnowing of projects.

One thing I needed to take a break from all those years ago was the soup kitchen. But I *liked* working at the soup kitchen and had deep, long-term commitments there. I didn't want to take a break, but nonetheless, I needed one. So, I made the difficult phone call to the soup kitchen. I needed a hiatus. They understood.

As you listen to your body, pay attention to the cycles of the seasons. Flowers are not always blooming. The moon waxes and wanes. You do not always have to be running full speed, nor always in hibernation. Get to know what your tendencies are. If you take care of yourself, you will be in a much better position to take care of others, the earth, and your magic. You can be open to the abundance of the universe, but remember, one of the Witch's tools is that of choice.

Over the next month or two, listen to your responses to the world. How can you best serve? Do you say "yes" to too much? Or do you refuse the gifts of the universe too often? Are you doing too much or too little? Are you using your talents and taking care of your physical and emotional health? If you listen deeply and look toward the route that feels most right, it will open in front of you. You will feed and be fed.

Abundant Earth

Another facet of earth and North is money. I would hazard to guess that many of us have trouble with money in one way or another. As we may have skewed attitudes toward our bodies, our culture also teaches us skewed attitudes toward money, and many of us have reacted to that in ways that end up not serving us. I have worked at extremes of the economic spectrum. Though I lived much of my life below the poverty level, I am currently middle class. Living below the poverty line partially stemmed from my working-class background but was more deeply rooted in a powerful sense that if I had enough for myself, it harmed another, taking away what they might need. This was coupled with my awareness of social injustice and inequality and a need to right the wrongs of the world. I hated money because I hated what I saw as a mechanism of control and oppression. Poverty itself became a status symbol to show my friends.

These days, I attempt to live more in balance, having pushed my edges and boundaries around money in many ways, probing the wound and trying to understand it. I worked full time on the Pacific Stock Exchange for four years, trying to learn something about our economic system and to challenge my prejudices and thinking. I worked for four years as a peep-show dancer to learn more about that way of relating to the confluence of money, sex, and power. Still further, I worked for four years full time in a soup kitchen, living on room and board and a small stipend, spending most of my time with the poor and disenfranchised. I learned different things about myself in each of these places, yet they all showed me a common human response: greed and need are everywhere, no matter who holds the economic advantage.

These days, twenty years after I first wrote this book, wealth inequity has grown into a staggering chasm and shows no sign of letting up. Life is harder for even more people around the globe. This makes it ever more important to change our relationship to greed and its siblings, scarcity and fear, endeavoring to shift them into a response of generosity. We can give back. We can smile at passers-by and enjoy the sun on our face. We can leave big tips.

There is one café where I often work at, and an unhoused person is often around outside. When they are present, I ask if they want coffee and a sandwich. They always say yes. This means that once a week, the café gets extra income from me, and the person gets some lunch. Can I solve homelessness? No. But I can do this small thing while also working for systemic equity and justice.

Let the antidotes to greed be simple. Engage in mutual aid. Share skills and resources. Be kind when you can. All of this is good magic.

Get out some paper and pen. Set a timer or clock alarm for six minutes. Begin to write down everything you think or feel about money and your relationship to it, how it affects the world, how it works (or doesn't) in your life. Start with the phrase, "Money is..." and move into

answering the question, "How do I feel about money?" Probably some things you already know will arise, but underneath that may be suppositions you were not conscious of. If you can observe something, it has the opportunity to change.

OPENING TO GENEROSITY

Just as energy follows breath, abundance and happiness follow generosity. This is the occult face of the old adage, "You have to spend money to make money." Magically, this phrase is not about investment, but generosity. Would that multinational corporations and billionaires learn this lesson. Whether they learn it or not, *we* can. We can try. We can spread a smile or a dollar, engage in acts of mutual aid, and lend a listening ear. We can collectively work to hold politicians, exploiters, and polluters accountable.

I like to also remember that multinational corporations, despite being legally treated as singular entities, are full of individual human beings, some of whom are probably reading this now. If I recall all the people sitting at desks or toiling in factories, I know that change is possible. If I am open to one person touching me and changing my life today, others can be, too.

How can we live to create abundance for all? Sometimes this means generous flow and sometimes more careful, less wasteful, resource management.

For one month, leave a bigger tip than you are used to at the local

café. Try smiling at five people a day and see what happens. Encourage the creative impulse of another. Set out a plate of food in gratitude for your ancestors. When the thought enters your head, "I don't have enough," or "I can't do that," try to turn that thought around. Just for that moment, focus on what you do have and what you can do. Then pass it on. What is true, right now?

Look at how you use natural resources such as water, time, gasoline, trees, and electricity. Look especially closely at their subsets—found in things like packaging, air conditioning, new paper usage as opposed to high post consumer waste content, bus or bicycle travel as opposed to car travel—then make your own internal list.

Have you already worked on changing your habits around natural resource usage to come in line with a more sustainable, healthier earth relationship? Let every interaction with human, animal, or vegetable, be an interaction that fosters connection. Connection follows generosity of spirit and action.

And last, how are you working toward economic equity and social justice? How are you helping build healthy and sustainable communities?

EMBRACING DEATH

Another important aspect of the North and the powers of earth is the strength of death in the cycle of life. Again, this is the juxtaposition of the stable cube with the moving pentacle: death is final and death is simply change. As a reminder of this, I have a ceramic skull in the office where I do my writing and publishing work. The skull is surrounded by all the books I've written so far, reminding me of the paradox of creativity and death. I am learning to embrace it all.

There are many ways to see these cycles, for life and death are all around us. You can look at the fly, caught in a web; it is dead, but it is also food for the spider, so it is life. See the bird, fallen beneath the tree, or the shriveled leaf on the otherwise green plant. Once the leaf is plucked, the green parts will grow stronger. The bird will decompose and eventually feed the tree. Our lives mirror these spirals in microcosm.

Years ago, I decided that since I was not a gardener, nor was I going to have a child, I needed to explore life's cycles in a different way. I began by doing hospice work, caring for the dying. I learned a lot about the powers of North: about death and the body. There

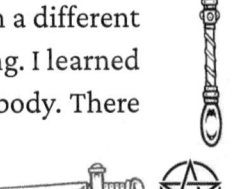

is a lot of strength in death: as the body fights the toxins that consume it, the spark of life strives to reach the surface. The body's functions continue in an increasingly erratic fashion, no longer trustworthy, but still quite present. A person calling for help, tangled in sheets, or needing to be cleaned up after a bout of diarrhea often awakened me in the middle of the night.

Through hospice work, I began to see the struggle within myself of parts that were dying to change yet still clinging to life. I also saw that when things are dying, they aren't necessarily graceful or pretty. I saw the ways in which I could resist change, awkwardly fighting and complaining against it, feeling out of my element and exposed, just like the people I cared for in their final days on earth. Despite this, I *always* end up running toward change, full tilt, near the end of every phase. And so new phases in my life are born, and I learn how to move in my new world.

What have you learned from your cycles? What is your pattern? Take a breath and ask yourself, right now, "What needs to give way so that something new can grow?"

Now reexamine your attitudes. Are you ready to unbind those that do not serve you and to release the energy they've tied up?

When situations have run their course, they often cause frustration or stagnation. We can choose to use outdated situations as a challenge to aid a new sense of practice, or we can choose to walk away from them, truly letting them go. Earth has the power to compost, to rest, and to leave space and food for something new to grow over time.

Are there people who were once friends, lovers, or colleagues who don't support your current life and practice? Can those relationships change, or should they be culled?

Learning about the importance of death and change doesn't always have to be about asking the big questions. Some things just fall away and new things enter in. What in your life can you cull? Are there drawers in your bureau, packed with papers you no

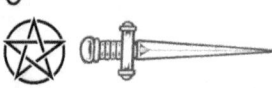

longer read or clothes you no longer wear? Are there projects that don't excite you but that still sap your energy because you have not taken leave of them? Is there an attitude you still carry that does not serve who you have become?

Take a breath. Open those drawers and begin to sort what is useful and what can be given away. Clean out your closet. Snip the dying leaves from your plants. Pull some weeds.

What are you willing to let rest, or to cull and let die to bring in the possibility of eventual new life? Winter calls. Death calls. No fear, only the cycle. Feel the skull resting beneath your face. Your bones support your life.

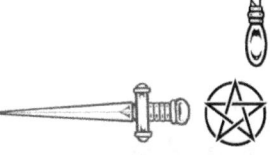

THE TOMB OF BIRTH

"*Die before you die.*"
—A Sufi Teaching

THROUGHOUT THIS BOOK we have been asked to look at our stories, at our bodies, at our sexuality, at our thoughts and perceptions. Hopefully, through this work, we have come to recognize the many parts of our selves that bump around inside of us. It is these parts, often called our personalities, which the Sufis speak of when they say you must die to yourself in order to live. In this way, the cycles of earth and North exist in our emotional states as well as in our bodies.

When we worked on the Self point of the Iron Pentacle, we saw that there were many masks to strip away, leaving only our core essence behind. You may have put a few layers back on since then, to function better in your everyday life. Other layers and masks of "self" may have crept back in over time. Take another

look. What part are you identifying with today? Who do you say you are?

Sometimes, we may find ourselves identifying emotions as self. We may be letting the emotional drama of a given situation take over as though it directly relates to who we are. We see this often when friends or associates want to relate the terrible injustice done to them at the hands of the person who made their latte in the morning, or at the line they had to wait in at the airport. They have begun to identify with the emotions brought up by those situations and taken them in, coating their personalities with indignation, and giving innocuous situations that could have been dealt with in ten minutes the weight of their day, and sometimes the weight of many years.

Can you catch these emotions as they rise, before they harden into a crust around your soul? I like to practice feeling the impatience, irritation, or indignation, then take a breath and remind myself of what the actual situation in front of me is. Is the airport full of people conspiring to ruin my day? No. Is the delay in service a personal affront designed to make me miss my appointments? Likely not. Does the person acting like a jerk online even know me? No.

We are not the center of the multiverse, rather, that is only the story we sometimes tell ourselves. By paying attention, we can feel our emotions and then put the stories to rest, to sleep in the tomb of birth. What is born from that tomb? Many things, including the possibility of being present in the situation and an abundance of energy not tied up in self-justification. Often greater patience and compassion are born as added bonuses.

The seed is in the ground, waiting. The bear sleeps in the cave. We sit, still as a mountain. Something gestates in the darkness.

When you find yourself harboring grievances, give them a cave to sleep in, instead. See what happens when you take a breath, feel your feet beneath you, and really look at the people around you. Send a breath through your heart. Engage your belly muscles, reminding yourself that you have a will and are not simply at the mercy of every stray action and emotion. Let the situations that frustrate you in the moment enter the Tomb of Birth. Feel the cool, cave-like quality surrounding you. Be still. Be still inside, for just one moment. One long breath. Remember that you have an essence deep inside that is not this emotion, not this situation. Die to this piece. Let it rest. It may not need to live, but you do. You cannot live fully if all of your life's energy is taken up by random situations and injuries of little consequence. Do you have to be right? No, but you have to be present in order to live.

From the tomb, something new and fine has a chance to be born now. Cultivate that which is soul-strengthening. As those other parts sleep, your essence can awaken.

FLOWING AND SPANNING

Carved into the Green Cube, the Pentacle glows, holding the energy of shifting change. Within the structure of your soul and body, the Iron and Pearl Pentacles meet, expanding your ability to grow into yourself and connect out with the world. These pentacles also connect to the elements swirling in your body. Iron and Pearl sing together within you, just as you sing, placed between earth and sky. You are child of earth and starry heaven, whole and complete unto yourself.

The pentacles work with one another, becoming multidimensional, feeding into each other, giving the concepts and energies depth and shine. By beginning with the Elemental pentacle, and layering in the tools, you can derive a great deal of help with your work in understanding the qualities of the Iron and Pearl Pentacles.

Flowing from water, Wisdom naturally flows from Passion, as Passion comes from the deep well of ocean and the refreshing waters of the cup. We cannot be wise about things for which no Passion has ever flowed. Air creates a Knowledge that comes naturally from Self. So much knowledge is helped by the develop-

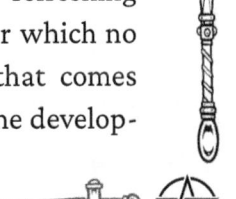

ment of self-knowledge. And the crystal tip on the wand is the key, the reflection, that instrument that catches the morning star, the first ray of sunlight, bringing the flash of knowledge into the self.

Fire lends will to the blade, lighting the fire beneath Pride and contributing to natural Law. Fire is the blade scything through the forest so that new things can grow. Earth is the cube, the cave of darkness, the pentacle of change. Power, to be stable like the cube, must also become fluid like the pentacle or it becomes brittle and breaks. True power is the basis for liberation. If we are not in our power, we will forever be subject to insecurity and the force of others. Spirit flows through Above, Below, and Center, creating the hub of the sphere. Life force is the core of Sex and Love vibrates from that space of connection and expansion.

Breathe deeply. Connect once again to the fiery star in the earth, calling it up your grounding cord and into your body. Begin to run the Iron Pentacle: Sex, Pride, Self, Power, Passion. Sex. Run this over and over, until the energy flows fast and clear, and you begin to tingle with it. Then draw the circle around yourself: Sex, Self, Passion, Pride, Power. Sex. Feel yourself glowing in the Pentacle of Iron. Take a deep breath. Let the energy lighten, beginning to vibrate up one octave, until it shifts into the energy of Pearl. Begin to run the Pearl Pentacle through your body: Love, Law, Knowledge, Liberty, Wisdom. Love. Run this over and over, until the energy sparkles, radiating and luminous. Then draw the circle around yourself. Love, Knowledge, Wisdom, Law, Liberty. Love. Feel it. Feel yourself full and glowing. Iron and Pearl. Call the Iron energy into your mind, your body, feel it like a bass note beneath the Pearl, supporting it, and the Pearl answering back, in harmony. Feel the energies sink into your body and rise outward. Iron and Pearl. Let them vibrate together.

You can take the meditation below point by point, feeling the interplay of the octave and the way the Iron energy makes room for Pearl to appear. You can also use the Devotional Dance move-

ments to feel the energies more fully and to sense the dance between the points.

Focusing on Sex, let yourself fill with Sex energy, then let it begin to shift, vibrating with Love. Feel how Love and Sex interact, supporting one another, life force feeding into the powers of creation. Feel Pride. Fill with the energy of Pride. Let Pride lay the foundation for Law. Feel them working together, vibrating within you, the confidence of Pride, not coddling weakness, and thus leading to the balance of Law based on worth and connection with life's flow. Fill with Self. Feel the "I am" within you, quiet or loud. Listen, let Self be answered by Knowledge. All that you know, all you are growing to know, comes from the strength of knowing yourself. Let Self and Knowledge dance together within your skin.

Now fill with Power. Feel the strength flowing into your body, feel how Power shifts within you, vibrating with Liberty. Liberty is only attained through the basis of Power, true power, Power within, Power with. This brings Liberty, and Liberty reinforces Power. The more liberation, the truer the Power. Now fill with Passion. Feel the desire that is keyed to your creation, what you want to bring into the world, and what draws you. This is the Passion that flows now into Wisdom: the overflowing cup of desire and intuition. Passion is fed by Wisdom and Wisdom is cultivated through the exercise of Passion. Feel that dance.

Feel yourself, red and silvery white, glowing cool and hot. Combusting yet not burning away. Feel the power in your hands, in your genitals, flowing through your feet. You are connected to the stars and the first acts of creation. Life arises from the spark of creation, and the pearl is born in the cauldron of the poet's heart. From the grit of your life comes burning beauty. Can you live with that? Then you are ready to be whole, in this moment.

Let the energies settle inside you, sealing them into your body by placing your right hand on your heart and your left hand on your belly. This balances all the points in the realms of compassion and will. Take a deep breath.

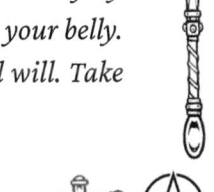

WALKING THE PENTACLES

I often use the Iron and Pearl pentacle points as a walking meditation. As I step, I chant "Sex, Love, Pride, Law, Self, Knowledge, Power, Liberty, Passion, Wisdom, Sex, Love..." interlacing Iron with Pearl as I activate the points in my body. As I say each set, I try to sense the place in my body where those points originate; for example, Self and Knowledge in my left hand. This keeps me connected to my body—moving through the world—cleansing and expanding myself to meet that which I can see, touch, taste, smell, and hear. In the past, I have used prayer beads to add another tactile layer to the experience. As hematite and pearl slip between my fingers, I am reminded that strength and luminosity connect me to my magic.

Using a string of beads, or simply using the words as a focus, spend some time moving with the pentacles, letting the concepts enter further into your body and soul.

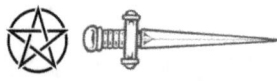

SPELL TO BECOME WHOLE

Stand or lie down in the star position, with arms outstretched and feet spread. Now take a breath and conjure yourself, saying:

By Sex and Spirit, I invoke Love.
By Pride and Fire, I invoke Law.
By Self and Air, I invoke Knowledge.
By Power and Earth, I invoke Liberty.
By Passion and Water, I invoke Wisdom.
By stepping into wholeness, I invoke Life.

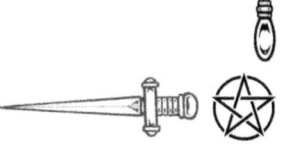

YOU ARE THE BODY OF THE EARTH

You are sacred, alive on the earth. Your body holds mystery and you know how to dance in the dark. Feel the power of the North in your bones. Now take a breath, and reach for the sky.

PART EIGHT
POWERS ABOVE: RISING AND DREAMING

CALLING ABOVE

What lies above you, calling to your spirit? What captures your imagination and feeds your dreams? Step out under the night sky and see the stars, birthed in space and dying in flashes of iron and heat. Yet all looks still and cool. All seems peaceful mystery. That is the paradox of your life and your connection to the life of stars. What shines in you? Look into the mirror. Burn brightly. Your soul is as vast as space.

. . .

WE CONTINUE INVOKING our sacred sphere by turning from the four cardinal directions and calling on the powers above. The Powers Above and Below are very important in some, but not all, Craft traditions. We do not live in a flat world, but one that stretches far around us—honoring the Powers Above and Below acknowledges this. The Powers of Above, Below, and Center all hold spirit in the Elemental pentacle. Spirit drives the hub of the wheel that becomes the sphere of life.

When we call the Powers Above into our sacred space, we allow ourselves permission to stretch beyond our comfort zone, beyond what we sometimes allow as being possible. This is the space of vast opening, exploration of new dreams and living in a world where much is not yet proven, leaving doors of perception wide open to our deepest senses and wildest imaginings. It is the place where science and fantasy meet and our souls can dance with the Gods.

In this section, we will look into the Star Goddess's mirror. We will gaze upon the powers of dreams and desire. We will dance in love's storm and travel to the stars, returning always to the cycles of earth, and to ourselves, more human and more divine. What is real? What is imagined? What is possible within us?

LOVING THE FACE IN THE MIRROR

Mirrors have been a traditional tool of seers, oracles, and priestesses throughout time. Whether polished bronze or a clear dark pool looked at under the full moon, mirrors have been gateways to vision and true seeing. The tool I personally use for the Powers Above is the Black Mirror of Space. This mirror holds our ability to stretch toward ourselves, to gaze upon our reflections and embrace ourselves in love. Mirrors can also help us by reflecting our true selves back at us.

Remember the Queen's mirror in *Snow White*? It was trying to show the truth, but the Queen didn't want to see it. The silver mirror can hold the harshness of the light. The black mirror can help us to see beyond the surface. It shows us what is hidden in shadow. Can you learn to gaze on each with love?

In Feri Tradition mythology, the Star Goddess—God Herself, a being beyond gender—gazed out into the vast blackness of space. She caught a glimmering, a glimpse, and began to move toward it. Where the edges of space curved, a black mirror formed. In it, She saw Herself and was struck by Her great beauty. She began to look upon Herself with desire and, full of this desire, began to make

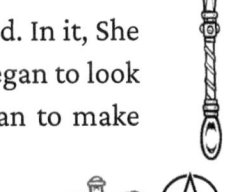

love to Herself. She was so beautiful and full of desire, that the image grew substance and stepped forth. God Herself came in ecstasy, and stars spun across the sky. The Milky Way is the product of Her joyous lust, and too, from Her love and lust, the Divine Twins were born. Brothers and Lovers, they wheeled out across the sky.

Brothers and lovers, they shift and change: sisters, siblings, male and female, female and female, male and male, neither and both, the paradox unfolds. Blood of blood and sex of sex. The ray of divinity, the impulse of creation, flowed out into the multiverse and thus were all the Gods born, and thus was born our universe, our earth. We are children of paradox, and so we hold the center spaces where all things meet in chaos and in form and so She blesses the center. Together we shine.

If we love ourselves, there is no end to what we can create. Self-loathing gets us nowhere. It hurts us and causes us to hurt others. Stretch up into space and feel how huge and beautiful you are. Breathe in. Know that you are loved, loving, gorgeous, and strong. You can fill space. You can shine.

GAZING AT THE SILVER MIRROR

One of the hardest things for many of us is to acknowledge that we deserve love and the good things that come our way. Just as we must take responsibility for our part in the difficult things in our life, we must take equal responsibility for the good. We must nourish ourselves and know that to continue to do our work responsibly requires a base of self-love. Other parts of the book have addressed this, but I'd like to offer another exercise to help us. This exercise comes in this section of the book because it requires preparation. It requires all of the work we have done on ourselves in years past. Seemingly simple on the surface, our cultural conditioning can make this exercise difficult to do with ease.

Use the following technique every day for one full cycle of the moon, or one month. If it still is not easy, contract with yourself for another cycle. You will begin to see changes in your life, in your ability to receive abundance and in your ability to give love with generous compassion. Remember: if you cannot receive, it becomes more difficult to give. Things in nature work in multiple ways, and the way of replenishment is one of them. A tree will not

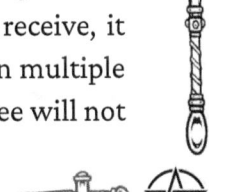

bear fruit if it has not received rain and sun and air. You will bear less fruit if you cannot receive love and support.

You will need a mirror and a candle to do the exercise below. A big mirror is better: one where you can see your whole face and head at one time is best. If you have a magic hand mirror, it is all right to use this. Your bathroom mirror will do the trick as well.

In a private space, light a candle. Take a deep breath. Look at yourself in the mirror. Really look. See how your face curves. Look at your eyes, your nose, your chin. Take another breath. Do you have wrinkles, pimples, fat? Look at that. Take another breath. As you breathe, let your stance begin to soften. Let any tension you are holding in your face, your shoulders, your back and belly begin to release. Let yourself grow soft. This is warrior work, this ability to be soft. Close your eyes for a moment if you need to. If you have fear, feel it. If you feel anger or sadness, let those be with you. Now, take another deep breath and blow some softness into those feelings.

As you continue to breathe, open your eyes if you have closed them. Look into your eyes in the mirror. Look deeply at yourself. Now, out loud, say, "I love you." Take a breath. Say it again. "I love you." Take a breath. You will now say it a third time, beginning with your name. "_____, I love you." On your next breath, take in that love. Take it in to any of the places that felt tense. Imagine that you can breathe it into your heart. If you have any excess energy or emotion, you can breathe it up to your God Soul, aligning your Triple Soul. Look in the mirror and say, "Blessed be."

RESTING IN THE ARMS OF LOVE

You can do this during the same time period as the silver mirror exercise, or you may want to do it in the moon cycle following. Please do it for the full month, which will allow you to relax and sink into the work. It may feel difficult, but for us to expand fully into our lives, we must expand our ability to receive and give love.

If you share a bed with a partner, you may want to tell them you will be doing an exercise and to not disturb you. Or you can just lie there, breathing and doing this exercise without telling them anything. It is not something that will be readily apparent to an outsider, except that your breathing may be deeper than usual. This exercise draws on the work we did earlier when we changed the color of our aura.

Before you go to bed, notice where the moon is in its cycle. Is it dark, waxing, waning, full? Let yourself feel the moon. Then go to bed. As you lie in bed, preparing for sleep, begin to breathe deeply. Let your body relax. Relax your neck. Let your back and butt sink into the bed. Tense your leg muscles and release them. Feel your tension drifting away as you sink into the bed, relaxing. As you breathe, begin to feel yourself

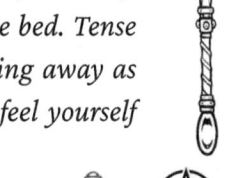

cradled in gentle arms. Let your aura begin to fill with a sense of warmth, safety, and love. Fill your aura with pink light. Let yourself feel cradled in the arms of God Herself. You are fed by love. You breathe in the love the universe has for you, child of earth and starry heaven. You are beautiful, unique, and wonderful. You are loved, wholly and without reservation or expectation. Let yourself relax into this love. You are surrounded by love. Let yourself drift to sleep, cradled in security, gentleness, and love.

THE GUARDIAN OF ABOVE

The Guardian of the spaces above can help you to reach beyond your comfort zone, by opening and connecting you to the forces that swirl high above you.

Take a deep breath, connecting to your grounding cord. Cast the blue sphere around you. Light a candle on your altar, violet or black. Look above you and breathe deeply. "Guardian Above, expand the swirling vortex and join this rite." Feel a breath upon your forehead. Open to the Guardian of Above. Begin to feel the presence coming closer to you. What does this Guardian feel like? Can you get a glimpse? The Guardian of Above. The force that births stars, spinning out that which forms us and shows us what is possible. This guardian wheels above you, shot with stars. Reach. Reach. Say the name, over and over. Feel the presence. Raise your hands above you and say,

Guardian Above,
Zenith of time and exploder of space.
Expand the swirling vortex and join our rites.
Teach us the ways of expansion,
And show us the beauty in vast possibility.
Let us open together,

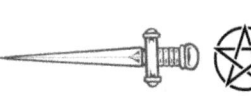

Let us open.
Touch our spirits, touch our souls.
May we grow beyond our borders.
May we vision evolution.
May we fly in the midst of love.
Welcome.

Take a deep breath. Feel the guardian above you, guarding all those spaces beyond and bringing them closer, huge and beautiful. Stay in this presence for a while—feeling, sensing, gazing. You may wish to write or draw what you sense. There may be a key to this presence. Listen for it. When you are done for this meeting, you may say:

Guardian,
Thank you for your presence.
Thank you for the gifts of reach and space.
May I touch the stars and rise to love.
Go if you must, stay if you will.
Hail and farewell.

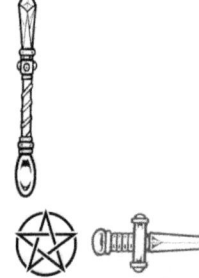

TRACKING YOUR NIGHT DREAMS

Our night dreams have many functions. They process the day's information and uncover fears and desires. Since we are working with the powers above, let us try to expand into the processes that happen when we are most unconscious, when our autonomic reflexes are taking care of our bodies. This may give us information to use when we are attempting to live our lives in waking states. Night dreams reflect our secrets, holding the power of the Black Mirror of Space.

Relax your breathing, feeling yourself sink more deeply into your bed, letting your breath flow down through your body. Before going to sleep, set your intention to remember one dream.

When you awaken, write down whatever images, thoughts, or sensations come to you. This may be an entire story or one word. What preoccupies you in your sleep? What fears or hopes arise? Just notice. Over time you may begin to see patterns that are helpful to your spiritual work.

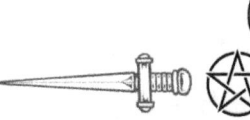

ENGAGING YOUR DAYDREAMS

What is your deepest wish? Do you feel you deserve it? We often have deep-seated patterns that keep us from realizing our wishes. Do the Self-Love cleansing in Part Two, and let those thought-forms begin to wash away. Let the Gazing at the Silver Mirror spell help you.

Begin to draw your dreams closer to you. What would your life really look like if you realized that dream? This is a step we often forget. Once we examine what that "reality" might look like, we might find that the dream is not what we want at all! Rather than something to work toward, it has just been a fantasy we use to escape our daily reality. To realize our dreams, we must first be open to them, then we must be willing and able to do the work to make the dream happen. This is not about winning the lottery; rather, it is about changing some of your attitudes and habits about money in order to find a job that is fulfilling for you and makes enough money for you to live comfortably. This is about taking singing lessons or scheduling time each week to write poetry. What do you want to do? What is one thing you will do this week to open that as a possibility?

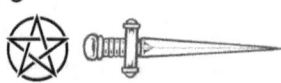

Once you have begun engaging your dreams, you are ready to stretch toward what you truly desire.

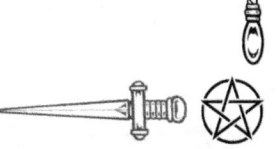

RISING TO MEET YOUR DESIRE

"*Everything worthwhile is dangerous.*"
—Victor Anderson

TO ENGAGE the Powers Above is to reach beyond ourselves.

If you work with magical guides or allies, you can call on them to help you here. There are also expansive deities that might help you stretch yourself.

One such figure is the magical Baphomet, who encompasses all gender polarities, and is both human and animal, physical and metaphysical, of earth and air. With the words *solve* written on one arm, and *coagula* on the other, it illustrates the dissolving and coagulation of the spiritual alchemical process. The Baphomet stands for synthesis, harmony, and unity. The Baphomet also spans the worlds above and below, guiding seekers with a flaming torch rising from their brow, illuminating the space above the crown where we encounter our God Soul.

Feri Tradition Craft has a relationship with a similar figure,

the Peacock Angel. The Peacock is the child of the Star Goddess. There are many stories about the Peacock, some lovely and some difficult. They have teaching for us, though, no matter what the story. They hold lessons about abundance and fear, lessons about there being enough for everyone: enough beauty, wealth, pride, and talent.

Many in Feri Tradition use the name Melek Taus, though that name comes from the Yezidi people, whose relationship with this entity is different than ours, despite strong resonances.

Expansive deities call on us to awaken to our true selves and live in pride. Ignoring our true nature gets us nowhere, it just keeps us asleep. We can claim our beauty, our darkness, and our illumination. What is fallen in us can be brought to light and to life. All of our parts must be met for us to be whole. The Peacock and the Baphomet are both symbols of this conflict and resolution.

In Feri Tradition myth, Melek Taus is created when the Divine Twins, in their forms as the serpent and the bird spirit, are married and joined in union.

This marriage and integration of bird and snake is found in other spiritual traditions that show the peacock eating the snake to conquer darkness. Manly P. Hall writes: "The peacock and the ibis were objects of veneration because they destroyed the poisonous reptiles which were popularly regarded as the emissaries of the infernal gods." An emphasis on *union* rather than destruction is an important philosophical shift, congruent with the Feri Craft dictum, "I would know myself in all my parts."

Within both the Peacock God and the Baphomet, earthiness and a sense of danger are wed with beauty and lightness. Cutting off what we do not like leaves us wounded half-people and, in that state, evolution becomes impossible. We can learn to love ourselves, in all our parts.

Feri Craft legend has it that the Peacock was walking in the

Garden of the Gods when he came upon the mirror of his Mother, the Star Goddess. He gazed into that mirror and exclaimed, "Ha! Behold how beautiful I am!" He shook his tail until the seven heavens were filled with thunder! There was glory in all the worlds.

The Peacock God awakens to his beauty and shakes his great tail. He cracks the sky, creating thunder to announce his presence. The Peacock God is beautiful and fearsome. Why is he fearsome? Because he dares to be beautiful and we fear that beauty. Why is he fearsome? Because he captures darkness in the eyes shimmering in every feather. Those are the eyes of the storm, and they are portals to other worlds, within us and between the realms. In myth, he is the fallen angel. Pride. But we can reclaim pride as he dared to claim his beauty. This can be dangerous to our parts that wish to remain hidden and small. It can also feel dangerous to relationships or a society that may wish to keep us in line. There is that which we fear within ourselves—darkness and conflict, glory and beauty—that we must face to be whole.

The power of desire is potent. In rising to meet it, we remove it from the realm of pure fantasy and free up the energy of action. Fantasy, while giving us hope, can also keep us static, becoming just another story that saps our life force. Fantasy that shifts into desire becomes the energy that feeds our work and infuses our lives with deep satisfaction. When it is rooted in fear, envy, or apathy, fantasy remains in the realm of "someday." The potency of desire brings us into the "now," freeing us up to walk more fully into our lives.

Here are a few things you can do to begin to engage the power of the expansive deities and your own desire. Remember, everything worthwhile is dangerous, though I also add, not everything dangerous is worthwhile. Your life is worth the effort of discerning which is which. Take a risk. You may just fly.

Expansive power must be tempered by compassion and will,

otherwise it can spiral out of control. This is another reason desire—and the Baphomet and Peacock—is feared as well as longed for. This power rests beneath the hand of the Star Goddess. Boundless pride and abundant will must both be held under the hand of love and creation. Pride and will are good but all things can fall out of balance.

Continue to look in your mirror and open your heart.
List all your desires, no matter how big.

- *What fills your nighttime dreams with fear? Cast a circle, call upon your allies, and turn to face that fear.*
- *Take a risk. Do something that is outrageous for you: buy a peacock-blue shirt and wear it to the office. Speak at a city council meeting about something that touches your heart. Go scuba diving. Say no. Say yes.*
- *Let yourself be sexy.*
- *Embrace your power.*
- *Admit to something that may fill you with shame. Admit to a secret desire that you may find unacceptable. Look at all your parts.*
- *Live as big, bright, bold, and beautiful as you can.*

SEEING BEAUTY'S BLACK REFLECTION

Gazing into a black mirror is not only a traditional way of scrying—seeing psychic visions—it is also a way to see our own faces in a new way. You can purchase a special black mirror in an occult shop or make your own by taking a picture frame and coating one side of the glass with high-gloss black spray paint or ink. You can also put a piece of shiny black paper or poster board cut to fit the frame and insert that behind the glass. Fill a shallow bowl with black ink or gaze upon your reflection in a window at night.

Black-mirror gazing comes from many esoteric occult and Craft practices. Let's try.

Set up a candle for your working. Align your Triple Soul. Ask the Star Goddess to help you see the parts of you that only emerge in darkness. Look at your reflection in the black mirror. Let your gaze soften. What emerges? Ask your reflection the question, "Who are you?" You might be surprised by the answer. This face may have answers to questions that your daylight face wouldn't even think to ask. Take a breath of courage. Listen. Look.

The Star Goddess loved Her reflection in the curved mirror of space. There is beauty in blackness, in secret spaces. Let yourself look upon it. Breathe in and out. Grow vast.

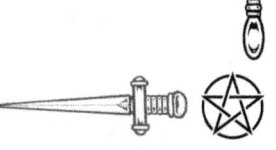

BALANCING IMAGE AND REALITY

The vastness of possibility may frighten or intimidate us. Most of us need to grow into ourselves. We have often been taught that we shouldn't be "too big for our britches," or we hold ourselves back for fear of what friends or family might say or think of us. We either feel too big, projecting a false image out in front of ourselves, or too small, trying to not be noticed in one way or another. Or we may be some combination of the two. Either way, we are in hiding.

To be truly large is to be in balance. When a person projects a "large" image, taking over conversations or entire rooms or projects, they are likely overcompensating out of fear and insecurity. The same is true for the person who hides, who never speaks, who asks for what they want by asking another person what *they* wants, who tiptoes into a room, thereby distracting everyone in it, instead of just walking in to get what they need.

What are your tendencies? How do you keep people away from you? How do you crush your passions and undermine your abilities? How do you try to crush others so they won't get ahead of you?

I remember struggling with myself, after years of dealing with

other people's projections onto my big, false, performing self. I was attempting to come into alignment, and was afraid that if I became more powerful, I would steamroll over others. My good friends, exasperated, kept saying, "Just go ahead and get bigger!" When I was finally able to begin that process, it was a relief to all. I became much more helpful to others, more effective in the world, and developed a greater store of generosity.

Some states are more tenacious than others, but you will not know what your capacity is until you make the attempt to grow.

Take a deep breath and imagine yourself as you would like to be. Imagine yourself as competent, confident, loving, and loved. Imagine yourself in your true power. Are you honest about what you can and cannot do? Spend one week stating your true abilities to yourself. Write them down as they come up. Share them with a trusted friend.

As you grow used to this practice, you can start taking more risks with this form of truth-telling. State your true abilities at work or in your community. The more accurately you can state what you can already do, the closer you are to stepping into your desires.

SPIRIT JOURNEYING

Since we are working in the realms above, held by the Star Goddess and infused with the confidence and pride, we can take another risk. We can step out of our physical bodies for a little while and, more importantly, practice coming back.

Many Craft and magical traditions use what I'm calling spirit journeying. This is also called astral travel. But why leave the physical body at all? Spirit journeying is another way of learning to walk in between rational spaces and into a whole *other* world. It is also a way to gather more information about the world we live in. It is not a method of escaping our lives; rather, it is another form of expanding more fully into ourselves and all the realms of the world.

If your impulse toward spirit journeying is to use it as a form of escape, I would wait and not use the following practices until you are more firmly rooted in what has come before in this book. Keep building foundational practices. If spirit travel does not open

you further to yourself and the realms you walk in, it will be of no help to your development in the long run. It is always good to question the motivations behind both our fears and our desires.

That said, this work can expand our knowledge of our emotional and psychic states and help us to get in touch with the unseen realms. There is travel on the inner planes, travel on the astral, and travel into other realms.

My former coven used astral travel as a way to build a space that was our own. We would journey together to our ethereal covenstead and do work, gather information, and meet with guides who could help us with our work. Sometimes people look different on the astral; this alone can give you a clue into your inner self. You may also have different skills, different clothing. Things on the astral and the inner planes often appear as symbols in ordinary consciousness. Discovering your internal symbols can be a key both to your personality and deeper essence. I used to have quite a nice set of armor on the astral! The state of the armor and how it changed was always a good reflection of how I was feeling emotionally and with my work in the physical world. Over my years of work, that armor disappeared. I no longer have need of it.

I have worked with a cross-tradition group of magical elders for two decades now. We do spirit work together monthly, meeting in a secret nook on the inner planes, deepening our work despite living a continent apart. There are many examples of this.

Other Witches often do magic in this way, when they've formed strong bonds with magical siblings who live in disparate places. They simply tune in at a certain time and date and travel to a common meeting place. Generally, they have agreed upon a method of entry, one example being to visualize a certain tree in a clearing, with a hollow in its base that acts is a portal to their space. After the journey, they then compare notes afterward.

Many of us probably believe we cannot do this, just as many

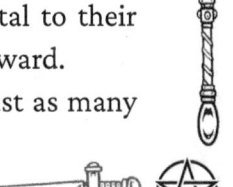

of us disbelieve our natural psychic or intuitive talents. I hope that these exercises will show you that the technique of spirit travel can be practiced and learned just like any other.

TRAVERSING THE BLUE SPHERE

I developed the following as an introduction to spirit travel that can help you feel safe in the unknown spaces the first times you try to journey.

Use the Casting from the Inside Out exercise from section two. Once you feel yourself encased in the bubble of your own personal blue sphere, imagine that there is a second layer, a membrane on top that can expand. Let that second layer ease out until you have the vast bubble of space around you. Now, imagine that your spirit self begins to rise out of your body, leaving the small blue sphere for the larger one. It is connected to your physical body by a silver cord that attaches firmly to your navel, like an umbilical cord. For some people this cord attaches to the base of their spine instead, further anchoring them to the physical body. Let this body rise until it is floating out beyond your physical self. Let yourself feel what it is like to float, then begin to fly. Let your arms reach out, and spin your spirit self like a skydiver wheeling through the sky. You can control your speed, velocity, and height. Experiment. Have fun.

Once you have been out for a while, imagine your spirit self floating back toward your physical self. Feel your spirit body sink lower and

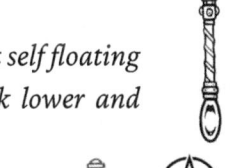

lower, penetrating the small blue sphere and gently easing itself back into your physical body. Feel your breath moving in your physical body. Inhale. Exhale.

Now let the larger sphere, the container you were floating in, begin to shrink back down, slowly, as you breathe. Feel it as it comes closer to your own sphere, behind you, below and above, to each side. Sense it. It grows close enough to touch your personal sphere, your own casting. There is a flare of blue as the spheres meet and merge fully. You are encased once again in the sphere you began with. Take a deep breath. Feel your physical body, feel your feet firmly beneath you and let your breath circulate from the soles of your feet to the crown of your head, running down your arms into your fingertips. Feel how the blue sphere has matched your Shining Body.

On a big breath, release the blue all around you, letting it return to the æther. You are left with just your aura and your expanded attention, which you can draw back into yourself if you like, just as in the Deep, Expansive Attention exercise. Or you can simply remain in this awareness, letting it fade as your attention is captured by other things. You can always return to it. Align your Triple Soul with any energy left over. Pull your earlobes, pat your thighs and arms. Say your name three times. Drink some water. Blessed be.

FURTHER ASTRAL TRAVEL

The following exercise is less complex than the last yet may feel riskier. I adapted it from my years of training with Victor Anderson and through working with other magical practitioners like Tom Johnson and Willow of the Night Hares Coven, and with the cross-tradition magical alliance I mentioned earlier.

I recommend practicing it a little bit at a time, practicing for five or ten minutes your first few times, and then working up to actual journeying. After you read through the exercise, I will offer suggestions for which parts to use as practice.

Prepare yourself and your space for this working. Gather some candles, or a lamp with diffused light. You want the room quite dim. You will also need a small dish of water, some water to drink, and some food, preferably protein and carbohydrates. As I stated in the section on North, sugar is not recommended, as it won't replace any of the fuel you will use on this journey.

You should have a soft blanket to cover up with, as when the spirit is journeying, the body can become cold, and if the blanket is too scratchy, it can act as a physical irritant to bring you back

into your body before you are ready. Before you begin, you should align your Triple Soul both as a way to make your journey easier and as a form of protection on the astral planes. Your working will be more successful if you are centered, whole, and aligned. You may cast a circle and call the Guardians if you wish. As a matter of fact, if you are first learning this work, formal casting is advisable.

If you have hematite, tiger iron, or an iron pendant or nail, you can place that on your altar to help call your spirit back to your body when it is time.

Lie down in a comfortable position in a dimly lit room. Imagine the contents of the room clearly, the rug, furniture, paintings, where the door is.... Now imagine that you hold a heavy weight in your right hand. Feel it there, solid and real. Now imagine that there is a helium balloon tied to your left hand. Feel the lightness and buoyancy as your hand gently rises. Feel the contrast between the weight and the lightness. Let these go. Now feel the heaviness of your physical body and the lightness of your spirit body. Feel your spirit body begin to separate out from the physical. First, let your spirit hands and arms begin to rise. Then feel your head and torso follow, until your spirit body is sitting up. Now allow your spirit body to stand up out of your physical body. Let your spirit body begin to travel wherever it wishes to go. Notice that at first, you can "see" the room you started out in, but it now glows with an etheric light.

You begin to move, perhaps rising to fly, perhaps walking with ease through this space between spaces. Choose a destination, perhaps into the next room, or a journey down through your neighborhood. Notice what you can see and what seems different from regular physical vision. Let your night senses open and let your psychic eye take in this new information. Once you have journeyed a short while, begin to feel the tugging of your physical body as it calls to you. Iron calls you back to your physical form, for you are human. Let yourself flow back toward where you began, journeying through all the places you passed on your trip outward.

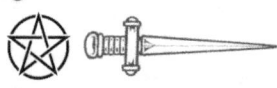

As you near the room where your physical body lies, feel it calling to you more strongly. Enter the room. Look down at your physical feet. Prepare to enter back into your body, slowly, gently, and easily. You will remember everything you did on your journey. Slowly enter, dropping gently back into your physical form. Feel yourself enter your feet, your hands, the back of your skull. Ease on down. Once you feel yourself fully in, take a deep breath from the crown of your head to the soles of your feet. Slowly open your physical eyes. Wiggle your toes and fingers. Pat your chest and belly. Dipping your fingers in the bowl of water near you, splash some on your face and rub some on the back of your neck, to make sure you are all the way in. Say, "I am body and spirit, emotion and mind/Present and whole, this instant in time." Sit up. Drink some water. Massage your feet and tug your earlobes. Eat some food to fully re-ground you in your physical form.

To acclimate yourself to this practice, begin by going through the technique up until the point where your spirit body is sitting up. Then let the spirit body lie back down into your physical body. You can do this several times, easing your way up and down, until you become used to the sensation.

If you are engaging in the suggested daily sitting practice, it will be of great help to your astral travel. If your mind tries to engage you with a nonessential worry while you are on your journey, your sitting practice will have taught you that you don't need to clutch onto the thought. It is just another automatic reflex like breathing or blood circulation. The thought can just move on past, not interfering with your travel. If you have *not* been sitting, your thoughts may actually grab you and plunge you back into your physical body, causing your journey to come to a jarring end. Sitting quiets your attachments to your mind, it quiets your body and, done long and often enough, it eventually quiets the rate and vociferousness of the thoughts themselves.

LOOKING UP AT THE SKY

We can have a relationship with our physical universe while remaining firmly in our bodies, standing on the ground. We do this by opening to our connections with the phases of the moon and sun in their seasonal dances. There are tides within our bodies that respond to the pull of the moon and our emotions respond to the waxing and waning of the year. Setting ourselves into alignment with these forces can help us remember that we, too, are part of nature, not separate from or above it. It is all around us and within us, too.

A Witch attempts to be in tune with the cycles of Nature. As creatures of Nature ourselves, we are affected by the sun and moon much as are plants, animals, or the tides. What happens to you when the earth obscures the sun? Or when the earth's shadow falls upon the moon? Begin to notice the sun phases where you live. Winter and Spring in Northern California are quite different from Winter and Spring in Delaware, Helsinki, or Lagos.

What are the signs you read that tell you when one season is flowing into another? When do you start to feel the strength of the sun? That is the time to begin putting plans into action. Begin

to tune into the phases of the moon. When you look in the night sky and see that the moon is on the wane, you may want to take time to cull—old habits, thoughts, or piles of clutter.

We can work with magic according to season or moon phase. The monthly moon phases also translate out into the larger year. Your work with deity and with your intent can use both cycles to complement the work you need done. Place yourself and your own cycles, emotional and physical, in concert with the cycles of the natural world.

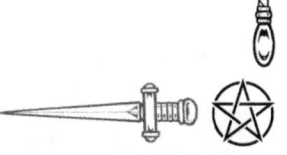

MOON PHASES

- *Waxing Moon: What do you want to draw in?*
- *Full Moon: What do you want to acknowledge as manifest in your life? What are you grateful for?*
- *Waning Moon: What do you want to cleanse and clear away?*
- *Dark Moon: Catch your reflection in the dark mirror. See the beauty in blackness.*

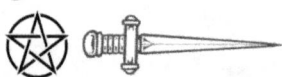

SUN PHASES

- *Spring into Summer: What have you planted that is growing?*
- *Summer into Fall: What are you growing and readying for harvest?*
- *Fall into Winter: What are you harvesting and what will lie fallow?*
- *Winter into Spring: What gathers in darkness, waiting to be born?*

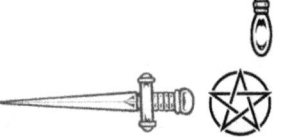

REACH

Oriented in your body, on the earth, yet gazing at the sky, breathe in your ability to expand. Breathe out and grow larger than you thought was possible. You are connected to the multiverse, spinning on this planet you call home. Get ready to reach down into the core of that home.

PART NINE
POWERS BELOW: LIGHTING THE DARKNESS

CALLING BELOW

Enter the spaces below your feet; the worlds below your consciousness. This is fecund space, where things grow in the darkness. Sink deeper. Feel the heat. There are things that swim here in the flames that are housed in the core of the world, the core of your inner spaces, where a bright star burns. Our tool here is the Cauldron, the bowl of your belly, cradled in the bones of your pelvis. The Cauldron: the Witch's tool of transformation. Light the fire below, and see what is cooking: What feeds you? Is it nourishing or poison? Light the fire within, let the dross burn away, let things that live in darkness

be lit by the shifting flames. Gaze into the fire of the Cauldron: What do you see?

A FIRE BURNS DEEP in the center of the earth. What exactly it looks like, we are not sure, but theory has it that it is hot iron, liquid and then solid, moving, pulling in, condensing, and reacting. There is a fire in the center of our selves. What exactly it looks like, we are not sure, but metaphysically, psychologically, energetically, I am betting it looks a lot like the center of the earth, part molten, part solid, and holding gravity.

This section continues the work of expansion we began with the Powers Above. In it, we will examine our shadow spaces. These spaces might contain things we have pushed down within ourselves: old, unexpressed anger; childhood traumas; feelings of inadequacy; a fierce desire that we don't feel we deserve to attain. The exercises that follow, coupled with the work we have already done, will help us to plumb these depths.

This is ongoing work. It does not and actually *cannot* be done all at one time. You may wish to augment this work with counseling, support groups, or a magical circle that gets together for the express purpose of helping each other through this work.

When patterns are hidden, they can exert a controlling force over us that we are barely aware of. Brought to the light, we can see what they are and work with them. The dark is powerful, not evil. Sometimes things need to grow there, to gestate until they are ready to come out into the world at large. Sometimes, however, we keep things hidden out of embarrassment or fear. The things we hold on to are human and sacred. Acknowledging that they are part of our lives gives us power. We can claim these hidden powers instead of letting them claim us. We can learn to walk at night without fear, for the night is part of our deepest selves.

In this section we will work with the Cauldron as a representation of the core fire. That energy will help us to face our fears, to claim our powers and responsibilities as warriors, and to gaze upon the unseeable.

THE CAULDRON

The Cauldron is both a symbol and practical tool. Witches were often portrayed as gathered around a large iron pot, cooking up potions and spells. This represents Hecate's Cauldron, the brewer of operative magic. The Cauldron also appears frequently as a source of inspiration, abundance and rebirth, especially in Norse and Celtic myth: the Dagda's Cauldron of Plenty; Cerridwen's Cauldron of Wisdom that must be stirred for a year and a day; Odhrerir, the Cauldron that holds the mead of poetry; the Welsh Cauldron of Regeneration.

The Cauldron is also a symbol of transformation—it burns old dross and feeds new life. It can be used to transform disparate ingredients into nourishing food. The Cauldron is a symbol of practical alchemy, where solid matter joins with water, heat is applied, and the two become something entirely new. Like the transformative power held in the tradition alchemist's alembic, the Cauldron's power shows the beauty of friction, of the Pythagorean harmonic of two notes played together forming a third, or Gurdjieff's reconciling force of grace that rises from a yes

met by a no. It is the third road that leads to faery, the place of paradox.

We have the ability to hold disparate things, to hold them until the very tension of the holding creates its own heat. Then something new can emerge within us. The Cauldron also holds the flames of change, the power of the Phoenix, the power of the great below and the shifting earth, the power of the great star that heats our core, creating the possibility of life. Are we open to that life? Can we let things burn, becoming fuel for a new desire? Can we burn for truth?

COOKING LIES INTO GIFTS

Alchemy is the art of blending disparate elements in the hope of creating a new substance. There is a cooking process that ensues here, a degeneration and transformation of the original ingredients. From this grows a new substance that was hidden as a seed in the original, disparate elements. I adapted the following technique to use the Cauldron as our alchemist's alembic to metaphorically "cook" what we throw in. In this exercise, the pot holds the flame *inside*, rather than resting on top of a fire.

For this you will need a small cast iron pot or a flameproof dish. Set it on several layers of hot pads, a metal trivet, or brick. Pour about an inch of Epsom salts in the pot. Saturate the salts with rubbing alcohol, allowing a quarter inch of alcohol to float above the salts. Center yourself and then throw a match into the pot. You may need to light the surface first, then let the match drop. Do not add alcohol to a flaming cauldron.

Once the fire is set, gaze into the flames. Breathe. Begin to throw conventions you are tired of holding into the flames.

Throw in lies you've been told and ways you act that feel false. Keep

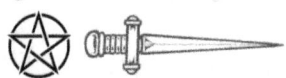

breathing and listen to your thoughts and emotions. Whatever rises, throw it into the fire. Once you feel done for the moment, take another deep breath and ask for a gift from the fire. Ask for whatever you need to keep looking at yourself and challenging conventions that don't fit your life. Do you need courage? Humor? A different education? An open heart? Passion? Ask for whatever you need. Let this rise up from your belly, not your head. Your belly holds your own cauldron fire. The cauldrons in your heart and head are lit from there. When you ask, pass your hand over the fire, as though you would cup a flame and draw it into you, receiving the gift of flame.

Now sit with this gift until the flames die down. If your pot is big, it may burn for a long time, in which case it is all right to put a lid on top. Let the pot cool, then run water in it to dissolve the salts and clean it. If it is cast iron, re-oil and season it by baking the oiled pot in your oven.

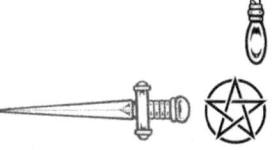

COOKING UP POSSIBILITY

Each phase of our work needs food, and various aspects need to be fed different foods. We may need praise, or we may need to cultivate discipline. We may require rest, or a better schedule in order to work more effectively. We may need courage, patience, or love. We may need more money or time, or a change in attitude to either of those.

Prepare a sacred stew or soup, cutting vegetables and adding protein consciously, pouring clean fresh water into the broth. What do you want to feed right now? Let each ingredient signify distinct aspects coming together to form nourishment for your soul. Stir them together.

Let the alchemy happen. Smell the changes being wrought by magic. Sit and stir in meditation as the soup cooks. Give thanks.

Eat and be well.

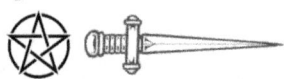

LEAPING THE FIRE

In spring, often on May first, it is traditional for many Pagans to jump a cauldron as a form of cleansing. Legend has it that herders would run their animals past bonfires to clear away the bugs and pests. In current Persian culture they leap the fire at Spring Equinox, asking it to take away any vestiges of Winter illness, and ask the fire for its life and heat. We can use this fire to cleanse our relationships and anything in us that needs transformation.

If you have the chance, build a small fire on the beach or in another fire-safe place. Use clean, uncoated wood free of nails. You can also use a small cauldron fire of Epsom salts and alcohol for this purpose. Charge the fire with your intention. Ask it to clear away sickness, depression, fear, anger, or anything else that you would like to begin healing or anything you would like enlivened with the power of fire. Leap the flames. Do it as many times, for as many reasons as you like. If you are doing it with friends, you can leap together to clear out anything in your relationship that keeps it from deepening. Let the flame lend you its cleansing, revitalizing power. Once you are done, douse the fire and clean up the space.

THE GUARDIAN OF BELOW

In order to reach deeply into ourselves and light the necessary fires, we may need some support. The Guardian of the Powers Below is a force of deep spaces and transformative fire. In the previous section, we stretched up. Now it is time to stretch down, deep. Both spaces may be well beyond our comfort zones. That is okay. We can ask the Guardians for help.

Take a deep breath. Cast the blue sphere around you. Light a candle on your altar, fiery red or orange. Turn toward the Center, open yourself to the power of the Guardian below, as you breathe deeply within yourself. Feel a breath upon your forehead. Open to the Guardian of Below. Begin to feel the presence coming closer to you. What does this Guardian feel like? Can you get a glimpse of it? "Guardian Below, open the glowing core and join this rite." *The Guardian Below, swimmer in the Cauldron of Fire, it is the burning star of heat and generation. Feel the presence. Introduce yourself.*

Guardian of the Powers Below,
Nadir of space and imploder of time.
Open the glowing core and join our rites.
Teach us the ways of cthonic life,

And show us the beauty that lives in secret worlds.
Let us plummet together,
Let us plummet.
Touch our spirits, touch our souls.
May we deepen beyond measure.
May our cells spark revolution.
May we glow with the heat of love.
Welcome.

Take a deep breath. Feel the Guardian beneath you, huge and beautiful. Stay in this presence for a while—feeling, sensing, gazing. You may wish to write what you sense. There may be a key to this presence. Listen for it. When you are done for this meeting, you may say:

Guardian,
Thank you for your presence.
Thank you for the gifts of lust and spirit.
May I touch the core of myself, and learn courage.
Go if you must, stay if you will.
Hail and farewell.

ENGAGING YOUR FEARS

"**F**ear *is a noose that binds until it strangles.*"
—Jean Toomer

LOOKING at that which is buried within is the key to our work with the powers below. We dealt with some of our emotions in the section on water. Now is time to turn to those emotions that many be buried even more deeply, sometimes wearing disguises or hiding themselves under still *other* emotions. I want to talk now about the emotions that often make us most uncomfortable, those that may feel harsh or unforgiving.

Whenever a harsh emotion rises inside of me—anger, irritation, shame—if I can look at it quickly enough, I often find an underlying current of fear. Once I discovered this, I began to examine the roots and patterns of fear in my life. This proved to be a potent tool for calling back both power and compassion and for dealing more honestly with other people. If I can admit that a fear drives my frustration with another, I can more readily talk to them about it, discovering the true source of our problems, rather than just foisting blame upon them. I often fear being seen as a fraud, or sometimes I'm just plain scared, like when a car comes too close to me when I'm trying to enter a crosswalk, and I feel a flash of anger because of it.

There are many fears that run our lives, both large and small. The following exercise deals with the small fears that keep us from moving ahead into what we really want for our lives. These fears can keep us from honest communication and often bolster the lies we tell ourselves.

Once you start bringing your fears to light, they may appear in layers over time. Your task is to face each one and name it. Your core pattern may not have fear at its root. What is it? Look at yourself. What are your manifestations? Whenever you feel discomfort, begin to look beneath it for the emotion at its root. Is it fear of anger, fear of losing face, fear of success? Though this exercise is talks of facing fears, if you find another deep emotion running your life, by all means, alter the exercise to reflect this.

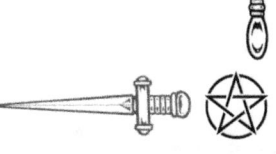

Naming Your Hidden Emotions

In the section on Air, I wrote about the power of naming. This is a step in regaining your life force. Truth feeds life force and lies bind it. Naming your fears—or other core emotions—loosens the ties of deception.

Carry a notebook with you and begin to jot down instances that cause you discomfort throughout the day. At first, this may be all you can do. Just this process of noticing instances of discomfort is a big step. Next, see if you can sense an energy or emotional current beneath the discomfort. This is step number two. Step three involves examining your notes at the end of each day, then at the end of a week and a month. See if a pattern emerges. This will give you a good insight into what is present beneath the surface of all your interactions with the world.

The final step, of course, is to name the pattern. Name the fear or fears and begin to face them, situation by situation.

When engaging with this piece of work, make certain to do a lot of cleansing, centering, and soul alignment. These can offer emotional ease and bring in compassion for ourselves and whomever else might be involved in the situation.

Our core fears or emotions may never leave us, but they can lessen, and don't have to control us.

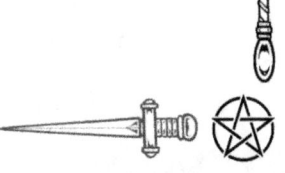

THE WARRIOR ETHIC

To face the flames below, one must have courage.

Calling upon our inner warrior helps us face our fears, and the things that cause discomfort inside and outside of us. We can learn to stand firm when uncovering old wounds or nurtured poisons. The warrior is supported by the powers of below, able to wade into the dark fire and come out the other side.

Warriorship can help us to practice non-violence. We can claim our ability to fight for what we love. If I don't claim my ability to fight and bring *that* to the surface through training and practice, my inner violence will control me, or other people's violence will.

All humans have a capacity for violence. If we do not train that, it tends to erupt in different ways. We can get caught up in gossip and backbiting. We become passive-aggressive. We squash our anger so it festers, causing us to hold grudges for years. We lash out inappropriately and cause damage to relationships. Most importantly: we do not walk and act with integrity.

The warrior's voice is a well-honed and honest voice. It does

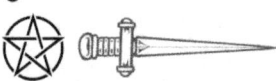

not shrink from looking at horror, yet is able, because of sheer human compassion, to realize a solution that will work for all, not just a dominant force or a minority with guns and an opposing agenda. Someone who has trained as a warrior is able to exercise perspective and keep a clear head and heart. This is difficult, but attainable. We can work on it.

NOT CODDLING WEAKNESS

"*Neither coddle nor punish weakness.*"
—Victor Anderson

We sometimes avoid the hidden spaces within, not out of fear, but because we are more comfortable not facing them. Both the warrior and the seeker plumbing the powers below must face discomfort. Along with the Feri Tradition tenet to not submit your life force to anyone or anything, is the dictum, "Do not coddle weakness." Coddling weakness *is* a submission of life force. So is punishing weakness. The powers below feed our life force just as much as the powers above feed our souls. Seeking to deny the powers below denies the potency of my life force.

When we coddle another, we are asking them to submit their life force to us, which is a sign of disrespect. Rather than trusting that they can handle our words or actions and grow from them, we instead assume that they are weak and need protection. Now, a person *may* need protection, comfort, and help, but to assume so

without asking does their spirit a disservice. Punishing weakness also helps no one; rather, it often cements a dangerous status quo.

Respect and compassion both help us treat ourselves and others in a more balanced, healthy way.

The exercise below deals with the many ways in which we coddle ourselves and ask others to support our weaknesses. It takes courage, honesty, and patience to engage in such self-scrutiny, but until we try, we will remain controlled by our complexes, addictions, and fears. Once we begin to do this work for ourselves, it becomes easier to not support others in their complexes and fears, and so we start to help the world.

How do you numb yourself and why? Experiment with not doing some of your usual mind-numbing or emotionally comforting things for one week and see how you feel. No TV or video games, no macaroni and cheese or pints of ice cream, no alcohol or marijuana. Try not engaging in whatever behavior you use to numb yourself and make everything all right. See what struggles this brings up in you and notice if any deeper information arises.

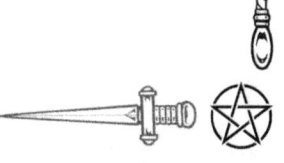

THE STORIES WE TELL

"*Self-justification is worse than the original offence.*"
—Sheikh Ziaudin

YEARS AGO, WHEN DISCUSSING OUR "STORIES," a Gurdjieff teacher told me his. It was one sentence: "I am a liar." At that time, I didn't really comprehend what he meant, but over time and with work on self, the truth of that statement has become all too clear. It really hit home one day when I was rewatching a segment of Alex Haley's *Roots*—decades after it was made—and simultaneously watching myself. I noticed the outrage that was rising and the emotions of "how could they?" in regard to the slave traders. I stopped myself from spiraling into that line of thought and really focused on what was happening both on the screen and within myself.

Then it hit me: "I am a liar."

In trying to distance myself from the actions of the slave traders, I was denying my own complicity in the self-justification

that upholds systems of domination. The slavers could carry on, being "good Christians" and engaging in "commerce," because they lied to themselves well enough. I began to realize how all humans use lies to prop up our lives. The lies keep us safe from seeing ourselves, and we then contract with other people to support each other's lies. And so, we coddle weakness and submit our life force over and over, never even realizing the magnitude of our inaction or action. These lies prop up a whole culture—advertising feeds these lies, government feeds these lies, and we become a society of cowards.

Begin to watch the ways in which you justify your behavior to yourself and others. How do you lie to yourself? Why? What purpose does it serve? How do you support the lies of others for the sake of friendship or keeping your job?

FACING THE RUST AND GILDED PENTACLES

I place these pentacles, shadows of the Iron Pentacle, with the Powers Below because the energies they hold are often hidden from us. The work with these pentacles come through the Reclaiming Tradition, my own work, and through Feri Tradition priest Steve Hewell. The points may vary among practitioners.

We need to call upon courage and the warrior's heart in order to face these pentacles. The points here can strangle or snuff out life force, but with help from the Guardian Below we can rekindle our own core fires and bring ourselves back into the balance held within the Iron Pentacle.

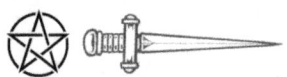

RUST AND GILDED

BOTH OF THESE pentacles arise when the Iron Pentacle is absent. I used to think that the points held in these stars were simply imbalances of the Iron points, but over time and through much work I came to comprehend that Impotence and Greed take over only when Sex is not present. Just as Pearl appears when Iron is *fully present,* so Rust and Gilded appear when Iron is *fully absent.* For example, Powerlessness and Force are the result of lack of Power. Let us look at these further and notice how they feel in our bodies, minds, and emotions. Some of these points may feel more familiar than others. Many of us spend more time in Rust than Gilded or vice versa, and still others of us bounce from one to the other. For example, we may experience what it feels like to be arrogant and then ashamed of it.

As an initial way to begin to explore your relationship and familiarity with these pentacles, we will try to feel them in our bodies. It is helpful to notice if any of the points feel like familiar patterns in our lives or are connected to stories we tell ourselves.

Start this exercise by running the Iron Pentacle through your body. Let it charge you up, feeling how the points respond to each other, building the energy. Then begin to let the points shift. Feel Sex leaving you, leading you into Impotence and then Greed. Feel Pride move away, into Shame and then Arrogance. What happens when Self is gone and only Deprecation or Egotism remain? When your Power is given over or taken from you, what do Powerlessness or Force feel like? When your Passion leaves you, feel the wake left behind and the Apathy or Obsession that rise up to take its place.

Once you have felt all of the points of Rust and Gilt in yourself, clear them out by running the Iron Pentacle through your body again, several times. Sex, Pride, Self, Power, Passion, Sex. If you still feel you need to release the Rust and Gilded points, take a Self Love Cleansing shower, or align your Triple Soul.

The points on these pentacles often insinuate themselves into our lives and end up wielding a great deal of control over our emotions and perceptions. These next exercises are ways to look at the Rust and Gilded pentacles in depth. I am not providing exercises for every point; rather, here are a few ideas to help you work with the points that are particularly absent or present in your life.

REACHING OUT OF BOUNDS

I designed this exercise, done with a partner, to help us tangibly feel what it is like when we are always doing things for someone else or doing what someone else is pulling us to do. This happens when we lack confidence and a strong sense of who we are and what need. This causes us to always be slightly off balance within, falling this way and that, reaching for approval, reaching to help another, reaching out beyond the boundaries set by who we really are. This state is indicative of many of the points on the Rust Pentacle.

If you cannot stand to do this exercise, experiment with doing it in a chair, or energetically instead of physically.

Face your partner. Balance on one foot, reaching way out, as far out as possible, using your free leg as ballast. Reach toward something not quite attainable. Reach for approval. Reach to fill someone else's needs or wishes in spite of what you may need. Reach. Feel what that is like. Is this a familiar feeling? Is there any emotional recognition brought up by this pose? Your partner will pull on you. Try to recover your stance. Reach. Your partner will push at you. Try to recover again. Reach. Stretch. Notice where your head is. Notice how low you have to

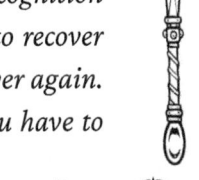
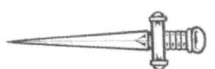

hold yourself in order to achieve any semblance of balance. Your partner knocks into you, blindsiding you. How long does it take you to recover? Breathe. Shake this pose and energy off of your body. Switch roles. You be the world, coming at your partner. You become the worries and duties that push and pull. What does that feel like? Breathe. Shake hands with your partner in thanks for the work.

AUTOMATIC WRITING

Drawn from practices done by both Victorian spiritualists and writing coaches like Natalie Goldberg, this exercise explores the absence of Pride. You can also experiment with using it to gain more information about any of the Iron points that feel weak, inactive, or absent in your life. Set a timer for five minutes and don't let the pen leave the page.

Begin writing out that which makes you feel ashamed, those things you have held secret for years because they were too painful to share with another, and you felt they made you look bad. Write about all the times you didn't speak up for yourself or another. Then write about those feelings of aggrandizement that make you arrogant, better than others.

Next, in a fire safe vessel, take the paper and burn it. As it burns, feel yourself without those things and start naming things you are proud of, no matter how small: "I am proud that I spoke up in class today. I am proud I defended someone who needed it. I am proud I acted instead of standing by. I am proud I walked to work instead of driving. I am proud I finished that poem. I am proud that I did what I needed to do. I am proud I volunteered today. I am proud to be who I am. I am proud that I am trying."

REBALANCING PASSION

This exercise encompasses both the Rust and Gilded pentacles. When we lack passion, we replace it with apathy or obsession. This exercise will help you to feel when your passion seems unattainable. It will help you look at the times when passion becomes obsession and it is all that you can see. Then it will bring you into a feeling of balance with your passion. I use Passion in the example below, but can substitute any of the Iron Pentacle points.

Take a deep breath. Drop into yourself, into your body. Relax. Breathe. Float down into yourself. Let your shoulders relax, face relax, legs relax. On each breath you relax more and more, drifting down, down into yourself. You are traveling in time. You are traveling through space. You are breathing. You are going to a time when passion felt very far from you. Passion was beyond your reach. Breathe. What do you long for? Where is it? What is it? Reach for it. It is just beyond you, drifting past your fingertips. Reach some more. No. You can quite grasp it. Are you bereft? Or do you feel relieved? Passion is so far from you. Do you even care? Is Apathy setting in? Are you still reaching toward

Passion, or would you just like to lie down for a while? Breathe. How do you feel?

Take a deep breath. Let time and space swirl around you once again. Let your longing settle. Breathe. Breathe in Passion. You are traveling to a time when Passion completely filled you. It was all you could see, feel, taste, touch. Your desire was as close as your nose, so close it almost smothered you. Obsession. Breathe. Feel it all around you. Are you exhilarated? Or do you feel lost, disconnected? Breathe. What you thought was Passion is so close, you are obsessed with it. Nothing else seems to matter. What is this longing? So consuming.

Take another breath. Let Obsession recede. Let time and space swirl around you once again. Breathe. Relax. Breathe in Passion. Draw it up. Draw up your desire. What do you desire right now? Breathe it in. Name it. Taste it. How does it make you feel? Let your Passion rise within you. Do not judge it. Open to it. Begin to move with it. It is near you, but not smothering. You can hold it, but it does not grip you too tightly. It is yours. And the cosmos sings to you: "Dance in the heat of your hearts desire.... Open the gate, the key is within, to the temple of the heart." Breathe, swim, dance, play. Passion. And you answer the cosmos: "I dance in the heat of my heart's desire, dance in the heat of my heart's desire...." Dance with your Passion. Dance your desire. Name it. Sing it. Claim it. You can have what you desire. Passion can fuel your work in the world. Your passion can heal you. You are whirling in it. You are centered. You are beloved.

Breathe. Let yourself rise to the surface of yourself. Begin to bring yourself back into ordinary space and time. Breathing. Let your body form around you, solid. Passion is still with you. Breathing. Open to the world in front of you. Open your eyes. Speak your Passion out loud. Write it in your journal. Begin to walk it, to live it, to love and work within it. It fuels you but does not consume you. It is your birthright. Blessed be.

IF BRITTLE, I WILL BREAK

This exercise allows you to experience what happens when you stand, stubborn and bullish, digging in your heels, unwilling to listen, to move, to talk it out. This is a posture of "I know that I am right, and no one will dissuade me." It seems like a strong pose, but it is very weak. It is the brittle bough that breaks rather than bending. This position is also out of balance and takes a long time to recover from when you get knocked off center. You are not really centered; actually, you are digging your heels into precarious ground. This state is indicative of the Gilded Pentacle. You will need a friend to help you with this exercise.

If you are physically unable to do this exercise, play with it energetically, instead.

Spread your feet about shoulder width, exactly parallel to each other. Dig in your heels. Straighten your legs. Puff out your chest. Ball your hands into fists. Put your chin up, defiant, arrogant, immobile. You are right. You know what is best and no one can tell you differently. Does this feel familiar? Do you recognize this pose? Your partner pulls on you. Try to recover. Get back in your pose. Your partner will push

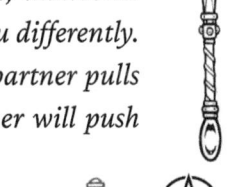

you, prod you, blindside you. Each time, recover your stance. Dig in your heels some more. Puff yourself up. Your partner knocks you off again. How long does it take you to recover? How does the stance start to feel to you after being thrown out of it over and over again? Breathe. Shake this stance and its energy off of your body. Switch roles. Become the world coming up against your partner. Become resistance, subversion, which wants to knock the king off of his throne. What does that feel like? Breathe. Shake hands with your partner in thanks for the work.

STEPPING FORTH

Once you have fully explored the Powers Below, the realms of yourself that are often obscured or hidden in shadow, you will be ready to step into the center of the sphere, the center of yourself. Open the gates to your soul.

PART TEN
CENTER: OPENING THE GATES

CALLING SPIRIT

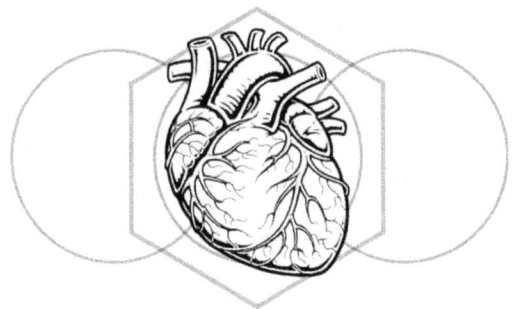

Open the gates! All the worlds stand before you now. You are stepping into primal time and space that bends to your passing. Meet yourself with a welcoming kiss. Here you give and here you can receive. The flower responds to your touch. You are becoming more alive. The tool here is the Black Heart of Innocence: the power of wildness, of innocence, and of truth without shame.

THE CENTER IS ALSO the Circumference of All. It is that shining edge I have spoken of, that becomes the central point, flipping our vision and expanding it in unusual ways. That which is central to our spirits is often not central to the culture outside us, but as we change ourselves, that which surrounds us changes. The paradox continues to unfold within us and without.

We stand now in the middle of the sacred sphere, surrounded by the Guardians of the Six Directions, encased in the mist of blue fire. Our hearts beat here, we are human and alive. In this space, we can become as large as the Guardians themselves, strong in spirit and love, forces of human nature, part Divine. Here we can be certain that we are emanations from the Star Goddess. We are large here, and small, connected to the tiniest particle and to the galaxies that wave out their births and deaths beyond our own.

The tool here is the Black Heart of Innocence. Of all the tools I learned from the Feri Tradition, this is the most internal. It is not a polished piece of jet or smoky glass sitting upon an altar, though some practitioners may have these too; rather, it is a living, breathing, beating state. It is your wild nature, sexual, honest, juicy, supple, and strong. Without the work that has come before, we would have small chance of accessing this state. It requires clarity, presence, divinity and full access to life force.

Spirit animates above, below, and center, filling our lives with connection. These three powers form a swirling axis: our DNA and the spiraling of stars. The center is mystery and magic, the confluence of core, depth, and height. Spirit combines all of the Elements of Life and a wild heart that is as spacious and expansive as the cosmos itself, encompassing realms both seen and unseen.

In this section, we will feel the beating of our hearts, and learn to tell the truth that resides inside. We will dance with our shadows, opening to love and forgiveness, unbinding our life force and standing, clean, fresh, honest, innocent, and wise.

AWAKENING YOUR BLACK HEART

"*To holding on, to knowing again that moment of rapture, of recognition where we can face one another as we really are, stripped of artifice and pretense, naked and not ashamed.*"
— bell hooks

THE BLACK HEART of Innocence is both a metaphysical concept and state of being. It exists within us in some form or another, yet a balanced, healthy relationship with it needs to be cultivated. Once realized, the Black Heart is the unfettered connection with everything. I am in the state of Innocence when fully connected with the life force. When I am centered, connected to the earth, and running energy fully through my body, I am accessing this state without thinking about it. Connected, we are honest, for there is no need to lie when we can simply *be*. This tool, this state, this energy, is held in the shape of the heart because the heart is the pump for the life force. The heart feeds all the parts of my body, as the life force feeds all of creation.

Some people mistakenly take this concept of honesty to mean that when they have something hard to say to someone, they need to blurt it out in a "Black Heart" moment. If I am thinking about it, chances are, I am not in a state of Innocence. The energy may be trying to emerge, for it is always with me, but if I am *trying* to use it, rather than letting it flow through me, it will come through twisted and distorted, not innocent at all, but manipulative and out of balance. When we begin layering suppositions or excuses over the original impulse, we render it harmful through its disconnection.

If I am running life force easily and in tune with my body, my breath, and my energy fields, I can be sitting with someone, truly listening, with my energy field connected with theirs in a state of true compassion. I can say many things from this state, coming from my heart, which, were I not connected to life force and to their Shining Body, would probably generate a "mind your own business" from them. But in this state, I can say hard things and they can be received because it is understood on a cellular level that they are coming from love, from my God Soul. This is the Black Heart of Innocence.

In the public sector, rather than one on one, the same "rules" apply, yet my ability to communicate is more dependent upon those listening, because it is harder to be linked fully, aura to aura, with each person in a group of ten to one thousand. One tool to help with this is Deep, Expansive Attention, which I explained in section three.

Another Innocent state is the joyous abundance of sexual energy released in sexual expression. This is not based on posturing, or acting, or trying to figure out what acrobatic thing would most impress a partner. I am not saying those things can't be fun, they can! All I am saying is, that in the state of the Black Heart of Innocence there is again that honest state where we are in

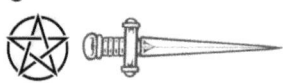

communication with the earth and/or another human being through all our auric, psychic, emotional, and physical senses.

Another facet of this are the times we walk along, feeling totally in love with every tree, sensing them as we pass. That too, is the Black Heart state.

Using all our tools, especially aligning our Triple Soul every day, is how we achieve deep comprehension of the Black Heart of Innocence. The following are exercises to help us get in touch with the life force pumping through our bodies, telling us we are alive and connecting us to all that lives around us. This is a jump start. In order to cultivate it, though, align your Triple Soul, run the energy of the Iron and Pearl Pentacles, clean your aura, and ground and center.

Cora Anderson often told me that the Craft is about living day to day. In becoming dedicated spiritual practitioners, we can free our energy and hum with life force.

THE EMPEROR HAS NO CLOTHES

We know the story: everyone supports the king in his delusion so as to uphold the status quo. The delusion is based on fear and insecurity on the part of the king and greed and grasping for power on the part of the tailors who are sewing his costly though elusive garments for the festival parade. We see that the garments are more expensive than their monetary value: they cost honesty, integrity, and the willingness to risk stating what one truly knows. We pay the price by squashing the whispering of the inner voice, the wisdom of God Soul, and the instinctive knowledge of our animal nature.

The lies can cost a whole society, once the lies are built upon and embedded into the fabric that weaves the culture together: commerce, law, art, and social status. The garments can also cost our vitality and our souls, as we are swaddled in falseness that breeds doubt. Where can one stand and breathe and see true colors? When can one speak?

It is the child—in all innocence, untrained in the ways that breed insecurity and secure of their place in the natural world—

who shouts the words that shatter the spell of lies. The king is naked, and so is the honesty of the Black Heart.

Listen to yourself when you have moments when something in you says: "That's not right!" You don't have to blurt out what you feel, but start to notice those feelings: When do they arise, in what situations? How do they make you feel?

When in an Innocent state in a larger group, we can become like the child that shouts out, "The Emperor has no clothes!" This is a valuable service to provide to a group, yet again, it cannot be manipulated, it cannot be forced, or otherwise it will simply be divisive. But if it is coming from a state of a pure heart and openness, connected to the forces running through all the earth, even anger can be helpful and cleansing and can act as a catalyst for positive change.

All too often, the world needs us to be that innocent child.

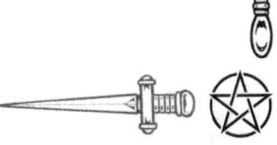

THE WAY TO YOUR BLACK HEART

I designed the following reading as a way to find a clear path to the innocent heart. It may uncover obstacles we face, or give us insight into what will clear the way. You may use cards, runes, ogham, or whatever oracle tool feels right.

As you shuffle or mix the cards or runes, ask, "What do I need to enter an honest, innocent state more fully, and to integrate it into my life?" Or you might ask, "What blocks me from my freedom?" This reading is a gateway into the self, which opens as we say, "I will be free."

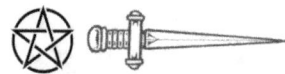

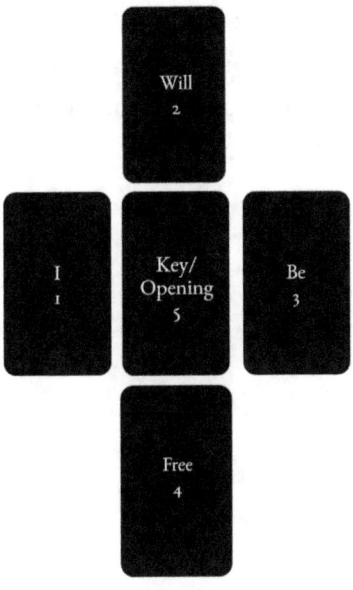

THE BLACK HEART READING

THE BEGINNING CARD IS "I" (1). This is you, right now, as you are. The next card, "Will" (2) is both a reflection of your potential and the condition of your will. It represents what you need to engage in your belly to move forward. This position may also hold what is blocked in you that needs to be made clean for your will to be strong. The "Be" (3) card is what you need to manifest, a state of "I am," of pure being not tied to personality. It may also represent what you need to move toward, but it is mostly an admonition to be, as you are, present and perfected in the moment. What is your being in this moment?

The final card of the sentence is "Free" (4). This card might be an image of what your freedom looks like, or an answer to the question, "How can I free myself?" What needs to happen for you to be free? The final card, the heart of the reading, is your Black

Heart (5), the key to your freedom. What opens the door to a life of honesty, innocence, life force, sexual connection, freedom from shame, living as a whole, balanced being in the world? Let this open you, and take you through.

GUARDIAN OF THE CENTER

Here stands the Guardian of the Center, who guards the gates of mystery. These gates are both outside of us and within. We travel into other worlds and we travel deeply past the gates of our souls. Here is a mystery; there is a Guardian of the Center, and the *Center Guardian is also ourselves.* The blue spark resides within us. The gates to each working and the other realms only open if we are fully present, clean, powerful, and innocent.

We are the key, and the gatekeeper.

Take a deep breath, connecting to your grounding cord. Cast the blue sphere around you. Light a candle on your altar, purple or black. Turn toward the center. Open yourself to the power of the Guardian there, as you breathe deeply. Feel your heart beating. Open to the Guardian of the Center. Feel yourself, fully present, and sense another presence close to you. What does this Guardian feel like? The Guardian of Spirit, of Sex, and of Love, holds the Black Heart of Innocence, opening primal space and shifting time. It shows us that the way through is the way within. Feel the presence. Introduce yourself and say:

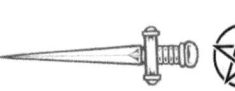

Guardian of the Gates,
Circumference and center of radiant all.
Unlock the spinning portal, join our rites.
Teach us the ways of love and innocence,
And show us the rush of the forces of life.
Let us open together,
Let us thrive.
Touch our spirits, Touch our souls.
May we fill with abundant growing.
May we vision the worlds as whole.
May we bring the worlds to love to love to love.
Guardian of the Gates,
Welcome.

Take a deep breath. Feel the Guardian there, standing in the center, beating in your heart, huge and beautiful, small and strong. You may wish to write or draw what you sense. There may be a key to this presence. Listen for it. When you are done for this meeting, say:

Guardian of the Gates,
Thank you for your presence.
Thank you for the gifts of spirit, sex, and love.
May I see clearly, and learn without shame.
May you always rest within me.
Hail and farewell.

FORGIVENESS AS A PATH TO POWER

The Black Heart is a state of perfection.

I used to feel that perfection was an end point, rather than a process of growth. From my childhood, I carried vestiges of fear and guilt, feeling that if I were "perfect" I would not get into trouble, that I would be loved and told that I was good. This is not perfection, but a trauma response, a state frozen in time, unable to respond to life as it appears. We may be perfect *in a moment*. But all power is dynamic—shifting and changing—if it freezes in place or time, it becomes brittle and will eventually crumble. Also, time shifts, so what is perfect in this second may not even apply to the conditions of the next.

Like power, perfection is mutable, not static and fixed. We are mutable and so are those around us. We can change. We can trade off succeeding and failing, being weak and being strong. Over time, I believe we can become more graceful in our changes and can listen more deeply. We can learn to forgive. We can learn that perfection is wholeness, including all things that are possible within us, not just eradicating what we see as flaws. Perfection is a state of shifting balance.

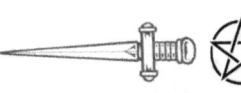

From this state comes a basis for strong ethics. This is not prescribed or legislated morality, but an ethical stance that examines each situation and then acts or judges accordingly. Can we forgive ourselves and each other and walk forward together? Can we invite our hearts into a perfect circle?

What can you forgive yourself for? What old mistake do you carry around inside yourself like a festering wound? Look at it, shining a light on it. Often, out of our own self-importance, we inflate our transgressions, and the longer we carry them, the bigger and heavier they become. Begin to let it go. Breathe in and say, "I forgive you." Others of us may do the opposite; we may downplay our mistakes by not taking responsibility for them, by blaming others, and by justifying our actions. This, too, wounds us, keeping us from living fully as adults in the world. We are forever children, crawling along, until we say, "I did that, and I am sorry." Only in being accountable can we truly claim adulthood.

This week, ask forgiveness of one person you may have hurt. Write a letter or make a phone call, whether it is something you did or said yesterday or fifteen years ago. Ask forgiveness. Say you are sorry. Take responsibility. Then notice the energy that is freed up by that act. Breathe it in. Expand.

Then strive to forgive yourself, as well.

THE RITE OF UNBINDING

I place this practice here, in the space of Center, because it has been core practice in my own life, secondary only to the Prayer for Alignment. It acknowledges that life force is central to living life in all its ordinary mystery. If we can unbind the life force tied up by years of training, by insecurity, anger, or sorrow, then we can expand our capacity to embrace paradox and to live with an open heart. I suggest doing this at least once a week at first, or daily if you need it.

This is a rite to loose what is bound, to heal what is hurting, to clean what is encrusted, and to forgive that which causes pain. We can carry huge quantities of tangled complexes, most of which remain invisible because of the dense knots we've tied, year after year. This rite helps us to let go, to unbind, to forgive and be forgiven, otherwise our life force will never be our own. Unbinding frees up our access to the Black Heart of Innocence.

This rite is syncretic. In it we find echoes from Huna's ho'o'ponopono rite, and from several global folk magic and Craft traditions.

The act of unbinding has been very helpful to me. I used to

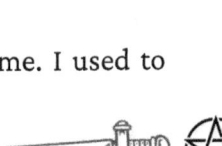

shrug off slights and hurts at the times in which they happened, saying they were "petty" or "no big deal." But then I would carry that bound up energy for years, always battling both the resentment and the thought that the resentment was beneath me. The Rite of Unbinding, like many of the practices in this book, helped me to move through emotions, feeling them and facing them with less anxiety. While I was in the heart of the process of unbinding old wounds, I did this rite daily. It helped me look at a situation, feel what arises, deal with it, and *let it go*.

Later, if we are still having a residual reaction—as emotions are both quick and tenacious—we can do this rite and further loosen the obstructions, so as to see, feel, and hear more clearly.

Victor Anderson used to ask those who came to him for help with a troubling situation, "Do you really want to be free of this? Do you want to be healed?" This is a key question, for we must also take action in the world to change the situation that caused the binding in the first place. This is true of all magic. But sometimes, just doing the external work does not always help us emotionally or energetically. I find it best to make external changes and do internal work simultaneously. This rite can become a tool for ongoing liberation.

For this rite you will need a glass holding as much water as you can drink at once without taking a breath.

Take a deep breath and let yourself begin to relax. Do the Prayer for Alignment (Section Three), breathing until you are full of life force, then tilt your head and breathe up to align your Triple Soul. Feel the energy rush back down into your body, settling you. Once you feel aligned, form your two hands together in a heart shape in front of you. Now begin to focus on what in you needs unbinding. What needs to be healed or forgiven? Begin to breathe it out into the space between your hands, imagining that it forms a small egg into the center of your hands. Do this in four long, even breaths, filling that egg in your heart with the bound up energy.

Once the egg is clear in your mind, release it with the syllable "Ahhhh," cracking the egg over your glass, releasing the energy into the water. Now pick up the glass. Holding it up, begin to intone the syllable "Ma," invoking the Star Goddess, the Mother of All. Imagine that the water turns into a swirling light of healing as you tone. Intone the syllable until all the breath is expelled from your lungs. Then inhale deeply, and drink the water down without stopping. Let the healing fill you, loosening all that is tight within you. Hold your belly and your heart, saying whatever it is you need to hear to settle the healing into your body. You are loved. You are on your way to freedom.

If a problem is particularly knotty, we can ask ourselves, "Do I want to be healed of this?" before intoning "Ma" to shift the bound-up energy into healing. If the answer is "Not really. Not right now," then pour the water out. Then bless a fresh cup of water and drink it to begin the work of replenishing our being.

Sometimes we need to do the first part of the Rite of Unbinding to get clear enough about the situation we're in to even be able to realize whether or not we want healing or forgiveness! This happens quite rarely, but regardless, even that action is always a step toward liberation.

Sometimes, we may need to do the Rite of Unbinding when not in a place to tone or break energy eggs over water. If you have water with you, simply say a prayer, breathe across the water, and drink.

Something similar can be done without water, as well. Years ago, while waiting for a ride to dance rehearsal, I was sitting in the parking lot outside the underground station, feeling the need to be cleansed of something that was weighing upon me. I began to gently rock and softly say, "May I be healed." I did this until I felt a peace descend. I aligned my Triple Soul with the energy I raised. When the energy settled, I looked down at the sidewalk in front of me. Resting on the concrete was a small, gold heart, a charm. I thanked the Gods for receiving my prayer. Magic works.

THE VIOLET PENTACLE

Some Feri practitioners use a Violet Pentacle to represent æther, or Spirit, which includes above, below, and center. Violet is the highest color on the light spectrum, before all things dissolve again into white. This also holds true for ultraviolet rays, which our eyes cannot see, but perceive as white instead. A honeybee, for example, might perceive a white flower as being different colors depending on how much ultraviolet light the flower is reflecting.

Metaphysically, violet represents our connection to the multiverse and the unseen. It is our gateway to expansion beyond the purely physical. While most Witches place the Pentacle in the North, because of its representation of the human body as part of Earth, some witches place it in the place of spirit and æther because æther is formed by all of the elements in combination.

Violet is close to lavender, and lavender often represents queer energy, that combination of the "blue is for boys" and the "pink is for girls." Queer means many things, which is why it is a term I use. It is all-encompassing, claiming gay, lesbian, transgender, bisexual, polysexual, asexual, gender fluid, and many others. As

fey-natured humans are often not wholly one gender or another, the lavender color honors and celebrates that, while the violet honors our ability to commune with the cosmos.

Cast the sacred sphere. Imagine a violet pentacle spinning above you and below you. See these pentacles open up the central, violet column in the center of the sacred sphere. This is the hub of Sex, Love, Spirit, and æther. Feel your spine stretch, feel your feet sink. Let yourself grow tall, deep, and vast, filled with violet light.

Now return to your regular physical state. See the pentacles recede, growing misty and less substantial. Dismiss the sphere, thanking any Beings you called in to help you with this work.

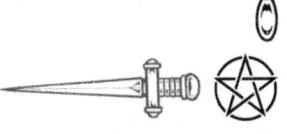

Honesty

Truth-telling is an important part of all spiritual work. In the previous section, we looked at our lies. Now it is time to look at our deepest truths. I place this work in Center because our truths come from connection to Spirit, to Nature, and to our own divinity. We do not learn in a vacuum, but in community, whether that is a community of humans or from communion with the natural world. Where are your teachers? Listen to their honesty and reply with some of your own.

Deep listening is required for truth-telling. Some of us are graceful at accepting criticism while other people may reach the end of their lives unable to listen at all to others. When are you able to listen deeply, and when are you not able to? What is the difference?

We must also learn to discern when criticism is being done in good faith, or from a wish to undermine or tear us down. Criticism in bad faith should never be listened to, except as an indicator that the person is not wholly trustworthy. Developing our powers of attention and intuition can help us with this assessment over time.

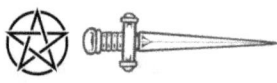

Has someone challenged you, or posed a difficult question to you lately? What emotions did that bring up in you? What questions of your own come up in response? Take a deep breath and drop your attention to your heart and then your belly. Let yourself relax. Begin to do a timed writing, not letting the pen stop until six minutes is up. Begin with the question or challenge at hand. Then let the words begin until you loosen up and the censor steps aside, letting your deeper truths flow to the surface. "I believe in this because…" "I acted in this way because…"

USING YOUR TOOLS TO SUPPORT TRUTH

In both the Elemental Pentacle and the sacred sphere, the space of Center is the home of spirit. All of the Elements of Life are present here. Stand firmly on earth, tempered by fire and water, as you breathe in air. Imagine it now. What gives you stability? What tempers you and makes you true? Feel all of that and breathe in life force, further strengthening your soul and your truth.

Just as Spirit gives us access to all of the elements, we also have access to all of our tools. Imagine that your tools can help to bolster your ability to perceive your truth and put it out into the world. Call upon the power of your own spirit—and let the tools speak to you.

The Wand: What grows when you tell your truth? Does your truth bring newness and a fresh way of thinking or speaking? If that which grows from what you say or believe is something that doesn't feel helpful to you or others, you may wish to reexamine it and see if there is a deeper truth at hand.

The Blade: What happens when you back up your truth with will and intention? Fill with your truth, and then breathe it across

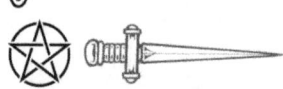

your blade. How do you feel marrying your truth with fiery will? What are the consequences of using your will to back up your truth? Imagine those consequences. Use this information to look at your truth and gauge its power and veracity.

The Chalice: Fill your cup with truth and drink it. Does it refresh and renew you or leave you feeling slightly ill? If the latter happens, look again. Perhaps there are vestiges of poison in what you are calling truth. Dive down another level and open up to compassion. Now what does the truth feel like?

The Green Cube: Stand on your truth. Will it support you? Does standing in your truth make you feel strong? Is there movement in it, as with the pentacle inscribed upon it, or does your truth risk becoming brittle?

The Black Mirror: What does your truth reflect? What is its shadow? How does your image of yourself or the world change by looking at your truth in the mirror of space?

The Cauldron: What fire does your truth light? Does it cook something nourishing or toxic? How does your truth feed yourself and others?

REVITALIZING BREATH

After working with the above exercise, you may feel a need to do the Rite of Unbinding and realign your Triple Soul. Both of these will aid your continued exploration into truth. You can also use the breath work we began in earlier sections. Below is an expanded way to use your breath to revitalize your connections to self, body and the Gods.

Take a deep breath. Every time you exhale, send a breath through a different part of your metaphysical body. Start with your root chakra, down at the base of your spine. Now send a breath through your sex. Send a breath through your belly, cleansing and activating your will. Next, breathe out through your heart. Exhale through your throat. Now, send a breath out through your third eye, the psychic center in your forehead. Last, breathe out through the top of your head, your crown, which connects you to the Gods. Repeat this process until these places feel clean.

Once you are done, say a prayer that you may walk, speak, live, breathe, and dream your truth. Take a breath and exhale from the soles of your feet to the crown of your head. Now draw in another breath and breath out through whatever place most holds your truth today. It

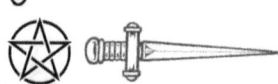

might be your sex or belly. It might be your crown or heart. Wherever your truth lies, send a breath to strengthen it. Next, find the center that feels weakest or most in need of your truth today. Take a big breath of life force in and exhale it out through that center to begin its activation.

Do this work for the next week and try to sense any changes within. Notice if you walk or stand differently. Notice if it seems easier for you to speak. Notice if you need extra cleansing or longer times of meditation. Do whatever you need to do to strengthen your ability to walk your truth.

INTEGRATION AND MOVING FORWARD

Integration expands our ability to remain conscious and strengthens our effectiveness in all of our work. Where are you in your life and work right now? Are you coping well, are you barely standing, or are you thriving? Has your capacity to hold and share power, truth, and compassion grown? Are you working at full capacity?

Whenever I am coming upon a time of increasing growth or increased responsibility, I strengthen myself by adding on to my spiritual practices. I sit with my God Soul, listening for longer periods, and I do more cleansing, especially using the Rite of Unbinding. I take extra care with my work on staying present in any given situation, using my posture and Keys to Remembrance as aids to this. I align my Triple Soul as often as possible. All of these lead me further into my own integration. Intention requires consciousness and I can only remain conscious when aided by actual, physical time spent doing my practices.

Integrity requires an awareness of all our parts. For example, if I am unconscious of my habits, I cannot act with integrity no matter how much I want to, because I hold no integration

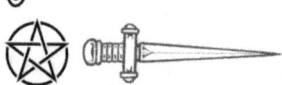

between my thoughts, emotions, and actions. I often find that misunderstandings about integrity crop up in our language, within phrases like "Their intentions were good" or "They meant well," when actually they intended and meant nothing, because they were not conscious of their words or actions. What people probably mean is, "They intended no harm." That is correct. They had no intention whatsoever.

Consciousness, intention, and integration are available to anyone and can help us to live more fully and truthfully. We just have to be willing to do the work. We have to seek out support and begin to move past the fears that keep us small, trapped in habitual behavior patterns.

In the place of Center, you can both deepen and expand upward. Take a deep breath and stand tall in the world.

There is often discomfort before the breakthrough, darkness before the dawn. Remember who you are and why you are working. When you integrate your practices and open to your central truths, your work opens up to include the whole world.

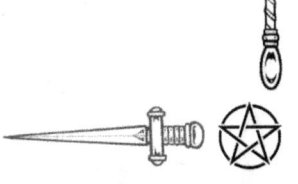

CIRCLES TO LOVE

This is similar to the Circles of Power exercise. It can be done alone or with a small group. If done in a group, the final circle, the circle of love, is one that everyone steps into at once. It is a circle that is meant to be shared. Step into the center of your heart.

MAKE sure you have enough room in front of you to take four big steps. Take a deep breath. Feel yourself grounded and centered. Align your Triple Soul. Feel yourself as you are, where you are. Are you afraid, overconfident, sad? Just notice. Breathe into any feelings you may have. Stand there in them. Stand as you are. Now, think, what would it take for you to live more freely, more honestly, and with greater access to your sexual energy? What would it take for you to grow in strength and compassion? Say a prayer for what you need.

When you are ready, step forward. You are stepping into the circle of courage. Let courage fill you. This will help you in all of your work. It will help you to keep opening to change, to risk, to the Black Heart of

Innocence. Feel the courage as it surrounds you and fills your body. Breathe it in.

When you are ready, take a deep breath. Step forward. You are stepping into the circle of acceptance. Feel acceptance surround you. Acceptance of your dreams, your fears, your mistakes, your body, your mind, your secrets, your hopes. Acceptance of yourself. Feel it. Breathe it in. Accept your journey. Accept that you can move forward. Breathe it in.

When you are ready, take another breath. Step forward. You are stepping into a circle of hope. Let hope fill and surround you. Breathe it in. Hope keeps you going. This is the hope of seeing a flower gently opening to spring sunshine. This is the hope you nurture for yourself that you may sometimes feel afraid to admit to anyone, or even to yourself. Take another breath. Prepare to enter the last circle. Step forward. You are stepping into the circle of love. Feel yourself surrounded by love. Let love fill you. Let it tingle around you. Stand in it. Breathe it in. Let it open your heart a little more. Breathe. Feel love moving through your whole body, through every part of you, through your Triple Soul, through your shadows, through your strength and fragility. Breathe love in.

If you are in a group, standing in this circle together, put your arms around each other. Feel the circle of love. Now, one by one, step into the very center. Let the circle enclose you. Everyone begins to tone love at you. Feel what it is to be surrounded by love. Take a breath. Receive it. Step back into the circle of arms and warm bodies. Let the next person step in. Let love fill you. Release it in a tone toward the person standing in the center. Feel what it is to share love with the world. Breathe it in. Love goes on and on.

Magic requires reciprocity. Energy must go out and come back in. If you are constantly giving and never receiving, you will soon run dry. Conversely, if you are constantly taking, the earth won't be able to hold you for long. Magic is a circuit requiring currents

that flow both ways. Breathe that in. Make that thought a part of your practice. Let us be open to one another. Let us care for each other and receive care. Let us give back to the earth as we receive the gifts of the earth. So mote it be.

PART ELEVEN
CLOSING THE SPHERE, OPENING THE WORLD

CALLING OUR SELVES

"Who is this flower above me, and what is the work of this God? I would know myself, in all my parts."
— Victor Anderson

YOU ARE ENTERING the space you already occupy. Your life is your own. You walk with the Gods, in concert with Nature. You are alive, fey and wonderful, human and Divine. You are stepping into

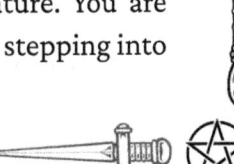

paradox where the world is both the same and new. Breathe deeply of this sacred air. It has surrounded you all along. How does it feel to truly be yourself? Celebrate your place in this new world.

Our lives are a continuous spiral. We move on, sometimes up and sometimes down, revisiting the same faces, voices, and patterns, all slightly changed. We gain the perspective of faithful practitioners, spiritual seekers who have found footing on a Path that can no longer be denied. Once we have set upon it, it continues for as long as we give and take breath—and beyond.

In this final, closing section, we will listen for our deep names, look upon our whole selves, and ask ourselves what evolution might look like. Then, we will step forward into our divinity, into our work. And the story continues.

This section closes the book and opens us to the possibility that our lives can include integrated practices that will carry us further within ourselves and simultaneously out into the world. One day at breakfast, in the midst of a spiritual discussion, I asked a friend, "What is your practice *right now*?" He answered, "Drinking water," then placed his glass on the table with a thunk.

The possibility of continuous practice is available to us all. In *The Way of the Pilgrim*, the Russian peasant walks all across the country searching for someone to teach him how to pray without ceasing. May our lives become such a practice, such a search, such a prayer. May we know ourselves, in all our parts.

How do you feel now, in this arm of your spiraling journey? How do you define yourself: Witch, artist, parent, writer, warrior, magician, activist, gardener, or priestess? Are you a dancer in the cosmos or a caretaker of the earth? Look at all of your talents and the responsibilities inherent in them. Are you up for the task of being fully yourself and continuing your sacred work in the world?

To become Siblings and Children of the Craft we must honor

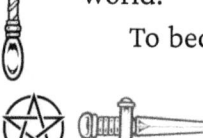

our commitments to be ourselves and to continue on our spiritual paths. We must also commit to others, for we cannot evolve alone. Sitting on top of the mountain can be helpful for a time, but we put our work to the test when we come down the mountain and engage, actively, in the world. Teaching children. Planting trees. Making magic. Speaking out for justice. Loving the world, as it is and as it could be.

LISTENING FOR YOUR DEEP NAME

Some people get spiritual names during formal initiations, others in a blinding flash. Some use their names for years, and some only for a short time, until the lesson sinks in. Some have secret names. All these names are useful to our magic. My public name came during my Reclaiming initiation. I lay in the bathtub arguing: "Goddess, can't I be called something else?" The answer was no. The name that kept being repeated to me, over and over, was Thorn. When the priestess came to take me to the next gate, she asked if I had my name and I replied, "Yes, but I don't like it!" Nonetheless, I was smart enough to realize there was a lesson there that I would learn only over time and with repetition.

So, I decided to make Thorn my my legal name, so I would hear it every day.

Take a walk in a wild place, or draw a sacred bath, and allow yourself time alone to listen. Call on the Guardians and any of the Gods you need. Let yourself relax into their presences, and into your own presence —your heart beating, your lungs filling and expelling air, your muscles moving. Let thoughts of your life drift

through your head. Where have you come from, where are you going? What does your work feel like, right now? After a while, let those thoughts quiet. Begin to listen. Ask the Gods for a deep name, a true name, a name that will be your key magically, and a name that describes your essence or will help you to grow. Relax. Drift. Listen. It will come.

You may have to repeat this process more than once. Your name may come to you a week after you have done your listening, while you are hiking in the woods, or it may be called after you on the street by a stranger, some misheard thing resounding in your ears. Open to it and learn from it. Names are powerful. Open to this new power.

ENGAGING YOUR WHOLE SELF

P oet John Keats said that the world is a vale of soul making.

All things in our lives can change and form us, strengthening our spirits and our life's purpose. But we must choose, every moment of every day, to heed the lessons life gives us. This is the ultimate in integration and the next step toward evolution—cultivating the ability to drink in each breath, each phone call, each second standing in line, each conversation with a coworker—of choosing awareness and waking instead of habit and comfort.

With the foundational tools in this book, you can use the world as a setting for your own development. The joys and irritations of life are invitations to grow and change, to develop something substantial and immortal. What is your challenge to yourself, right now? By bringing your whole person to the task, worlds will change.

EVOLUTION AND COMMUNITY

Our challenge is to maintain spiritual practice amongst others: coworkers, family members, or spiritual communities. Part of the work of Evolutionary Witchcraft is changing how we relate to one another. In doing our personal work, we must not lose sight of the health and well-being of the world at large: of issues of economic justice or environmental protection. What is harder for many of us, however, is dealing with our close communities—in coven, ritual-planning group, activist group, PTA, family—with compassion, patience, and honesty. This is hard and constant work and the tools in this book are available to help.

If we grow impatient, we can ground and center, getting back in touch with our breathing. We can use the aura work and soul alignment to help communicate more effectively. If we are about to enter into mud-slinging, we can look in the mirror first and speak the words there. If we want to engage in malicious gossip, we can practice truth-telling face-to-face first.

The more we practice, the more we can grow together, becoming open to listening and talking and building a healthy

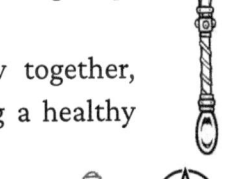

and sustainable community. Dominant culture does not teach us these skills. We have to learn them, practice them and, in love, begin to teach each other.

How do you function in community? How do your communities function? Are there practices you engage in that facilitate communication? How does your vision for you own life connect with your hopes for community?

RITE OF INTENTION AND DEDICATION

This ritual will both express your intention to dedicate to your path and to further your work and training. It can also help you to find the right teacher to help you when the time comes. I recommend making an amulet or choosing a stone, necklace, or charm to mark this rite and carry as a reminder of your work, wish, and intention.

Cleanse your working space. Build an altar; gather candles and offerings for the Fey, allies, and the Gods.

Bathe yourself, do the Rite of Unbinding and align your Triple Soul. Now set up your space to work ritual.

Ground and center and say, "Holy Mother, in Whom we live, move, and have our being, from You all things emerge and unto you all things return." Cast the sacred sphere. Ask for the presence of the Guardians, the Fey, and whatever Gods you wish to be present for this rite. Thank them, and make your offerings.

Standing in your sacred sphere, say "I, (your name), call upon my will and state my intention to dedicate my life to the unfolding of mystery and to gaining knowledge of myself. In the presence of these Gods and Guardians, and my allies, I dedicate

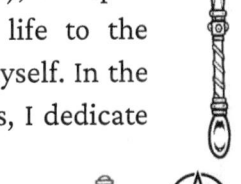

myself to walking the path of integration, joining my soul's work with the spirits of Nature and the Gods."

Breathe your intention into your amulet or stone, giving it power. You may also sing, drum, or dance to raise energy to channel into your sacred object.

Bask in the power of the Gods and Guardians, breathe in life force, and align your Triple Soul. When you are ready, thank all that you called into your sphere and draw the energy of the blue fire back into your blade. Ground and center once again, exhaling by pushing the energy down through your feet and up through your head about a foot. Send another breath out to your aura. Your rite is complete.

You are now fully dedicated to your spiritual life and to expanding your relationship with your magic.

REMEMBER, YOU ARE DIVINE

There is a wonderful story from the Hindu tradition about Krishna as a boy. He and his friend are playing ball at the edge of a lake. The ball inevitably is thrown into the lake by a wild pitch. Krishna dives in to retrieve it. In this lake, he encounters the seven-headed hydra, Kaaliya, who both guards and poisons the small body of water. A fight ensues between the serpent and the blue God, and they struggle together until Kaaliya holds Krishna, trapped and gasping for air, at the bottom of the lake.

Krishna's friend shouts down to him, "Krishna, remember, you are a God!" Upon hearing this, Krishna fills again with the breath of life, his strength returns, and he soon gains the upper hand. He gains control of Kaaliya and, rising to the surface, dances on top of the serpent's many heads. He threatens to kill Kaaliya for poisoning the waters of the lake, but Kaaliya's wives intervene, and the serpent himself says, "It is my nature to give off poison." Krishna decides then to banish Kaaliya to the great ocean, where there is so much room for Kaaliya that it will be impossible to poison it.

This story teaches two important lessons. The first is about the importance of peers, friends, and community. In community, we can remind each other of our divinity. When one person is feeling upset, another can say, "Remember, you have tools you can be using to help yourself. Remember, you are a God." The reminder that we hold the Divine within us helps us to do our work. If our community members devolve into vicious gossip, for example, one of us can remind the group of our stronger, kinder natures. Then we can rise back up to the surface and breathe clean air again, instead of choking on our own toxic fumes.

The second lesson of the story is that of creating space for that which we find difficult to bear. If we are envious, angry, or grief-stricken and feel like we cannot bear to look at ourselves or the situation at hand, we try to create more room for the feeling. We can stand in fear, for example, and take a deep breath. Upon exhalation, imagine our energy body expanding, creating more space for the strong emotion to flow. Once we do this, we feel more ease and less trapped. We expand our ability to bear our own pain—and the pain of the world—and to face our fears.

In order to take in either of these lessons, we must be willing to both look at the pain or sickness and be willing to change our relationship to it. These exercises are not about getting rid of the pain or eradicating the sickness, but about bearing both and seeking out that behavior which is most helpful to us and to our communities.

When have you needed a reminder of your own divinity? Do you need one now? Take a moment to align your Triple Soul. If you are in a meeting where people are growing fractious, take a deep breath and encourage others to do the same. Then point out a common goal or ideal you may all be seeking. This is a reminder of the stronger, kinder nature of the group, and is supported by your own inner divinity.

When have you been overcome by grief, fear, envy, or anger? Take a breath into that state, that memory. Make space for your emotions so

they do not have the power to freeze or poison you. Breathe now. Feel your energy body expand as you exhale. Remind yourself that you can hold more humanity than you sometimes know. You are part of God Herself.

We can continuously expand into our own Godhood. As I learned from Victor Anderson: God is Self. Self is God. God is a person like myself.

SEEKING A THIRD PATH

Throughout this book, you have been asked to expand your capacity to hold energy and emotion and then join these practices with recognizing your Godhood. This work will make you ready to find your rightful place in the world.

The following is the third part of the cauldron exercises we did earlier. This piece fits into finding your true work in the world. It may also remind you of the work we began with our blades, walking between choices, engaging our wills. This also strengthens us, helping us to find what our purpose is, and what the best path toward it may be. Having recognized our conflicting voices and warring desires, we can truly listen to the deeper voice created by our alchemical powers, and find what the Gods and our hearts really want us to do. Walk strongly and sit still. This work takes a warrior, a Witch, an artist, an alchemist. Are you ready?

When you think of your desire, your dream, your work, or even your pain, what in you says "yes" and what in you says "no"? Usually, we try to go with one voice or another. An adept, however, sits between those two voices, tempered by the heat created in the tension of not

answering. Take a breath. Hold "yes" and "no" in your body and your heart. Sit with it. Do not act. Something will arise, a third path, which will lend energy to your work.

Remember, the third path leads to Faery and to magic, a place both beyond where you think you are and, paradoxically, deeper within.

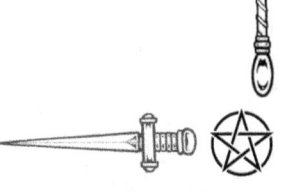

FINDING YOUR WORK

Living fully as seekers and priests requires us to give context to all of our actions. How are we living our lives? What do we read, eat, listen to, or create? How do we structure our days and nights? These sorts of questions always bring us around to asking, "What is our work?"

What *is* your true work? Sometimes this question emerges slowly over time. It requires every listening tool in this book to sense what your work might be and it requires as much presence and attention as you can bring to bear in order to step into your work fully and effectively. In section five, we worked with developing our will. "What is the work of my Divinity?" asks us what our deeper will is, our True Will. Are you ready to discover this? Can you open to its unfolding?

Ask yourself: What do I long for? How can I be of service? What feeds me? If I could do anything with my time, what would I be doing?

As the way opens in front of you, so your work will unfold. The more you diligently practice integration, the clearer your work will become. After many years of work on self, in community, and

many years of growth, I began to say this prayer: "May I do my work. May I do the work of the Gods." My true work, which I had always felt inside, but which had always been a struggle to bring into life, suddenly opened up with ease and dizzying speed. If I had not put in all of those years of preparation, would the same thing have happened? I don't think so. The preparation laid the foundation for the prayer. Yet without the prayer, and the intention to remain open, my true work may have taken longer to manifest.

What is your prayer? Right here and now? What is your work in this moment? Take some time to sit with these questions, to pray about these questions. You may want to do some divination: get a Tarot reading or do some scrying. Drop into Deep, Expansive Attention and do some automatic writing. Start with the words: "What is my work?" or "I would know what my true work is." Open up to the Gods and see what happens. Ask the Star Goddess to give you vision and clarity.

Your path opens now in front of you. Take a breath and look at yourself. Gather your energy, step into your power, and evolve. May you know yourself in all your parts.

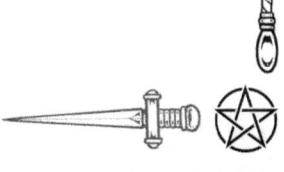

CLOSE THE SPHERE AND OPEN THE WORLD

Our work is done and always beginning. Take your sacred blade in hand, and as we began together by casting the sacred sphere, so shall we close it. Thank the Faery ones and ancestors for their help. Thank the Gods and Guardians, honoring their presences. Once all are thanked, you may say, *"Guardians of Mystery, Go if you must, stay if you will. Hail and farewell!"*

Now point the tip of your blade toward the powers below, and then sweep your blade up to the powers above. Imagine the blue fire flowing back into your blade. Moving then from North to West to South to East, release the sacred sphere and send a spark of that fire spinning out, using your magic to re-enchant the world. The rest of the blue fire will remain held in your blade until you need the containing sphere once again. Where you started this journey by making one small room sacred, you now have the ability to walk within a sacred world.

While you do the above actions, you may say this closing cantrip I wrote many years ago:

My knife gathers the flame

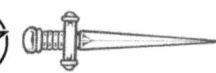

Back deep within.
The forces we have called,
Now outward spin.
Earth, water, fire, and air
Have taken part,
Within this space
Of magic, will, and art.
Unto their rightful homes
We bid them speed,
Until next time we call
To them in need.
And may the Gods
Now bless each waiting heart,
For merry we have met,
And merry part.

Holy Mother, in Whom we live, move, and have our being, from You all things emerge, and unto You they must return.

May your life be blessed. May you grow in knowledge, strength, and love.

May we evolve within ourselves, and together, help humanity evolve to be better suited to care for this beautiful planet, and for the cosmos in which we spin.

Acknowledgments

One thousand blessings to my Kickstarter backers, and blessings on all of my students, teachers, and colleagues. The world is richer and more magical because you are in it.

Thanks to Dayle Dermatis, editor extraordinaire, and Maxine Miller for the amazing artwork. Thanks also to the talented Mat Auryn for the kind foreword.

Thanks as always to my family, both chosen and found.

And finally, thank you to Spirit, my contact, my guides, and the Gods and Goddesses, for walking with me.

May the way be open.

APPENDIX: USEFUL BOOKS

Along with Thorn's companion book, *Stars of Power*, here is a brief list of other books:

Cora Anderson, *50 Years in the Feri Tradition*
 Victor H. Anderson, *Thorns of the Blood Rose*
 Victor H. Anderson (with additional material by Cora Anderson), *Etheric Anatomy: The Three Selves and Astral Travel*
 Marcus Aurelius, *Meditations*. A classic Stoic Pagan text helpful to any engaged in self-development.
 Rabbi David Cooper, *God is a Verb: Kabbalah and the Practice of Mystical Judaism*. Easy to understand information on the Jewish view of the Triple Soul.
 Mat Auryn, *Psychic Witch*. Quickly becoming a classic resource, this is an excellent book on exploring energy magic and your psychic self.
 Phyllis Curott, *Witchcrafting: A Spiritual Guide to Making Magic*. An good source of practical magic.
 Ivo Dominguez Jr., *Casting Sacred Space* and *Spirit Speak*. Two

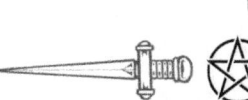

powerful books on magical practice by the founder of Assembly of the Sacred Wheel. Highly recommended.

Lon Milo Duquette, *The Magic of Aleister Crowley: A Handbook of the Rituals of Thelema*. Thelema provides interesting parallels to many of the concepts in this book, including not coddling weakness or submitting life force, developing will, and getting in touch with Sacred Dove, akin to Crowley's Holy Guardian Angel.

Epictetus, *A Manual for Living*. Another classic Stoic text helpful for those engaged in work on self and developing will.

Orion Foxwood, *The Faery Teachings*. Work in folkloric Faery practice.

Mary Greer, *Women of the Golden Dawn: Rebels and Priestesses*. For an interesting history of the early Golden Dawn, which set the stage for much contemporary magic, I recommend this book.

Manly P. Hall, *The Secret Teachings of All Ages*. A reader-friendly reprint of a grand source for religious and metaphysical research. Skip the misinformation about Islam and dive into the other informative segments.

bell hooks, *all about love: new visions* This is just one that I like for meditations on love, honesty, and innocence. Helpful for Black Heart work and reclaiming Sex and Love.

Ronald Hutton, *Triumph of the Moon: A History of Modern Pagan Witchcraft*. An excellent history of Witchcraft.

Wynn Kapit and Lawrence M. Elson, *The Anatomy Coloring Book*. A simple source for discovering your physiology. Body awareness is a must for any spiritual practitioner.

Eddie Lenihan, *Meeting the Other Crowd: The Fairy Stories of Hidden Ireland*. The title says it all. For those of you interested in stories of the Faery world.

Eliphas Levi, *The History of Magic*, translated by A. E. Waite. A good source for any serious student of the Occult.

Audre Lorde, *Sister Outsider*. See especially "The Uses of the Erotic" for insights into reclaiming sex as sacred life force.

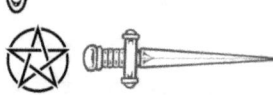

APPENDIX: USEFUL BOOKS

Jacob Needleman, *Money and the Meaning of Life*, and *Time and the Soul*. These books can help with the work in Chapter Six.

M. Macha Nightmare and Starhawk, *The Pagan Book of Living and Dying* This is the only book I know of, of its kind.

P.D. Ouspensky, *In Search of the Miraculous: Fragments of an Unknown Teaching*. A key book to help understand human automatism and how to become more self-aware and less of a machine.

Wendy Palmer, *The Intuitive Body: Aikido as Clairsentient Practice*. Holds good exercises to get one in touch with one's body as a holistic and psychic force.

Candace B. Pert, *Molecules of Emotion: The Science Behind Mind-Body Medicine*. Dr. Pert has written an interesting entry into non-dualistic science that shows how integrated consciousness really is.

Gershom Scholem, *Kabbalah: A Definitive History of the Evolution, Ideas, Leading Figures and Extraordinary Influence of Jewish Mysticism*. Scholem writes an excellent text for those wanting to further understand the Triple Soul.

John Shirley, *Gurdjieff: An Introduction to His Life and Ideas*. Gurdjieff's work has had a great influence on my thinking and is helpful to students of magic. This is a good introductory book, a little more story oriented than Ouspensky's more technical book.

Starhawk, *Dreaming the Dark: Magic, Sex and Politics*. A great book on merging spirit and politics.

Starhawk, *The Spiral Dance: The 20th Anniversary*. A Witchcraft powerhouse, first published in 1979. Includes a lot of Feri material.

Jean Toomer, *Essentials: Jean Toomer*, edited by Rudolph P. Byrd. Reflections on the spiritual life. Not Witchcraft, but quite insightful, written by a Gurdjieff student and writer of the Harlem Renaissance classic *Cane*.

If you want to get weekly musings from Thorn in your inbox, or buy books directly from the author, please visit thorncoyle.com and thorncoylebooks.com
Also, reviews are always welcome!

About the Author

T. Thorn Coyle worked in many strange and diverse occupations before settling in to write books full time.

Author of the *Bookshop Witch Paranormal Cozy Mystery* series, the *Pride Street Paranormal Cozy Mysteries*, *The Steel Clan Saga*, *The Witches of Portland*, and *The Panther Chronicles*, Thorn's multiple non-fiction books include *Sigil Magic for Writers, Artists & Other Creatives*, *Kissing the Limitless*, *Make Magic of Your Life*, and *Evolutionary Witchcraft*. Thorn's work also appears in many anthologies, magazines, and collections.

An interloper to the Pacific Northwest U.S., Thorn drinks a lot of tea, pays proper tribute to the neighborhood cats, and talks to crows, squirrels, and trees.

Connect with Thorn:
www.thorncoyle.com

Also by T. Thorn Coyle

NON-FICTION

You Are the Spell Book and Oracle Deck

Sigil Magic for Writers, Artists, & Other Creatives

Crafting a Daily Practice

Evolutionary Witchcraft

Kissing the Limitless

Make Magic of Your Life

FICTION

The Witches of Portland

By Earth

By Flame

By Wind

By Sea

By Moon

By Sun

By Dusk

By Dark

By Witch's Mark

The Bookshop Witch Paranormal Cozy Mysteries

Bookshop Witch

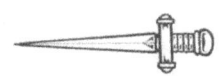

Haunted Witch

Tarot Witch

Running Witch

Hallows Witch

Solstice Witch

The Pride Street Paranormal Cozy Mysteries

Sushi Scandal

Flower Frenzy

Muffin Murder

Hairspray Horror

Dandy Distress

The Mouse Thief

Mouse's Folly

Mouse's Fight

The Panther Chronicles

To Raise a Clenched Fist to the Sky

To Wrest Our Bodies From the Fire

To Drown This Fury in the Sea

To Stand With Power on This Ground

The Steel Clan Saga

We Seek No Kings

We Heed No Laws

We Ride at Night

Short Story Collections

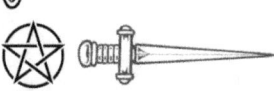

A Hint of Faery

A Touch of Faery

A Spark of Magic

A Flame for Yuletide

A Hope for Winter

A Time for Magic

A Speculation of Stars

A Speculation of Hope

A Speculation of Time

Risk It All: Queer Stories of Love, Suspense, And Daring

Thresholds: Queer Stories of Love, Suspense, And Daring

Ghost Talker

Cats and Other Creatures

www.ingramcontent.com/pod-product-compliance
Lightning Source LLC
LaVergne TN
LVHW021339080526
838202LV00004B/237